The VINEGAR Collected Works Book

D1611323

by Emily Thacker

Published by:

Tresco Publishers

718 - 12th Street N.W.

Canton, Ohio 44703

U.S.A.

The Vinegar Book
©1993, 1994, 1995, 1996   Tresco Publishers

The Vinegar Book II
©1996   Tresco Publishers

The Vinegar Home Guide
©1996   Tresco Publishers

The Vinegar Diet
©1997   Tresco Publishers

ISBN: 1-883944-27-9

Printing 12 11 10 9 8 7 6 5 4 3 2 1

First Edition   Copyright 1998   Tresco Publishers

Table of Contents

SECTION ONE – THE VINEGAR BOOK

SECTION TWO – THE VINEGAR BOOK II

SECTION THREE – THE VINEGAR HOME GUIDE

SECTION FOUR – THE VINEGAR DIET

The Vinegar Book

Dear Reader,

I can't begin to tell you how many kind readers have written to me, asking when the sequel to *"Home Remedies from the Old South"* would appear . Your letters have been a real encouragement! Many of you have also shared your remembrances -- and commented on the Old South remedy which you found to be most useful.

One theme kept reoccurring in your letter. Readers, from all across the country, related how Apple Cider Vinegar has been a part of better health and easier cleaning.

In reading my mail, it seems as if many readers feel Apple Cider Vinegar is practically an instant remedy for all the ills of human kind! Some believe it is a liquid cure-all -- a tonic to extend life, promote good health, and provide needed vitamins, amino acids and trace elements. Faith in the power of Apple Cider Vinegar dates back to about the time of the discovery of the apple. And, some of the claims made for it seem a bit extravagant.

Do I feel Apple Cider Vinegar is a remedy for all the ills of this world? Well, probably not.

But vinegar does contain a multitude of essential trace elements, many of which science has not decided a value for. The importance of trace elements continues to be uncovered by medical researchers. And evidence continues to mount that pure, natural foods are our best source for both minerals and vitamins. Newest findings show the number of elements and compounds in a good Apple Cider Vinegar make the ingredient list of most multivitamins look paltry by comparison.

So perhaps the future will reveal how vinegar helps promote good health. And for sure, it is a good, safe, recognized cleaner. It is kind to the planet and it protects the environment.

If you want to radiate good health and well-being for as many decades as possible, you should look very carefully at your diet and lifestyle. How you conduct your life can ensure a more radiant, abundant future. Most illness in individuals over 50 is due to degenerative diseases: arthritis, cancer, and cardiovascular disturbances like heart attacks and strokes. And most physicians agree these are diseases which are affected by what you eat and how you live.

Through the ages, many have felt Apple Cider Vinegar could play a part in a healthy lifestyle. You cannot control your medical history or genes. They create within you certain tendencies and weaknesses. But you can control some of your future. You control what you eat and how much exercise you get. This is the only body you have, so you better take care of it. And that's what this book is about -- some preventive maintenance.

Beyond that, much of what this book does is relate history. The interpretation must be left to you, the reader.

Do remember, old-time remedies have value but they cannot take the place of medical advice. When you are sick, you should seek the guidance of a competent medical practitioner. For everyday healthy living and cleaning, you may want to try some of these old-time ways with vinegar.

Emily

Chapter One

Stay Young Forever

So you want to live forever!

Apple cider vinegar contains the healthy goodness of apples, concentrated into a teaspoon of golden liquid. It is packed with essential amino acids and healthful enzymes. And so it comes as no surprise that some individuals have claimed this natural storehouse of vitamins and minerals will cure all that ails mankind — and even extend life and youthfulness.

Is apple cider vinegar an instant remedy for all the ills of this world? A magical nostrum? A mystical elixir? A liquid cure all? Some believe it is something very close to this!

Traditional medical systems are sickness oriented — designed to respond to illness. But good health, and extending the prime of life, begins with a body which is maintained, every single day, by good eating and health practices. A healthy, ageless body requires a diet rich in a wide assortment of nutrients. And the safest way to get adequate nutrients is to supply the body with a varied diet. It should meet all known nutritional requirements and be enhanced with lots of trace elements.

Perhaps this is why apple cider vinegar has the reputation of being an almost magical tonic — one of the most healthful, nutrient filled fluids known to mankind. A teaspoon of this golden liquid supplies a generous portion of the building blocks needed to be a healthy person. This potent substance is endowed with a multitude of vitamins, minerals and essential amino acids.

Scientists know humans need very tiny amounts of hundreds of as yet largely unidentified compounds. Nutritional researchers are constantly discovering minerals, enzymes, amino acids, and other substances and essences the body needs for complete health. Exactly how the body uses trace elements remains a medical mystery. Nor has science identified the amount needed of most of them.

Doctors do know a tiny deficiency, a missing milli-micro-gram of an important element can result in sickness, premature aging, or damage to the mind. The best advice nutritional scientists can give is to eat a diet of assorted foods, making a broad spectrum of nutrients available to the body.

Since the beginning of time mankind has sought the magic elixir which bubbles from the fabled "Fountain of Youth." For most of us, apple cider vinegar may be as close as we'll ever come to such a universal remedy. Because, you see, the secret to eternal youth is already ours. It is simply to be vital and able to enjoy a zestful, vigorous, life every single day we live.

So, it is no wonder apple cider vinegar is a time-honored prescription for those who want to retain vitality and good health well into old age. Through the ages it has been prescribed as an aid in maintaining general health, preventing disease, controlling weight, easing the discomfort of coughs, colds and breathing difficulties, and settling a disturbed digestive system.

Because old-time remedies (such as those in this book) are handed down from parent to child to grandchild, over many generations, changes occur. Families develop their own variations. Yet, there is one constant theme: some small amount of apple cider vinegar, taken each day, somehow brings better health and longer life. Some of these old-time beliefs about what apple cider vinegar could do follow (remember, these are only folk remedies, not scientifically proven cures!):

LIVE A LONG, HEALTHY, VITAL LIFE

Ensure long life and health by drinking vinegar every day. Simply add a tablespoon to a full glass of water and drink it down.

The way to stay healthy and alert, well into old age, is to combine 1 teaspoon of vinegar, 1 teaspoon of honey, and a full glass of water. Take this tonic 3 times a day, 1/2 hour before meals.

For a long, vigorous life, filled with robust good health, sip a vinegar tonic, very slowly, before each meal. Mix together and begin drinking immediately: 1 cup warm water, 2 tablespoons apple cider vinegar, and 1 teaspoon honey.

The most palatable way to take a daily dose of vinegar is to add a small dollop of clover honey to a tablespoon of vinegar and a teaspoon of olive oil. Mix it all together and drip this healthy dressing over a small bowl of greens.

A health promoting salad dressing can be made from 1/4 cup vinegar, 1/4 cup corn oil, and 1/8 cup honey. Mix well and serve at the evening meal to keep the whole family in good health.

Memory can be greatly improved by drinking a glass of warm water before each meal, with a teaspoon of apple cider vinegar stirred in.

FIGHT GERMS

To relieve the pain of a sore throat caused by a cold, mix together 1/4 cup honey and 1/4 cup apple cider vinegar. Take 1 tablespoon every 4 hours. May be taken more often if needed.

Ease the discomfort of a sore throat and speed healing by sipping occasionally on a syrup made of 1/2 cup apple cider vinegar, 1/2 cup water, 1 teaspoon cayenne pepper, and 3 tablespoons honey.

A vinegar gargle can ease the pain of a sore throat. Just gargle with a glass of warm water to which a tablespoon of apple cider vinegar has been added. Repeat as needed. This also acts as a great mouthwash!

Soothe a dry night cough by sprinkling the pillowcase with apple cider vinegar.

A small amount of vinegar, taken every day, keeps the urinary tract nice and acidy. This is useful to reduce the likelihood of getting a kidney or bladder infection.

To chase away a cold, soak an eight-inch square of brown paper (cut from a paper grocery bag) in apple cider vinegar. When the paper is saturated, sprinkle it with pepper and bind to the chest with cloth strips, pepper side of the paper next to the skin. After 20 minutes, remove the paper and wash the chest, being careful not to become chilled.

LOOK BETTER, FEEL BETTER

The most marvelous tonic for the feet is to walk back and forth in ankle deep bath water to which 1/2 cup apple cider vinegar has been added. Do this for 5 minutes, first thing in the morning, and for 5 minutes before retiring in the evening. Hot, aching feet will feel cooled and soothed.

If troubled by the itching and peeling of athlete's foot, soak socks or hose in vinegar water. Mix 1 part vinegar with 5 parts water and soak for 30 minutes before washing as usual.

A full head of healthy, richly colored hair can be ensured, well into old age. You need only to start each day with a glass of water to which has been added 4 teaspoons each of apple cider vinegar, black strap molasses, and honey.

Apple cider vinegar is helpful in melting away excess pounds. Simply drink a glass of warm water, with a single teaspoon of apple cider vinegar stirred in, before each meal. It moderates the over-robust appetite and melts away fat.

Now, whether vinegar actually burns up fatty calories, reins in the over-lusty inclination for partaking of provisions, or simply fills one up with tart vinegar-water, the results are the same. You eat less and the pounds melt away!

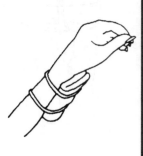

Asthma can be relieved by combining the advantages of accupressure with the benefits of apple cider vinegar. Use a wide rubber band to hold gauze pads, which have been soaked in vinegar, to the inside of the wrists.

Heavily soiled hands can be cleaned, while giving them a soothing treatment. Simply scrub with cornmeal, moistened with apple cider vinegar. Then rinse in cool water and pat dry.

You can banish dandruff and make hair shiny and healthy if you rinse after every shampoo with: one-half cup apple cider vinegar mixed into two cups of warm water.

Use a vinegar and water rinse to eliminate frizz from over-permed hair. It also brightens dark hair and adds sparkle to blond hair.

Ensure soft, radiant skin and prevent blemishes by conditioning the skin while sleeping with a covering of strawberries and vinegar. Mash 3 large strawberries into 1/4 cup vinegar and let it sit for 2 hours. Then strain the vinegar through a cloth. Pat the strawberry flavored vinegar onto the face and neck. Wash off in the morning. Skin will soon be free of pimples and blackheads.

Corns and calluses will fall away, overnight, if you treat them with a vinegar compress. Simply tape 1/2 of a slice of stale bread (which has been soaked with apple cider vinegar) to the offending lump. By morning the skin will look smooth and new.

Ladies can protect their skin from the ravages of the summer sun by applying a protective of olive oil and apple cider vinegar. Mixed half and half, this combination helps prevent sunburn and chapping.

Age spots (some call them liver spots) can be gotten rid of if you wipe them daily with onion juice and vinegar. 1 teaspoon onion juice and 2 teaspoons vinegar should be mixed together and applied with a soft cloth. Or, 1/2 a fresh onion can be dipped into a small dish of vinegar and then rubbed across the offending skin. In a few weeks the spot will begin to fade.

Itchy welts and hives, swellings, and blemishes can be eased by the application of a paste made from vinegar and cornstarch. Just pat it on and feel the itch being drawn out as the paste dries.

Relieve the discomfort and unsightliness of varicose veins by wrapping the legs with a cloth wrung out of apple cider vinegar. Leave this on, with the legs propped up, for 30 minutes, morning and evening. Considerable relief will be noticed within 6 weeks. To speed up the healing process, follow each treatment with a glass of warm water, to which a teaspoon of apple cider vinegar has been added. Sip slowly, and add a teaspoon of honey if feeling overtired.

EASE PAIN & SUFFERING

Headaches will fade away if you follow this simple procedure: add a dash of apple cider vinegar to the water in a vaporizer and inhale the vapors for 5 minutes. Lay quietly and the headache should be relieved in 20 minutes.

Hiccups will disappear if you sip, very slowly, a glass of warm water with 1 teaspoon of vinegar in it. This works even better if you sip from the far side of the glass!

An unsettled stomach will calm down if you sip quietly on a glass of very warm water, to which has been added 1 tablespoon honey and 1 tablespoon vinegar. This is also good for easing gas.

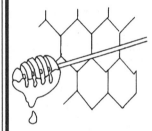

If a headache will not go away, try a paper bag hat. Soak the bottom of the open edges of a brown paper bag in apple cider vinegar. Put the bag on the head (like a chef's hat) and tie it in place with a long scarf. The headache should be relieved in 45 minutes.

Those plagued with nighttime leg cramps can find relief by supplementing meals with a glass of water, fortified with apple cider vinegar.

Prevent leg cramps by combining 1 teaspoon honey, 1 teaspoon apple cider vinegar, and 1 tablespoon calcium lactate in 1/2 glass of water. This is taken once a day.

Soothe tired or sprained muscles by wrapping the afflicted area with a cloth wrung out of apple cider vinegar. Leave it on for 3 to 5 minutes and repeat as needed. For extra special relief, add a good dash of cayenne pepper to the vinegar.

Banish the discomfort of nausea or vomiting by placing a cloth wrung out of warm apple cider vinegar on the stomach. Replace with another warm cloth when it cools.

Chapter Two

Vinegar Fights Disease*

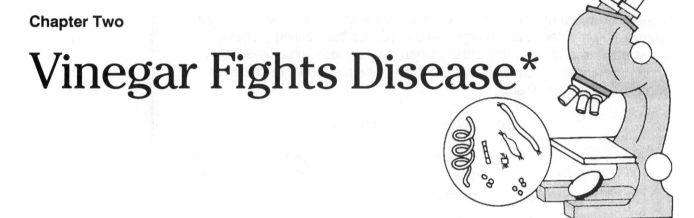

Apple cider vinegar enthusiasts can recite a long list of ailments it is reported to be able to cure or prevent. It is claimed vinegar can banish arthritis, forestall osteoporosis, prevent cancer, kill infection, condition the skin, aid digestion, control weight, preserve memory, and protect the mind from aging.

On the pages which follow, some of the most recent findings of medical researchers, and the way this research impacts on vinegar therapy, are recorded. Also included are some of the more enduring traditional remedies.

Tannins are naturally astringent preservatives

Cider is a blend of juices pressed from chopped apples

Can apple cider vinegar possibly do all that is claimed for it? One answer may be: "Yes, because it is such a marvelous combination of tart good taste and germ killing acids." Vinegar is fermented from sweet apple cider, and takes its honey-gold color from tannins which flow from ruptured cell walls of fresh, ripe apples. When these naturally occurring, colorless preservatives, come into contact with air they develop the rich, golden color we associate with cider. This is called enzymatic browning. It contributes to the distinctive flavor of cider, a flavor with more spunk than simple apple juice.

Vinegar is made when fresh, naturally sweet cider is fermented into an alcoholic beverage (hard cider). Then it is fermented once again. The result is vinegar.

Apple cider vinegar contains more than thirty important nutrients, a dozen minerals, over half a dozen vitamins and essential acids, and several enzymes. Plus, it has a large dose of pectin for a healthy heart.

When apple cider vinegar is exposed to heat and air, it gives off some hints of its character. Take a healthy sniff and what you inhale is the 'volatile' part of vinegar — the portion which will evaporate easily. Scientists

*Please remember, if you have a specific illness, or take medication regularly, discuss the effects of adding vinegar to your diet with your doctor.

recently analyzed this small part of what vinegar is. They found 93 different volatile components they were able to recognize, plus others as yet to be classified! Vinegar has:

7 Hydrocarbons	7 Bases
18 Alcohols	3 Furans
4 Acids	13 Phenols
33 Carbonyls (4 aldehydes and 29 ketones)	
8 Esters (plus 11 lactone esters)	

The exact composition of a particular vinegar depends on what it was made from. Even apple cider vinegar varies with the kind and condition of the apples in it. Partly because of this, medical scientists do not always know exactly how or why it promotes healing. They do know it is both antiseptic and antibiotic.

VINEGAR'S EARLIEST MEDICAL USES

An early Assyrian medical text described the treatment for ear pain as being the application of vinegar.

In 400BC, Hippocrates (considered the Father of Medicine) used vinegar to treat his patients. This naturally occurring germ killer was one of the very first "medicines."

Vinegar was used as a healing dressing on wounds and infectious sores in Biblical times.

"Thieves Vinegar" got its name during the time of the Great Plague of Europe. Some enterprising thieves are said to have used vinegar to protect them from contamination while they robbed the homes of plague victims.

Vinegar is credited with saving the lives of thousands of soldiers during the U.S. Civil War. It was routinely used as a disinfectant on wounds.

VINEGAR AND THE SKIN

Historically, infections on the face, around the eyes, and in the ears have been treated with a solution of vinegar and water. It works because vinegar is antiseptic (it kills germs on contact) and antibiotic (it contains bacteria which is unfriendly to infectious microorganisms).

More recently, vinegar has been used to treat chronic middle ear diseases when traditional drug-based methods fail. One treatment

Vinegar has acetic acid, plus iso-butyric, lactic + propionic acids.

Cider contains phosphorus, potassium, chlorine, sodium, magnesium, sulfur, calcium, iron, flourine + silicon.

National Center for Health Statistics says ear infections are the most frequent diagnosis made by children's doctors.

13

currently being prescribed for ear infections at Ohio State University's hospital is irrigation with vinegar.

Doctors are currently considering the possibility of treating some eye infections with diluted vinegar. Right now, they are using it as a hospital disinfectant. One example of this use is at Yale-New Haven Hospital. When after-surgery eye infections became a problem, their Department of Bacteriology solved the problem with common vinegar. The hospital began routinely cleaning the scrub-room sink with a 1/2% solution of ordinary household vinegar. It worked better at eliminating the offending bacteria than the commercial product it replaced!

Two old-time remedies for treating mild burns were to douse the hurt with apple cider vinegar or to let a snail crawl over it. If you don't have a friendly snail around, you may want to try dabbing a bit of apple cider vinegar onto the painful area. Vinegar is particularly useful for neutralizing alkali burns.

Relieve itchy skin, too, by patting on apple cider vinegar. If the itch is near the eyes or other delicate areas dilute the vinegar, 4 parts water to 1 part vinegar. For a full body treatment, put 2 or 3 cups in the bath water. A handful of thyme can help, too.

Dampen a gauze square in apple cider vinegar and apply, gently, to ease rectal itching.

Use a cloth moistened in vinegar to clean armpits. Do not rinse it off and it will eliminate offensive odors for several hours.

Cool the burning of a sunburn by bathing in a tub of lukewarm water, to which a cup of apple cider vinegar has been added. Anytime a sprain or ache needs to be soaked in very hot water, a splash of vinegar in the water will make the water seem cooler.

One reason vinegar is so very helpful in treating skin disorders is that it has a pH which is nearly the same as healthy skin. So, applying vinegar helps to normalize the pH of the skin's surface.

VINEGAR, FIBER AND CHOLESTEROL

Vinegar contains a treasure trove of complex carbohydrates, as well as a good dose of that mysterious stuff called "dietary fiber." Both complex carbohydrates and dietary fiber have been recommended by the U.S. Surgeon General to help build resistance to cancer.

Ear infections heal faster if the ear is washed out with vinegar

About fibers ... yes, there are different kinds of fibers. Some are water soluble and some are not. A water soluble fiber soaks up water (adding bulk) but also has the power to interact with the body. Insoluble fibers soak up water (adding bulk) but do not interact with the body in the same complex way soluble fibers do.

When vinegar is made from fresh, natural apples it contains a healthy dose of pectin. Pectin is a soluble fiber. It dissolves in water, making it very available for the body to use. In addition to soaking up water, it slows down the absorption of food and liquid in the intestines. Therefore, it stays in the body longer than an insoluble fiber.

An insoluble fiber, such as wheat bran, rushes through the system. Particularly, it rushes through the intestines. This gives it laxative properties. Wheat bran may also produce large amounts of gas.

As pectin (apple cider vinegar fiber) works its slow, gentle way through the digestive system it binds to cholesterol. Then pectin pulls the cholesterol which is bound to it out of the body. Less cholesterol in the body makes for a reduced risk of cardiovascular problems, such as heart attacks and strokes.

VINEGAR AND DIGESTION

Apple cider vinegar is very similar to the chemicals found naturally in the stomach. Because of this, it has traditionally been hailed as an aid to digestion. And so, by improving digestion, it is felt it will improve the overall metabolism of the body.

Those who regularly imbibe of this elixir feel it helps cuts and abrasions heal faster, as well as speeding up the healing of more serious wounds.

Vinegar is considered by many to be able to attack and kill harmful bacteria which has invaded the digestive tract. This may lessen the likelihood of the body developing toxemia and other blood-borne infections.

Some doctors suggest regular vinegar use to prevent food poisoning. They recommend its use when visiting questionable restaurants or foreign countries. The usual dose is to take 1 tablespoon of vinegar, 30 minutes before meals. It can be mixed with a glass of water, vegetable juice, or any other beverage. Honey added to vinegar and water makes the taste more palatable for most people.

A vinegar experiment anyone can try is to use it to make legumes more digestible, and so less gas producing. Just splash a little vinegar in the pot when cooking dried beans. It will make them tender and easy on the digestive system.

Vinegar adds fiber + is low in fat, salt + sugar.

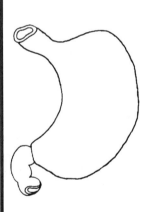

VINEGAR, BETA CAROTENE, AND CANCER

Aging, heart disease, cancer, and cataracts are symptoms of the harm done to the human body by free radicals, the "loose cannons" of the cell world. They damage chromosomes and are probably responsible for many of the physical changes associated with aging.

Free radicals roam through plants, animals, and humans, bouncing from cell to cell, damaging each in turn. Antioxidants absorb free radicals, making them harmless. Beta carotene, a carotenoid found in vinegar, is a powerful antioxidant.

Carotenoid occurs naturally in plants such as apples. Vinegar's beta carotene is in a natural, easy to digest form. One example of how this antioxidant contributes to maintaining good health is the way it protects the eye from cataracts. Cataract development is related to oxidation of the eye's lens. This happens when free radicals alter its structure. Studies show that eating lots of antioxidant containing foods decreases the risk of forming cataracts.

A correlation between eating lots of foods containing beta carotene and a lower risk of cancer has also been documented. Researchers, in more than 70 different studies, agree beta carotene lowers the risk of getting cancer. They include those at the State University of New York at Stony Brook, the University of Western Ontario in Canada, Tufts University, and Johns Hopkins School of Medicine.

In addition to giving cancer protection, beta carotene boosts the body's immune system. It works by attacking the free radicals which destroy the immune system.

Carotenoids are also the body's raw material for producing vitamin A, another potent antioxidant. They act together to protect from cancers associated with chemical toxins. According to National Cancer Research in England, when the body does not get enough vitamin A, it is particularly susceptible to cancers of the respiratory system, bladder and colon.

Old timers have long recommended taking a teaspoon of vinegar, every day, in a tall glass of vegetable juice. With all we now know about fiber and beta carotene, this may turn out to be very good advice!

VINEGAR AND MEMORY*

Memory loss is one of the most common and costly diseases of the elderly. Its price to this country is $44 billion a year, which is only the cost

Carotenoids probably protect plants from solar radiation.

A diet high in beta carotene helps prevent cataracts & cancer

* For more information about saving your memory, see the Order Form for Mind Power . . . Memory Magic!

16

in dollars. The real cost is in disrupted lives. Quality of life is ruined for those with memory loss, and often for their loved ones as well.

The three most common causes of memory loss are: Alzheimer's disease, multiple strokes (multi-infarct dementia) and alcohol abuse. Many other elders endure mental impairment caused by poor nutrition and reactions to prescription drugs.

Too often memory loss in individuals who are over 55 is treated as if it were irreversible or inevitable. Yet, information continues to pile up which proves memory loss can be successfully treated. More and more doctors are echoing the words of one specialist:

"...several of the causes are treatable, resulting in an arrest or actual reversal of the symptoms."

Diet is an important factor in control of risk factors for memory loss, and to reverse damage which has already been done. Good nutrition can decrease the likelihood of stroke by lowering cholesterol. It can also protect the mind from some of the worse causes of loss of mental function. The Journal of the American Dietetic Association puts it this way:

"Some forms of dementia — those due to excessive alcohol intake or vitamin deficiency — may be entirely preventable and partially reversible through diet."

Dementia which is associated with excessive alcohol intake is particularly treatable. The Journal goes on to say:

"In all types of dementia, adequate nutrition may improve physical well-being, help maximize the patients' functioning, and improve the quality of life."

Some studies indicate nutritional deficiencies are a problem for 36% of the over 80 year old population. And, nearly half of all nursing home patients have been shown to have some vitamin or mineral deficiency. These lower than normal levels of vitamins and minerals are important because they contribute to loss of mental ability. For example, memory loss is more frequent in patients who have lower than normal blood levels of vitamin B-12 and folate.

Apple cider vinegar supplies a balanced dose of vital amino acids, vitamins, and minerals that both the mind and body need for good health.

The worst of the mind robbing diseases associated with aging is Alzheimer's disease (AD). Some studies show AD sufferers are particularly short of calcium, thiamin and niacin. And low serum B-12 levels have been reported in up to 30% of elderly patients with this kind of dementia. Almost every patient in a recent study of nutrient deficiencies showed complete recovery when given B-12 therapy. Folate supplements also proved valuable.

Thiamin deficiency is another nutritional cause of chronic memory problems. If the diet is sufficiently short of this nutrient, nerve cell loss and hemorrhages in the brain can result. Experts continue to remind us:

"...dietary modification may play an important role in the control of several ...diseases that may produce a dementia..."

The more we learn about good nutrition and the importance of getting an assortment of vitamins and minerals each day, the easier it is to understand old-time reliance on apple cider vinegar. One grandmother suggests this way to a healthy old age:

"Stir a teaspoon of apple cider vinegar and a teaspoon of honey into a glass of water and drink it with your meal. Do this 3 times a day to remain bright and alert all your life."

Treating malnutrition with megadoses of vitamins is being tested, with mixed results. Sometimes it is difficult to get the balanced dose a particular individual may need. And, there is always the possibility of doing harm by giving too many vitamins, or of giving an overdose of minerals. Vitamin therapy can also be expensive.

It is much better to prevent nutrient shortages by eating a balanced diet. And, for balancing the diet, it is hard to match the nutritional storehouse contained in a tablespoon of apple cider vinegar.

VINEGAR AND ARTHRITIS

Arthritis sufferers spend $8 to $10 billion each year searching for relief - relief that, too often, does not come. Those who are feeling the pain of arthritis will try almost anything to be free of the disease. This often results in large sums of money being spent on supposed cures which do not improve health, relieve chronic pain, or stop the progression of the disease.

The Select Committee on Aging's Subcommittee on Health and Long Term Care (House of Representatives, 98th Congress) calls the marketing of supposed arthritis cures a $10 billion a year scandal. In reporting on this, the Journal of the American Dietetic Association notes that both medical and nutrition authorities agree on one important fact about arthritis care:

The only specific treatment for arthritis is "weight control ... and a nutrient-dense diet ...."

This respected journal goes on to explain the conclusions nutritional scientists have drawn from studies of the eating habits of arthritis sufferers:

Sometimes the patient's diet is found to be "... grossly deficient in some nutrients."

Perhaps this helps to explain the long-standing belief by many that apple cider vinegar can play an important part in relieving the pain and slowing the progression of arthritis. At the very least it is less likely to hurt the one taking it than some of the more outrageous chemicals which have been advertised as being able to ease the symptoms of arthritis. And, in addition, it is inexpensive!

The time-honored vinegar recipe for dealing with arthritis is 1 teaspoon honey and 1 teaspoon apple cider vinegar, mixed into a glass of water and taken morning and evening.

Others believe the proper dose is to drink a glass of water, with 2 teaspoons vinegar in it, before each meal (3 times a day).

Another tonic which has often been recommended for those who suffer from arthritis' discomfort combines vinegar with celery, Epsom salts, and citrus (for vitamin C). Combine in a saucepan:

1/2 grapefruit	2 stalks celery
1 orange	4 cups water
1 lemon	

Cut the celery and fruit (including the peelings) into chunks. Simmer in water, uncovered, for 1 hour. Press the softened foods through a jelly bag and then stir in 1 tablespoon vinegar and 1 tablespoon Epsom salts. Drink a full glass of water, morning and evening, to which 1/4 cup of this tonic has been added.

With any of these vinegar regimens, expect it to take about a month for relief to begin. For more immediate results, many doctors say a gentle rubdown may help. One old-time liniment combines vinegar and oil with egg whites:

Epsom salts, which contain magnesium sulfate, have long been used to fight inflammation

Magnesium Sulfate is called "Epsom Salts" because it was once obtained by boiling down water from the English town of Epsom.

2 egg whites	1/2 cup vinegar
1/2 cup turpentine	1/4 cup olive oil

Mix all the ingredients together and use right away. Gently massage aching joints with this mixture, then wipe it off with a soft cloth. (Most all medical authorities would recommend leaving the turpentine out of this remedy, as it can cause skin irritation.)

VINEGAR AND IRON

Children, adolescents and adult women of child-bearing age should be sure to consume generous amounts of foods that are high in iron. The U.S. Surgeon General stresses that iron deficiency is a special problem for those in low-income families.

Others who should be sure they are getting lots of iron in their diets are high users of aspirin. Aspirin frequently causes intestinal blood loss, making the person at risk for iron deficiency.

One long-standing solution to low iron intake is to cook in iron pots. Each time one of these pans is used, some iron leaches into food. The higher the acid content of foods, the more iron will be absorbed into food. Adding a splash of vinegar to meats, sauces, and stews will raise their acid content. This increases the amount of iron they leach from iron pans.

To prevent anemia, the body needs iron, B-12, folate and a wide range of other nutrients. Apple cider vinegar delivers many of these nutrients, in an easy to digest and absorb form.

VINEGAR AND CALCIUM

Calcium is the most abundant mineral in the human body. Besides its well-known part in forming bones, calcium is necessary for many other parts of the body to work properly. Although only 1% of the body's calcium is found outside the skeleton, without this small amount muscles do not contract properly, blood clotting is affected, and neural function is seriously impaired.

Calcium absorption is affected by the amount of certain other substances in the body. For example, a diet too rich in phosphorus can cause calcium not to be absorbed properly. Or, eating too much protein can interfere with calcium absorption. Then, even if enough calcium is eaten, the body cannot draw it out of food and use it.

15 to 20 million Americans currently suffer from osteoporosis

Osteoporosis is literally, porous bones!

Each year over 300,000 women suffer fractured hips. 200,000 will never return to normal life. Nearly 45,000 will die within six months of the fractures from complications. Other thousands find their spinal column begins to collapse, reducing height and producing the back deformity known as a widow's hump. Osteoporosis is a major factor in these disabling fractures.

As the body ages it is less and less efficient at pulling calcium from food. Complicating this is the fact that with age, people tend to take in less and less calcium. Some of this is because many older individuals develop lactose intolerance, causing them to drop calcium-rich dairy products from their diets.

And so it comes as no surprise that many individuals find their bones begin to shrink as they get older. As osteoporosis advances, bones decrease in both size and density. The result is porous, fragile bones that fracture easily. It is a serious health problem, causing deformity, disability, and pain.

Bones, you see, are living tissue. They are constantly being rebuilt and replaced. Whenever there is a shortage of calcium in muscles, blood, or nerves, the body pulls it from bones.

Apple cider vinegar contains a trace of needed calcium. It can also be used to dissolve calcium in soup bones. Several recent scientific reports show that when vinegar is added to the water in which soup bones are cooked, it leaches calcium from the bones and deposits it in the soup stock!

Some time-honored ways to combine vinegar and calcium, and some new ways medical research validates vinegar's use follow.

To make a delicious, low calorie, calcium-rich chicken soup you will need:

1/2	cup vinegar	2	bouillon cubes
3 lbs.	chicken bones	2	slightly beaten egg whites
3/4	cup tiny pasta	2	tablespoons chopped parsley

Begin with a gallon of water and at least 1/2 cup vinegar. Gently simmer 2 or 3 pounds of bones (chicken wings are a good choice) for about 2 hours, uncovered. Strain the broth and skim off all fat. Strip the meat from the bones and add the chicken, pasta, and bouillon cubes to the stock. Bring to a boil and cook for 10 minutes. Remove from heat and immediately dribble the egg whites into the hot liquid, stirring continuously. Mix in the parsley and serve. This soup is low calorie, healthy, and it adds calcium to the diet!

Cramps, gas and diarrhea after eating milk products are symptoms of lactose intolerance.

The inability to digest lactose, a sugar in dairy products, increases with age.

As little as one tablespoon of vinegar per quart of water can make a difference in the calcium which is pulled from boiled soup bones. A stronger vinegar solution (such as that used above) results in even more calcium being added to soup!

Another way to add calcium to the diet is to crumble feta cheese over torn greens. Use spinach, collards, beet tops, and kale, in addition to lettuce leaves. Sprinkle on a mixture of 2 tablespoons apple cider vinegar, 2 tablespoons honey, and 2 tablespoons water.

Newest research describes calcium supplements as being useful in the prevention and treatment of osteoporosis. And so, many doctors and nutritionists recommend them. Calcium supplements are prescribed for those with calcium deficient diets, elders who do not metabolize calcium adequately, and for those with increased calcium needs (this can include postmenopausal women). This calcium is usually added to the diet by taking calcium tablets, or in the form of antacid tablets.

The US Pharmacopeia Convention sets standards for drugs. It says a calcium tablet should dissolve in a maximum time of 30 minutes. An antacid tablet should be completely broken down in 10 minutes. If a tablet takes longer to break up than the recommended time, its usefulness is seriously impaired.

Studies estimate that more than half of the popular calcium supplements on the market do not meet the recommended timetable. Yet, calcium supplements can only be properly used by the body if they disintegrate in a reasonable length of time after being taken.

A simple to use vinegar test can tell you whether or not your calcium supplement dissolves in time for your body to digest it properly:

• Drop the calcium supplement tablet into three ounces of room temperature vinegar.

• Stir briskly, once every five minutes.

• At the end of 30 minutes the tablet should be completely disintegrated.

Tests by medical researchers found that times varied widely among the most popular brands. One brand of calcium supplement tablet broke up, completely, in three minutes. Another popular brand tablet was still mostly intact after 30 minutes.

15 to 20 million Americans are affected by osteoporosis. This contributes to the 1.3 million bone fractures, every year, that occur in

Research indicates cooking longer than 2 hours doesn't add much extra calcium.

The average adult diet includes only about 50% of the recommended level of calcium.

individuals over 45 years old. Over the years, this adds up to a lot of disability. For example, one out of every three women over 65 has at least one fractured vertebra. When these tiny back bones crack, they can cause disabling pain.

Hip fractures are an even bigger problem. By 90 years of age, one out of every six men and one out of every three women will have suffered a fractured hip. One out of each five hip fractures leads to death. Long term nursing care is required for many others. All told, osteoporosis costs this country more than $10 billion every year.

As the body ages, the stomach produces less acid. Some believe this fact contributes to calcium shortages in elders. After all, acid is needed to dissolve almost all calcium supplement tablets. One solution may be to take calcium supplements with an old-fashioned vinegar tonic. It not only has acid for dissolving calcium, it adds the bit of extra calcium which is in vinegar!

VINEGAR AND BORON

Have you had your boron today? If you began the day with apple cider vinegar your body is probably well fortified against boron deficiency. This critical trace element is needed for good health and strong bones.

Boron is a mineral which is necessary for both plant and animal life. When it is not readily available to plants, they do not grow properly. Some become dwarfs and others crack and become disfigured. The human body does not make strong, straight bones when it is missing from the diet. One reason for this is that boron plays a critical role in the way the body uses calcium. Without boron, calcium cannot form and maintain strong bones.

When vinegar releases its boron into the body, all sorts of wonderfully healthy things begin to happen. Boron affects the way steroid hormones are released. Then it regulates both their use and how long they stay active in the body.

How boron builds bones is just now beginning to be understood by scientists. One of the few things they do know is it makes changes in the way the membrane around individual cells works.

The boron and hormone connection is vital to bone formation. Blood and tissue levels of several steroid hormones (such as estrogen and testosterone) increase dramatically in the presence of boron. Both of these are needed to complete the calcium-to-bone growth cycle. This

Beware: bone meal sometimes recommended as a calcium supplement, may contain toxic amounts of lead!

23

relationship between hormones, boron, and calcium helps to explain why estrogen replacement is about the only treatment for osteoporosis.

Some other trace elements necessary for maintaining bone mass are manganese, silicon, and magnesium. Some doctors recommend supplements of all of them for post-menopausal women, even though no one knows exactly how they work. Many feel boron is useful for treating a lot of the ailments (such as arthritis) that doctors are not able to treat successfully with drugs.

We do know that apple cider vinegar supplies boron, as well as manganese, silicon, and magnesium to the body. Even more important, it does so in a balanced-by-nature way.

JAPANESE RICE VINEGAR AND HEALTH

Taking vinegar and honey as a life enhancing tonic is more than merely an American custom. In Japan it is an old favorite, too.

Japan's most famous vinegar is made from rice. The bulk of Japanese commercial vinegar is made from wine leftovers. The sediment left from the production of the rice wine called "sake" is used to make industrial vinegar. These dregs, called "lees," produce a vinegar which is similar in nutrient value to our white vinegar.

The rice vinegar which is used for cooking and healing remedies is made directly from brown rice. Belief in the healing nature of this deeply colored rice vinegar has come down through thousands of years of Japanese culture.

Some ways of using vinegar that have endured for centuries - and some of Japan's newest research into the healing power of rice vinegar follow:

According to the Japan Food Research Laboratories, vinegar made directly from brown rice has five times the amount of amino acids as the commercial product made from lees. Perhaps the healthful benefits of rice vinegar are because of the 20 amino acids it contains. Or maybe it is the 16 organic acids which can be found in it.

The bottom of the bottle of even the best rice vinegar will have a fine rice sediment. When these grounds are disturbed they give the vinegar a muddy appearance. This dark residue is considered to be the mark of a high quality rice vinegar.

Recent research by Dr. Yoshio Takino, of Shizuka University in Japan, proved vinegar helps to maintain good health and slow down aging by helping to prevent the formation of two fatty peroxides. This is important to good health and long life in two important ways. One is associated with damaging free radicals. The other with the cholesterol formations which build up on blood vessel walls.

In Japan, vinegar is used to produce one of that country's most potent folk remedies. Tamago-su, or egg vinegar, is made by immersing a whole, raw egg in a cup of rice vinegar. The egg and vinegar are allowed to set, undisturbed, for seven days. During this time the vinegar dissolves the egg, shell and all.

At the end of one week the only part of the egg which has not been dissolved is the transparent membrane, located just inside the shell. The Tamago-su maker splits open this membrane and dumps its contents into the glass of vinegar. This piece of the egg is discarded and what remains is thoroughly mixed.

A small amount of this very powerful egg vinegar is taken three times a day, stirred into a glass of hot water. It is believed it will assure a long, healthy life. Traditionally, Samurai warriors considered egg vinegar tonic to be an important source of strength and power.

Vinegar is used as a bleaching agent on white vegetables. It also prevents enzymatic browning. When foods do not darken in air, they do not develop the off-taste associated with browning. Rice vinegar is also used in salad dressings, marinades, sauces, dips, and spreads.

Rice vinegar (like all vinegars) is a powerful antiseptic. It kills, on contact, dangerous bacteria such as salmonella and streptococcus.

The sushi industry is largely dependent on vinegar's ability to prevent germs from growing on the raw fish. It is sprinkled on the fish, included in dipping sauces, and used as a preservative.

Vinegar acts as a tenderizer on meats and vegetables used in stir-fry dishes.

Japanese housewives add a little rice vinegar to summer rice to prevent it from spoiling.

Vinegar, added to fish dishes, helps to eliminate the traditional fishy odor. It also helps get rid of fish smells at clean up time.

Enzymatic browning gives apple cider its color + tang.

Without vinegar, there would be no sushi!

Chapter Three

Where Did Vinegar Come From?

3,000 years before barley is grown to make beer—

4,000 years before all of Mesopotamia is engulfed in a disastrous flood—

5,000 years before wheeled vehicles appear in Sumeria or the Egyptians learn to plow—

—An enterprising householder prepares some fresh, naturally sweetened juice and seals it tightly in a stone jar. In a short time it ferments into the mildly intoxicating brew we call wine.

A very special day soon follows. The wine is left open to the air. A second fermentation takes place. Vinegar is created!

Imagine the surprise of the poor soul who took the first sip of this new brew. All the alcohol in the wine had turned into a sharp tasting acid! Had a partially filled wine cask been unknowingly set aside and left uncared for? Had a servant carelessly left the wine uncorked? Or could it possibly be ... did someone suspect the possibilities?

I've got the feeling vinegar has been around as long as apples!

No one knows for sure how it chanced to happen, but vinegar entered the world. And the event was momentous! Vinegar was found to be an almost universal preservative and cure-all. Vegetables submerged in this wonderful liquid kept their fresh color and crispness. Fish remained edible long after they should have rotted. Festering sores, when doused with it, began to heal. It only followed that mankind would confer an exalted status to this amazing concoction.

Our word "vinegar" comes from the French "vinaigre" - "VIN" for wine and "AIGRE" for sour. And that is just what it is: wine that has gone sour.

Although vinegar can be made from most any mildly sweet liquid, the most miraculous claims for health benefits are those linked to vinegar made from apple cider. So, unless literature specifically says otherwise, references to vinegar usually came to mean apple cider vinegar.

Once the ancient world recognized vinegar's value for healing and health, the intentional production of this amazing elixir began. Because vinegar could do so many miraculous things it is not surprising that the souring of apple cider into vinegar was often an elaborate process, with overtones of magic.

Vinegar making was, for thousands of years, more an art form than a science. The physical steps for making vinegar were often augmented with incantations and seemingly superfluous steps.

We now know the complicated recipes of the mediaeval alchemists were not needed. These early recipes owed their success to the accidental infection of their brews with organisms needed for fermentation. It was exposure to air which brought vinegar into being!

WHAT IS VINEGAR?

Technically, vinegar is an acid liquid made from wine, cider, beer (or most any mildly alcoholic beverage) by what is called an "acetous fermentation." What this means, is that alcohol mixes with oxygen in the air. The alcohol then "disappears." (Actually, it is changed into acetic acid and water.)

Acetic acid is what imparts the characteristic tart, puckery taste sensation to vinegar. The acetous fermentation which creates it is due to a tiny microorganism, the vinegar bacillus. This bacterium occurs naturally in the air, everywhere, and is why early vinegar producers were successful.

It was not until 1878, nearly 10,000 years after vinegar making began, that a microbiologist named Hansen correctly explained the chemical process which creates vinegar. He accurately described the three species of vinegar bacilli. These tiny creatures gobble up alcohol and excrete acid. The process where alcohols are changed to acids is called fermentation.

Fermenting is thought by many to endow the end product with a special ability to heal. It is also thought to sharply increase nutritional values. While the primary reason for fermenting foodstuffs was, originally, to keep them from rotting - the result can be better tasting than the original - just ask any pickle fanatic.

Vinegar contains dilute acetic acid. It also has the basic nature and essential nutrients of the original food from which it was made. For example, apple cider vinegar has pectin, beta carotene, and potassium from the apples that were its origin. In addition, it contains generous

Acetous fermentation is how alcoholic liquids, like beer or wine, yield acetic acid.

Don't confuse acetic acid ($C_2H_4O_2$) with vinegar - its often made from wood shavings.

27

portions of health-promoting enzymes and amino acids. These complex protein building blocks are formed during the fermentation process.

Claims for the curative and restorative powers of apple cider vinegar are legendary. Some believe this fabulous liquid is capable of solving the most vexing and tiresome of human afflictions. It has been said to lengthen life and improve hearing, vision, and mental powers.

Devotees claim it will help heartburn, clear up throat irritations, stop hiccups, relieve coughs, deal with diarrhea, and ease asthma.

Over the centuries vinegar became a commonplace remedy for many ills.* It was also found to be useful in cleaning, cooking, and food preservation. Some examples of ancient recipes for health, well-being and sanitation follow:

Ye may ease the rasping of the evening cough by sleeping with the head on a cloth which has been steeped in vinegar.

An aching throat will be eased by rinsing it with water which has been made to blush by the addition of vinegar.

Difficult breathing may be eased by wrapping strips of white cloth, well dampened with vinegar, around the wrists.

Ye may purify the waters of the body by sipping a tonic of goodly vinegar, mixed with clear running water.

Those who sup regularly of the miraculous vinegar will be blessed with a sharp mind for all their life.

Bumps, lumps, and knots of the flesh may be relieved by the timely application of a binding soaked in the best vinegar.

Itching of the flesh may be relieved by the frequent application of vinegar.

Alleviate the discomfort of aching in the lower limbs by wrapping the afflicted area with a cloth wrung out of apple cider vinegar. When the binding begins to dry, renew it with fresh vinegar.

* For more old-time healing ways, see the Order Form for Home Remedies from the Old South.

Make the suffering of one who speweth up their food less grievous by covering the belly with a well washed cloth, well soaked in warm vinegar.

Before scrubbing garments, sprinkle them with vinegar to make the task lighter. This will also make the fabric more agreeable.

Vinegar and salt added to washing water will drive bugs from garden foods.

Saddles and boots may be cleaned with beeswax, soap, oil, and vinegar. Carefully work beeswax into warm vinegar, then add soap and oil. Heat until the ingredients are thoroughly mixed and cool before using.

Soak venison (or other fresh flesh) in vinegar and water before cooking. This will make it palatable and soft for the teeth.

Coarse, sinewy vegetables become more toothsome if, before cooking, they are allowed to rest in water laced with vinegar.

HERB VINEGARS

Those of the ancient world quickly learned to combine vinegar with beneficial plants for maximum medicinal value. Herb vinegars have been in use for thousands of years. Yet, the virtues of healing herbs are only now beginning to be understood by the scientific community. Some examples of vinegars considered to be both healthful and antiseptic follow (see the Cooking With Vinegar chapter for directions on preparing herb vinegars):

DANDELION adds its mild laxative nature to vinegar's natural antiseptic qualities. It also has an anti-inflammatory effect on the intestines. This is an old time remedy for ailments of the pancreas and liver, said to ease jaundice and cirrhosis. It is also a diuretic, and as such is considered useful in lowering blood pressure. (Dandelion is rich in potassium, a mineral some other diuretics pull out of the body.)

MYRRH has long been considered of particular value in maintaining a healthy mouth. Swish this vinegar around in the mouth to hasten healing of sores and to soothe red, swollen gums. This will also sweeten the breath. Ancients used it for treating chest congestion.

SAGE vinegar not only adds its delicate hint of flavoring to meats, it tenderizes them. Splashed into soups and dressings, it serves up a tranquilizer for frazzled nerves.

PEPPERMINT, like all the mints, settles and calms the digestive system. Use a couple of teaspoons of peppermint vinegar, added to a glass of water, to ease stomach cramps, diarrhea, or gas. Add a teaspoon of honey and it is one of the best tasting cures for indigestion. Mix this herb vinegar with others to intensify their flavor and effectiveness.

ROSEMARY, the herb of remembrance, combines with healthy, amino acid laced apple cider vinegar to treat maladies of the head. It boosts the function of mind and memory, relieves tension headaches, and eases dizziness.

EUCALYPTUS is the source of the eucalyptol which makes some cough drops so effective. Steam from vinegar which has absorbed the aromatic oil of this herb helps to clear a stuffy head or a clogged respiratory system. A popular over-the-counter salve for relieving the stiffness and swelling of arthritis and rheumatism carries the distinctive aroma of eucalyptus.

WORMWOOD is quite bitter. This vinegar is best used externally, as a deterrent to fleas and other insects, or applied as a wound dressing. For insect control, sprinkle it liberally onto infested areas of rooms.

RUE was once given as an antidote for poison mushrooms and toad-stools, as well as the bite of snakes, spiders, and bees. Bitter, aromatic rue vinegar was once sprinkled about to ward off both witches and contagious diseases.

LAVENDER makes a vinegar that is pleasantly aromatic and useful for fighting off anxiety attacks. The haunting scent of lavender has long been associated with headache relief and calming of stressed nerves.

THYME vinegar is a good addition to meat dishes, as it both flavors and tenderizes. Applied to the body, it acts to deter fungus growth.

SPEARMINT is one of the gentler mints. A bit of spearmint vinegar in a glass of water calms the stomach and digestive system. It also relieves gas and adds a tangy zing to iced tea.

CLOVE vinegar is especially good for stopping vomiting. Its use dates back more than 2,000 years (to China) where it was considered an aphrodisiac.

Eucalyptus is more than just Koala bear food!

Cloves are the dried bud of the clove tree.

When herb vinegars are used for medicinal purposes, the usual dose is one to three teaspoons added to a full glass of water. They can also be sprinkled into meat and vegetable dishes or splashed on salads. The very strong vinegars, and the very bitter ones, should be used sparingly, and only for external purposes.

Natural, organic vinegars are not the same as commercially processed and pasteurized products. In its most natural state vinegar is alive with living organisms. These naturally occurring creatures, as well as some enzymes and vitamins are destroyed when vinegar is processed in a high heat process, such as pasteurization. Descriptions of a couple of these little inhabitants of the vinegar barrel follow:

Vinegar eels are frequently found in vinegar. This species of nematode worm is a natural part of many vinegars. These curious creatures can be seen near the surface of a vinegar which has been exposed to air. They resemble tiny thread worms, and are considered a harmless part of vinegar.

Vinegar flies (of the genus Drosophila) lay eggs which hatch out into larvae that live comfortably in vinegar. They thrive on this acid brew, but are not a particularly appetizing addition to vinegar!

Fortunately the vinegaroon - a large scorpion - doesn't live in vinegar! It just smells vinegary!

Chapter Four

Vinegar's Historic Development

As vinegar's virtues became known, its production spread throughout the world. Vinegar's use can be chronicled down through the ages in many different times and cultures. It has been used for everyday cleaning and for specific medical ailments for at least 10,000 years. And sometimes, vinegar can be said to have actually changed the course of history. Some of the more intriguing vinegar uses, as well as some vinegar hints for today, follow.

THE ORIGINAL HOT ROCKS

Was vinegar the world's first bulldozer? Without vinegar, Hannibal's march over the Alps to Rome may not have been possible! The chronicles of this historic march describe the essential role vinegar played in the task of getting Hannibal's elephants over the perilous mountain trails.

Frequently, the tortuous passage across the Alps was too narrow for the huge elephants. Hannibal's solution was for his soldiers to cut tree limbs and stack them around the boulders which blocked their way. Then the limbs were set afire. When the rocks were good and hot, vinegar was poured onto them. This turned the stones soft and crumbly. The soldiers could then chip the rocks away, making a passage for both the troops and elephants.

You may not have an immediate need to relocate a boulder so your elephants can cross a mountain range, but you may want to try some of these ways to ease cleaning chores:

Renew old sponges by washing them in vinegar water, then soaking them overnight in 1 quart of water with 1/4 cup vinegar added to it.

Use vinegar to clean away mineral buildup on metal. Just add 1/4 cup to a quart of water for cleaning metal screen and storm doors and aluminum furniture. Add extra vinegar if your water has a particularly high mineral content.

Eyeglasses will clean up and be free of streaks when wiped down with water to which a splash of vinegar has been added.

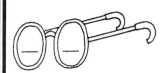

Clean and freshen the microwave oven by boiling vinegar water in it. Mix 1/4 cup vinegar and 1 cup water in a small bowl and heat for 5 minutes. This will remove lingering odors and soften baked on food spatters.

Wipe down wood cutting boards with full strength vinegar. It will clean them, cut grease, and absorb odors.

A splash of vinegar added to rinse water will keep glasses from water spotting. It kills germs, too.

Clean and freshen the garbage disposal by running a tray of ice cubes, with 1/2 cup vinegar poured over them, through it once a week.

Make a brass and copper cleaner by combining equal parts of lemon juice and vinegar. Wipe it on with a paper towel, then polish with a soft, dry cloth.

Use vinegar and hay to revitalize iron pans which have rust spots. Fill the pot with hay, add 1/4 cup vinegar and enough water to cover the hay. Boil for 1 hour and wipe the rust away. Rhubarb may be substituted for the hay.

Clean pewter with a paste made of 1 tablespoon salt, 1 tablespoon flour, and enough vinegar to just barely make the mixture wet. Smear it on discolored pewter and allow to dry. Rub or brush the dried paste off, rinse in hot water, and buff dry.

Keep drains clean by pouring in 1/2 cup baking soda, followed by 1/2 cup vinegar. In about 10 minutes, run hot water down the drain. Keep drains odor-free by pouring 1/2 cup vinegar down them once a week.

Wipe all kitchen work surfaces down with full strength white vinegar to clean them and to prevent mold.

Add a generous splash of vinegar to hot water and use it, with a little soap, to disinfect baby's toys. Be sure to rinse well.

Add a cup of vinegar to a bucket of floor washing water for cleaner floors. Or, after the usual washing, rinse floors with clear water, to which a

cup of vinegar has been added. There will be no soap scum to dull the finish.

1/4 cup vinegar added to a load of laundry, along with the usual soap, will brighten colors and make whites sparkle. This will also act as a fabric softener, and inhibit mold and fungus growth. Helps to kill athlete's foot germs on socks, too.

Vinegar is a good addition to the laundry tub when new clothes are being washed for the first time. It will help to eliminate manufacturing chemicals and their odors.

A vinegar rinse will also stop static cling and reduce the amount of lint that settles on clothes. Some laundry stains can be soaked out in equal parts of milk and vinegar.

A little vinegar and salt added to the water you wash leafy green vegetables in will float out bugs and kill germs.

When 1/4 cup linseed oil, 1/8 cup vinegar, and 1/8 cup whiskey are mixed together, they make a nice furniture polish. Dirt seems to disappear as the alcohol evaporates.

Wood scratches can be repaired with vinegar and iodine. Mix equal parts of each in a small dish and apply with an artist's paint brush. Add extra iodine for a deeper color, more vinegar for a lighter color.

A good saddle soap can be made from 1/8 cup liquid soap, 1/8 cup linseed oil, 1/4 cup beeswax, and 1/4 cup vinegar. Warm the beeswax, slowly, in the vinegar. Then add the soap and oil. Keep the mixture warm until it will all mix together smoothly. Then cool until it is solid. To use, rub it onto good leather, then buff to a high shine.

Polish leather with a mixture of 2/3 cup linseed oil, 1/3 cup vinegar, and 1/3 cup water. Beat it all together and apply with a soft cloth. Then buff with a clean rag.

THE MOST EXPENSIVE MEAL EVER

The world's most costly meal began with a glass of vinegar. When asked to think of the most expensive beverage, vinegar may not come immediately to mind. Yet it may take the prize for most expensive drink in history!

Cleopatra, queen of Egypt, made culinary history when she made a wager that she could consume, at a single meal, the value of a million sisterces. To many, it seemed an impossible task. After all, how could anyone eat so much?

Cleopatra was able to consume a meal worth so very much by dropping a million sisterces worth of pearls into a glass of vinegar. Then she set it aside while banquet preparations were made. When the time came to fulfill her wager, she simply drank the dissolved pearls!

Cleopatra won her bet because she knew vinegar was a pretty good solvent. If you do not have an overwhelming urge to dissolve a few thousand dollars worth of pearls, you may want to apply vinegar's remarkable ability in some of the following ways:

Brushes hardened with old, dried-in paint may be softened by boiling them in vinegar. Simply cover them with boiling vinegar and let them stand for 1 hour. Then heat the vinegar and brushes until the vinegar comes to a gentle boil. Simmer for 20 minutes. Rinse well, working the softened paint out of the bristles. For extremely heavy paint encrustations, you may need to repeat the process.

Most any old wood glue can be softened for removal. Simply wet the glued area down with vinegar, and keep it wet overnight. Even some of the newfangled, super-duper, hold-it-all glues can be scraped away if they are soaked overnight in vinegar.

Simmer 1/4 cup vinegar in a pot of water, uncovered, to clear the air of lingering cooking odors. Add 1/2 teaspoon of cinnamon to the water for an extra special air cleaner.

1/2 cup vinegar in dish washing water cuts grease and lets you use less soap.

Make a good metal cleaner by combining 2 tablespoons cream of tartar and enough vinegar to make a paste. Rub it on and let it dry. Wash it off with plain warm water and dry with an old towel. Metal will gleam.

Clean faucets and fixtures with 1/3 cup vinegar and 2/3 cup water. Use it to polish and shine, or brush it into the shower head to remove mineral buildup.

One million sisterces was many years' wages for a workman.

Combine 1/4 cup liquid soap, 1/2 cup vinegar, and 2 gallons of water to make a great floor cleaning solution.

Caution: vinegar can dissolve preexisting wax on furniture and floors. Use very small amounts to clean and shine, stronger solutions to remove wax buildup and heavy dirt.

Remove ink stains from clothes by soaking them in milk for 1 hour. Then cover the stain with a paste of vinegar and cornstarch. When the paste dries, wash the garment as usual.

Brass and copper will sparkle and tarnish will melt away if wiped down with 2 tablespoons catsup and 1 tablespoon vinegar. Polish until completely dry with a clean cloth.

Clean and polish soft leather with a vitamin enriched solution. Heat 1/2 cup vinegar to the boiling point. Drop in 3 vitamin E capsules and let stand, undisturbed, until the capsules dissolve. Add 1/2 cup lemon or olive oil and blend well.

Soak or simmer stuck-on food in 2 cups of water and 1/2 cup of vinegar. The food will soften and lift off in a few minutes.

Pewter cleans up easily if rubbed with cabbage leaves. Just wet the leaves in vinegar and dip them in salt before using them to buff the pewter. Be sure to rinse with cool water and dry thoroughly.

Apple cider vinegar removes soap scum from more than just shower walls. Dilute it half and half with water and use it to rub down your body after bathing. It will leave your skin naturally soft, pH balanced, and free of soapy film. It also acts as a natural deodorant.

Nail polish will go on smoother, and stay on longer if you clean your fingernails with white vinegar before applying the polish.

Perspiration stains in clothes will fade if soaked overnight in 3 gallons of water, to which 1/4 cup vinegar has been added. Use full strength vinegar to remove stains caused by berries, fruits, grass, coffee and tea.

Dissolve chewing gum and remove stuck on decals by saturating them with vinegar. If the vinegar is heated, it will work faster.

Clean hairbrushes by soaking them in 2 cups of hot, soapy water, with 1/2 cup vinegar added to it.

Car chrome shines up fast if polished with vinegar!

Keep a dish or two of vinegar sitting around when painting. The vinegar will absorb the paint odors. For a long painting job, fill a bucket with hay and drizzle 1 cup vinegar over it. Let this set for 15 minutes. Then add enough water to cover the hay. This will clear the air and keep the room smelling fresh for a couple of days.

OTHER HISTORIC VINEGAR MOMENTS

The Babylonians, back in 5,000 B.C., fermented the fruits of the date palm. Their vinegar, therefore, was called date vinegar and was credited with having superior healing properties.

You may know that vinegar is mentioned eight times in the Bible. (Four references are in the Old Testament, and four are in the New Testament.) But did you know there was a Vinegar Bible?

One famous version of the Bible is called the Vinegar Bible. In 1717 the Clarendon Press in Oxford, England printed and released a new edition of the scriptures. A mistake was soon discovered. In the top-of-the-page running headline of the 22nd chapter of the book of Luke, the word "vineyard" had been misprinted.

Instead of "vineyard" the printer typeset the word as "vinegar." The edition was quickly dubbed the "Vinegar Bible." And this is the name by which Clarendon's 1717 edition is known today.

Even poets have commented on vinegar. Lord Byron (1788-1824) called vinegar "A sad, sour, sober beverage..."

Well, puckery or not, vinegar's virtuous traits abound. Vinegar cleans by cutting grease. This makes it useful for melting away gummy buildup. It also inhibits mold growth, dissolves mineral accumulations, freshens the air, kills bacteria and slows its regrowth.

Many folk recipes combine vinegar with other household supplies. Chemical company copies of old-time cleaners use synthetic chemicals that are not always as environmentally safe as more natural, organic compounds. Among the more popular substances which have traditionally been used in combination with vinegar are baking soda, borax, chalk, pumice, oil, salt, washing soda, and wax. To vinegar, add:

- Baking soda to absorb odors, deodorize, and as a mild abrasive.
- Borax to disinfect, deodorize, and stop the growth of mold.

It's been at least 10,000 years since the natural souring of wine created the first vinegar.

37

- Chalk for a mild, non abrasive cleaner.
- Oil to preserve and shine.
- Pumice to remove stains or polish surfaces.
- Salt for a mild abrasive.
- Washing soda to cut heavy grease.
- Wax to protect and shine.

PLEASE NOTE: Some ingredients, when added to a vinegar solution, will produce a frothy foam. This is a natural chemical reaction, and is not dangerous in an open container.

**DO NOT SEAL A FOAMING VINEGAR MIXTURE
IN A TIGHTLY CAPPED CONTAINER!**

A collection of useful formulas for cleaning and polishing with vinegar follow:

Make your own kind-to-the-environment air freshener. Put the following into a pump spray bottle: 1 teaspoon baking soda, 1 tablespoon vinegar, and 2 cups of water. After the foaming stops, put on the lid and shake well. Spray this mixture into the air for instant freshness.

Vinegar is an excellent window cleaner. Just mix 1/4 cup vinegar into 1 quart water and put it in a spray bottle. Spray it onto windows and wipe off immediately with clean, soft cloth.

An excellent furniture polish can be made from vinegar and lemon oil. Use 3 parts vinegar to 1 part oil for a light weight polish. (Use 1 part vinegar to 3 parts oil for a heavy duty polish.) An oil and vinegar combination works well for cleaning and polishing. This is because vinegar dissolves and brings up dirt and oil enriches the wood.

Dusting will go much faster if your dust cloth is dampened with a mixture made of half vinegar and half olive oil. Give furniture a nutty fragrance by cleaning with vinegar to which a little olive oil has been added. When the vinegar evaporates, the wood is left clean and beautiful - and smelling good!

Appliances sparkle if cleaned with a vinegar and borax cleaner. Mix 1 teaspoon borax, 1/4 cup vinegar, and 2 cups hot water and put it into a spray bottle. Spray it on greasy smears and wipe off with a cloth or sponge.

Clean brass and copper with 2 teaspoons salt, 1 tablespoon flour, and enough vinegar to make a paste. First, mix the salt and flour together. Next, add vinegar until a thick paste is formed. Then use the paste to scrub the metal, rinse, and buff dry. Add some extra salt for hard jobs, or some extra flour for a softer paste.

Counter tops will shine if wiped down with a mixture of 1 teaspoon liquid soap, 3 tablespoons vinegar, 1/2 teaspoon oil, and 1/2 cup water.

Once a week clean, disinfect, and deodorize wood cutting blocks. Rub them with baking soda. Then spray on full strength vinegar. Let sit for 5 minutes, then rinse in clear water. It will bubble and froth as these two natural chemicals interact.

An excellent toilet cleaner can be made from 1 cup borax and 1 cup vinegar. Pour the vinegar all over the stained area of the toilet. Then sprinkle the borax over the vinegar. Allow it all to soak for 2 hours. Then simply brush and flush.

Clean windows with 1/4 cup cornstarch and 1/4 cup vinegar. Mix well and quickly dab it onto windows. Let it dry and rub off with a clean cloth. Glass will sparkle.

Make your own instant window cleaner! Combine 1/2 teaspoon liquid soap, 1/4 cup vinegar, and 2 cups water. Soak a sponge or small cloth in this mixture, then wring it out. Store the window cloth in a glass jar with a tight fitting lid until needed. Then simply wipe spots and smears from dirty windows. They will clean up without streaks - no mess, no fuss.

Shine and clean painted surfaces with 1 tablespoon cornstarch, 1/4 cup vinegar, and 2 cups hot water. Wipe or spray it on and wipe the paint dry immediately. Rub until it shines.

Preserve leather shoes and clean off dirt by rubbing them with a vinegar based cleaner. Mix together 1 tablespoon vinegar, 1 tablespoon alcohol, 1 teaspoon vegetable oil, and 1/2 teaspoon liquid soap. Wipe it on, then brush until the shoes gleam.

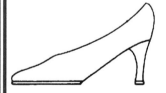

Water scale build up on glass shower doors can be removed with alum and vinegar. Mix 1 teaspoon alum into 1/4 cup vinegar. Wipe it on the glass and scrub with a soft brush. Rinse with lots of water and buff until completely dry. (Alum is aluminum sulfate.)

Soft vinyl surfaces are best cleaned with 1/2 cup vinegar, 2 teaspoons liquid soap, and 1/2 cup water. Use a soft cloth to wipe this mixture onto vinyl furniture, then rinse with clear water and buff dry.

Remove light carpet stains with a paste made of salt and vinegar. Dissolve 2 tablespoons salt in 1/2 cup vinegar. Rub this into carpet stains and let it dry. Vacuum up the residue.

Remove heavy carpet stains with a paste made of salt, borax, and vinegar. Dissolve 2 tablespoons salt and 2 tablespoons borax in 1/2 cup vinegar. Rub this into carpet stains and let it dry. Vacuum up the residue.

Stainless steel cleans up nicely if scrubbed with baking soda which has been dampened with just a little vinegar.

As with all cleaning products, test these old-time solutions to cleaning problems before using them. Always try them out on an inconspicuous area of rugs, upholstery, or clothing.

Cleaners you make yourself cost pennies, instead of the dollars super market cleaners cost. And, what is much more significant, the compounds you put together are safe, natural, and easy on the environment. Commercial equivalents cost more and may be more damaging to the environment.

Using vinegar to clean and disinfect is more than the inexpensive choice from a simpler time. It is the natural choice!*

For more old-time cleaning ways, see the Order Form for Home Remedies from the Old South.

Chapter Five

Vinegar Making

For thousands of years apple cider vinegar has been made in much the same way. First, cider is made from an assortment of whole, fresh apples: they are washed, chopped, and pressed.

When the sweet apple juice has been collected, it is allowed to age, sealed tightly away from the air. Natural sugars are fermented to produce alcohol. This "hard" cider is then allowed to ferment once again, while left open to the air. This time, the alcohol changes to acid.

Originally, the commercial production of vinegar was a by-product of the wine producer and the brewer. Vinegar brewing, as a separate industry, dates from about the 17th century. First established in France, it quickly spread to other regions.

Vinegar can be made from any liquid containing sugar, if there is enough sugar. Apple juice is one of the oldest fluids used to make vinegar, but grape and date palm use goes back thousands of years. Other popular vinegar sources are: molasses, sorghum, berries, melons, coconuts, honey, maple syrup, potatoes, beets, grains, bananas, and even whey.

Wine vinegar has many of the same nutritional benefits as apple cider vinegar. After all, it begins with naturally ripe, vitamin and mineral packed fruit. Wine vinegar will vary in color, depending on whether it was made from red or white wine. Vinegar's flavor, strength, and nutritional makeup depends on what it is made from. Sometimes "vinegar" is concocted from acetic acid (made from wood), colored with caramel, and then called vinegar. This is incorrect (and illegal) labelling. Acetic acid does not have the food value or aroma of genuine vinegar.

ALEGAR

One of the old-time vinegars made from a grain base is called alegar. Technically, it is a kind of malt vinegar. Malt is barley (or other grain) which

There's even a vinegar tree (Rhus typhiora) with acidy berries for vinegar making.

Vinegar made from ale is called alegar.

is steeped in water until it germinates, then dried in a kiln for use in brewing. This malt is fermented into an alcoholic beverage called ale. Ale has less hops than beer, so it is both sweeter and lighter in color.

The color of alegar varies from pale gold to rich brown. The intensity of the color depends on how the grain was roasted and dried. Medicated ales have been used for hundreds of years in Europe.

When wine or cider (from grapes or apples) is fermented, the result is called "vine-gar." When ale (from barley or other grain) is fermented, the result is called "ale-gar."

MAKE YOUR OWN VINEGAR

The are as many ways to make vinegar as there are apples, kinds of fruit, and people. If you have never tackled the operation, you may want to begin with the first apple cider vinegar recipe below. Then, experiment with some of the other ways to make vinegar.

Vinegar making requires two separate, distinct fermentations. The first, called alcoholic (or vinous) changes natural sugars to alcohol. The second, called acid (or acetic) changes alcohol to acetic acid. It is important that the first fermenting be completely finished before the second is begun.

You can hurry the first fermentation along by adding a little yeast to the cider, and by keeping it warm. At around 80° the liquids will convert very fast. To speed up the second fermentation, add a little mother-of-vinegar to the mix. And, the more air the mixture gets during this second part of the process, the faster it will convert to vinegar.

Caution: Mother-of-vinegar (it starts the second fermentation) must not get into the liquid until practically all the sugar has been converted to alcohol.

The vinegar bacterium is present wherever there is air. This is why any wine which is spilled at a winery must be mopped up at once. Bacteria could get started in the wine and sour it all! If a winery makes both wine and vinegar, separate rooms are used for each. And, barrels from vinegar making are never used for storing wine.

APPLE CIDER VINEGAR

Begin by making a good, tart cider. Combine sweet apples for aroma, tart ones for body, and a few crab apples for luck. The more sweet apples

Some people use peelings, cores, and windfalls.

The vinegar bacterium is called an acetobacter.

you use, the stronger the vinegar will be. This is because the high sugar content of sweet apples produces more alcohol to change into acid. The more tart apples in the mix, the sharper the flavor will be.

Chop the apples and when they turn golden brown, crush them in a cider press. Collect the cider in a glass jug. Never use store-bought apple juice to make vinegar. It contains preservatives, and may have been pasteurized, and so it will not ferment properly!

Next, cap the cider jug with a small balloon. It will expand as carbon dioxide is released, while keeping air away from the mix. When the sugar is all changed to alcohol, it becomes hard cider. This takes 1 to 6 weeks, depending on the temperature and the sugar content of the apples used to make the cider.

It is not necessary to add yeast, as wild yeasts are always on apples surfaces and in the air. If a grey foam forms on the top of the cider, it is excess yeast, and is harmless. Just skim it off.

Finally, pour the hard cider into a wide crock, so there is a larger surface area than in a jug. Put a cloth over the top to let in air, while keeping out dust and bugs. Vinegar will be created in a few months.

Wild spores floating in the air will start the fermenting process, but adding mother-of-vinegar to cider will hurry the conversion along. Simply smear a slice of toast with mother and lay it gently on the surface of the cider. Vinegar making works best if the ingredients are kept at around 80°. If the temperature gets much higher, the bacteria needed for fermenting is killed. If the temperature gets much cooler than 80°, the wild spores become dormant.

OTHER OLD APPLE CIDER VINEGAR RECIPES

Put cut up apples in a stone crock and cover them with warm water. Tie a cheesecloth over the top and set in a warm place for 4-6 months. Then strain off the vinegar. For faster action, add a lump of raw bread dough to the crock.

Let sweet apple cider stand open in a jug for 4-6 weeks and it will become vinegar.

Place apple and peach peelings, and a handful of grape skins, in a widemouthed jar and cover these fruit leavings with cold water. Set in a warm place and add a couple of fresh apple cores every few days. When a

Carbon dioxide forms when sugar converts to alcohol.

Cider for vinegar should have at least a 10% sugar content.

scum forms on top, stop adding fresh fruit and let it thicken. When the vinegar is good and strong, strain it through a cheesecloth.

Make vinegar in a special hurry by adding brown sugar, molasses, or yeast to cider.

OTHER VINEGARS

Let a bottle of wine stand, open to the air, in the summer sun. In about 2 weeks it will turn into a nice vinegar. Make winter vinegar by letting wine stand open to the air for about a month.

Put 2 pounds of raisins in a gallon of water and set it in a warm place. In 2 months it will become white wine vinegar. Just strain the vinegar off and bottle it. Make some more vinegar by adding another 1/2 pound of raisins to the dredges and going through the process again.

Make a deeply colored honey vinegar by pouring 1 gallon boiling water over 5 pounds of strained honey. Stir until all of the honey is melted. Then dissolve 1 cake (or package) of yeast in 1 tablespoon of warm water. Spread the yeast on a dry corn cob (or a slice of toast) and float it on the top of the honey-water. Cover the container with a cloth and let it set for 16 days. Take out the corn cob, skim off the scum, and strain the liquid. Now let it stand for a month or so, until it turns into vinegar.

Dark honeys ferment much faster than light ones. Add a cup or two of fruit juice or molasses to honey to speed the change to vinegar.

Because the sugar content of honey varies a lot, you may want to check and see if your water to honey ratio is correct. Do this by dropping an egg into the mixture. It should float in the liquid, with only a small spot showing above the surface. If the egg sinks, add more honey. If the egg floats too high, add more water. This method should assure you that the specific gravity of the mix is about 1.05, the best for making good honey vinegar.

For an extra special, clover-flavored, vinegar add a quart of freshly washed clover blossoms to the honey and water mix. Dandelions add a unique taste to honey vinegar. Just add 3 cups of blossoms to the honey and water. Be sure to strain it before using!

Raspberry vinegar can be prepared by pouring 2 quarts of water over 1 quart of freshly washed red or black raspberries. Cover lightly and let stand overnight. Strain off the liquid and discard the berries. Now prepare 1 more quart of fresh raspberries and pour the same liquid over them. Let this set overnight. Do this for a total of 5 times. Then add 1 pound of sugar to the

Color + flavor of this vinegar depends on the kind of honey used.

A Baume hydrometer will read between 7 and 8.

44

liquid and stir until it is dissolved. Set the mixture aside, uncovered, for a couple of months. Strain before using.

MOTHER OF VINEGAR

"Mother" (or "mother-of-vinegar") is the term used to describe the mass of sticky scum which forms on top of cider (or other juice) when alcohol turns into vinegar. As the fermentation progresses, mother forms a gummy, stringy, floating lump. Mother is formed by the beneficial bacteria which creates vinegar.

Sometimes mother from a previous batch of vinegar is introduced into another liquid which is in the process of becoming vinegar. This use, as a starter for new vinegars, is why the gooey scum on the top of vinegar is called "mother-of-vinegar."

Sometimes, as mother begins to form, it is disturbed and sinks to the bottom of the container. If it falls into the vinegar it will die, because its oxygen supply is cut off. This dead, slithery blob is called a zoogloea, and is worthless. Mother sinks for two reasons. One, if the vinegar making container is jolted, the film can get wet. This makes it too heavy to float. Two, if too many tiny vinegar eels develop in the liquid, their weight, as they cling to the edges of the developing mother, will weight it down.

Over the ages, traditional vinegar makers developed a deep reverence for the rubbery mass of goo we call mother-of-vinegar. Often, some was saved from a batch of vinegar. Then, it was transferred carefully to new batches of souring wine to work its magic.

Over time, this cultivated mother developed special flavoring abilities. It is still handed down, from generation to generation, and guarded as a secret ingredient in special vinegars. Tiny bits of the old mother are lifted out of one batch of vinegar and put into new batches.

Mother-of-vinegar may also form on stored vinegar supplies. This slime is not particularly appealing, but its presence does not mean the vinegar is spoiled. Skim it off and use the vinegar. While mother may not seem to many to be a particularly appetizing snack, some claim it is endowed with nearly miraculous healing properties. Some old-time mother-of-vinegar remedies follow:

Scoop the stringy mass of mother-of-vinegar from the bottom of a barrel that has held vinegar and save it for treating infectious diseases. Preserve it by mixing it half and half with honey. One small teaspoon of this honey and mother mixture, taken twice a day, gives protection from infectious diseases and parasite infestation.

Dip out a goodly spoonful of the moldy mother-of-vinegar from the top of a vinegar barrel and eat it very slowly. This healthy slime will relieve joint pains and headaches caused by infections.

Rashes caused by infections may be made to go away by nibbling on the mother which floats on a good vinegar. And, a bit of mother-of-vinegar, taken each day, prevents most infectious diseases.

Take a bite or two of mother-of-vinegar, morning and evening. It will keep grievous germs and nasty parasites away from the body.

Grow your own mother-of-vinegar by combining 1 cup of vinegar and 1 cup of fresh cider. Let this set, open to the air, for a few days (or weeks, depending on the temperature). The scum which forms on the surface is mother-of-vinegar.

HOW STRONG IS YOUR HOMEMADE VINEGAR?

Homemade vinegars can vary. What follows is one way to determine the percent of acid in a batch of vinegar. You will need 1/2 cup water and 2 teaspoons baking soda, mixed together. Plus, 1/4 cup of the water in which a head of red cabbage was cooked.

1. Put 1/2 cup water into each of 2 clear glasses.

2. Add 1/8 cup cabbage water to each glass.

3. Use a glass dropper to put 7 drops of commercial vinegar into one glass of the cabbage flavored water.

4. Put 20 drops of the soda water into the same glass and stir well (stir with a plastic spoon, not metal). The water will turn blue.

5. Now mix 7 drops of your vinegar into the second glass of the cabbage flavored water.

6. Add baking soda water to your vinegar (and cabbage water), 1 drop at a time. Stir after each drop. Count the drops.

7. When the color of your vinegar water turns the same shade of blue as the commercial vinegar water, the acid content of the two glasses will match.

8. To find the percent of acid in your vinegar, divide the number of drops of soda water you added to it by 4. For example, if you added 20 drops of soda water to your vinegar, divide by 4 and find that the acid content is 5%. (The same as most commercial vinegars.) The more soda water it takes to make your vinegar match the color of the commercial vinegar you are using as a control, the stronger your vinegar is.

A wine testing kit will also check the acidity of vinegar.

Determining vinegar's strength this way is called titration!

46

Chapter Six

In A Pickle
And Proud Of It!

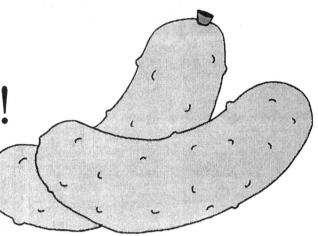

It's the law: if the label says pickled, then the product must be put up in vinegar!

Our world would be very different without vinegar's lively flavor to perk up humdrum foods. Each year, Americans use hundreds of millions of gallons of vinegar. It is used alone, in pickling, and in innumerable condiments.

The best vinegars begin with healthful, natural foods. Inexpensive vinegar, intended for industrial use, is sometimes fraudulently sold for preserving foods.

Cheap imitations are made from liquid sulfite waste from paper mills and acids from petrochemical sources such as oil, coal, and natural gas. Because grain and spirit vinegar is so much cheaper than food-grade vinegar (such as apple cider vinegar) there is a lot of financial incentive for businesses to use it.

There are also differences in the way taxes and import duties treat different grades of vinegar. Quality vinegar, from expensive food-base sources such as fruit juices, honey, maple syrup, apples, grapes, or even sugar cane or corn rates a higher tax.

Different tax treatment dates way back in time. In England, the Revenue Acts established during the reign of Charles II charged different duties on beer and on vinegar- beer.

Besides the differences in nutritional values, grain and spirit vinegars do not compare in taste to good, high-quality vinegars. A quality vinegar has a sour taste, without being bitter.

Charles II reigned in the mid 1600's!

Sour tastes are one of the sensations the body is most able to detect. The sensitive sides of the tongue (the area where sour is registered) can detect one sour part in 130,000. But it is even more sensitive to bitter flavors. The tongue can detect one bitter part out of 2 billion. This sensitivity is a safety measure, to alert the body to poisons. It also makes cheap vinegars unpleasant to the tongue.

Good, sour, acidy vinegar causes saliva to flow. This increases our ability to taste and enjoy other foods. It also aids digestion.

Pickling is one of the most basic, and easiest ways to preserve edibles. It works by increasing food's acidity. Expect a batch of pickled vegetables to last a month or two in the refrigerator. Or, over a year if they are canned.

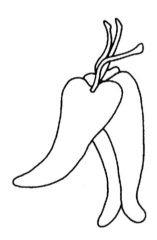

Because pickles are already partially preserved, they do not have to be canned in a pressure cooker. A boiling water bath provides enough heat to seal and sterilize them. Care does need to be taken in choosing containers. The high acid content reacts with some metals, such as aluminum and iron. It is better to use enamel, glass, or stainless steel pans.

Even the water which is combined with the vinegar can affect the quality of the pickled food. Water high in iron or sulfur will darken foods. Be sure food to be preserved is of high quality, not bruised or damaged.

PERSONALIZING TASTE

Everyone has their own idea of what the perfect pickle should taste like. There are several things you can do to adjust the taste: vary the kind of vinegar used, add or delete sugar, or change the spices.

There are some things you do not want to do in your quest for preserving the perfect pickle. Do not combat vinegar's tartness by diluting the vinegar excessively. This will lower the acid content of the mixture and could result in spoiled pickles.

It is better to mask tartness by adding extra sugar. Since sugar helps to preserve the food, doing this will not create a risk of spoilage. Use brown sugar and the entire batch will change to a darker color. Use honey and the flavor will be heavy and rich.

The salt used for pickling should always be "pickling salt" or "kosher salt." They are both free of the iodine and starch often found in table salt. Iodine in the salt will darken the pickles, and the starchy anticaking additives in table salt will cause the liquid to be cloudy.

Make simple cucumber pickles, or be creative and preserve eggplant, cauliflower, carrots, beans, onions, okra, Brussels sprouts, squash, beets, or asparagus. Even fruits can be pickled.

Flavor your mix with oregano, bay, red pepper, turmeric, mustard seeds or dry mustard, garlic, basil, dill, peppercorns, bell peppers, hot peppers, onions, or garlic.

BASIC PICKLING

Always use firm, young veggies, because they make the crunchiest pickled food. And never store cucumbers for pickling in the refrigerator. They deteriorate if stored below 50°.

For best taste, cut off the blossom ends (opposite end from the stem) of cucumbers. There are concentrated enzymes in the flowering end of the cucumber and they can soften pickles.

Never boil vinegar for pickles any longer than absolutely necessary. Acetic acid evaporates at boiling temperatures, leaving a vinegar which is too weak to do a good job of preserving.

Slice lots of cucumbers and a few onions. Arrange them in a crock, in layers. Sprinkle salt over each layer. Add very cold water and let them set and become very crisp. While the cucumbers and onions soak, mix sugar, vinegar, and spices in an enamel pan. Bring the liquid to a boil and immediately remove from the heat. Drain the brine off the cucumbers and onions. Add the pickles to the hot spiced vinegar. Put the mixture into clean jars and boil. When cool, set the jars away for a few weeks before beginning to use the pickles.

And remember, pickles pick up the flavor of whatever they are marinated in. This is what gives them their flavor. Traditionally, pickled foods are served at the beginning of a meal because they stimulate the flow of saliva and gastric juices. This makes other foods taste better.

Exact amounts of spices, salt, sugar, and vinegar will depend on your own judgement. What tastes great to one person will be too tart, or too sweet, or too garlicy to another. Do not be afraid to experiment. Some pickling recipes are included in the Cooking With Vinegar chapter.

You can pickle a peck of Hot peppers in a flash.

Pickled foods are sturdy, able to withstand a lot of variation in the way they are processed. However, occasionally things do go wrong. The finished product is not perfect. Too strong or too weak a vinegar solution, or the wrong balance of sugar or salt can result in pickles that are not crisp and crunchy. Contact with minerals can cause pickles to turn unusual colors. Use the following information to identify the cause of pickling problems.

WHAT CAN GO WRONG WITH PICKLED FOODS?

If:	Pickles will be:
Pickling solution (vinegar) is too strong	Tough
Brine is too weak	Soft
Table salt is used (it contains starch)	Cloudy
Pickling solution is too strong	Shriveled
Too much sugar	Shriveled
Too much salt	Tough
Cucumbers are old	Hollow
Cooked in a copper kettle	Off Color
Insufficient time in brine solution	Slippery
Water has a high mineral content	Off color
Cooked too long	Mushy

Chapter Seven

Cooking With Vinegar

A splash of protein, a dash of carbohydrate, and lots of vitamins and minerals - that's vinegar! A vinegary person is thought of as one who is ill-natured and sour. A vinegary food is apt to be one which has been changed from ordinary to gourmet. Vinegar's unique flavor perks up the taste of foods and keeps them safe from bacteria. Vinegar comes in dozens of kinds and flavors. Some ways to make and use flavored vinegars follow, along with a few other interesting vinegar facts and recipes:

Vinegar's acid softens muscle fiber in meat so it is tenderized. It also works on fish such as salmon, and on lobster, oysters, fruits, and vegetables.

Vinegar helps digest tough cellulose, so use it on coarse, fibrous, or stringy cooked vegetables such as beets, cabbage, spinach, lettuce, and celery. Sprinkle it on raw vegetables such as cucumbers, kale, lettuce, carrots, and broccoli.

Splash vinegar into bean soups, or use herb vinegar on pasta or bean salads to give robust flavor without salt.

Because meat fiber is broken down and tenderized by vinegar, less expensive cuts can be used in most recipes. They are healthier, since these are the cuts with the least fat.

Unless directions indicate otherwise, all flavored vinegars are made by adding flavoring agents to apple cider vinegar and allowing it to age.

Hot Pepper Vinegar
Add 1/2 ounce cayenne pepper to 1 pint of vinegar. Shake every other day for 2 weeks. Strain before using.

Spicy Vinegar
1	quart vinegar	1	teaspoon cloves
1/2	cup sugar	1	teaspoon salt
1	tablespoon cinnamon	4	tablespoons grated horseradish
1	teaspoon allspice	2	tablespoons celery seed
1	tablespoon mustard		

Combine all ingredients and bring to a boil. Pour over pickles or sliced, cooked beets.

Celery Vinegar
1 teaspoon salt
2 cups chopped celery
1 quart vinegar

Boil for 3 minutes and seal it all in a glass jar for 3 weeks. Strain and use.

Chili Vinegar
Add 3 ounces chopped chilies to a quart of vinegar. Cap for 2 weeks and strain. For a supper hot vinegar, increase steeping time.

Cucumber-Onion Vinegar
Slice very thin, 2 pickling cucumbers and 1 small onion. Add 1 pint boiling vinegar, 1 teaspoon salt and a dash of white pepper. Seal into a glass jar for 5 weeks and then strain. Allow sediment to settle and pour into a clean bottle and cap. Onion may be left out for a light vinegar that is especially good on fruit.

Horseradish Vinegar
Grate 1/4 cup horseradish into a quart of boiling vinegar. Seal for 3 days and then strain out the horseradish. Or, prepare an easy vinegar by simply putting a few large pieces of fresh horseradish in a bottle of vinegar. After 2 weeks, begin using the vinegar, without removing the horseradish. It will increase in strength over time.

Onion Vinegar
Peel three small onions and drop them, whole, into 1 quart vinegar. Wait 3 weeks. Remove the onions and use the vinegar, very sparingly. A few drops will be enough to season most foods.

Nasturtium Vinegar
1 quart nasturtium flowers
2 cloves garlic
1 quart vinegar

Combine and age for 6 weeks. Strain and use. May be improved by adding 2 peeled cloves of garlic.

Flower Power Vinegar

Add a flower scent to any vinegar by dropping in a few drops of scented oil. Or, add 1/2 cup of strong herb tea to a quart of vinegar.

Strawberry Vinegar

Crush 1 quart of strawberries into 1 quart of vinegar. Let set for 2 days, lightly covered; strain through doubled cheesecloth and discard the berries. Pour the same vinegar over another quart of berries and mash them. After 2 more days, strain off the vinegar and add 2 pounds of sugar. Boil for 10 minutes. A couple of tablespoons of this vinegar in a glass of water is cooling and refreshing.

Tarragon Vinegar

Put 1/4 cup tarragon leaves in a pint bottle of vinegar and let set for 8 weeks. Use on cooked and raw vegetables.

Garlic Lover's Vinegar

Separate and peel all the cloves of a large garlic bulb. Put them in a quart of vinegar and allow to steep for 2 weeks. Strain off the vinegar and discard the garlic. Only a few drops are needed in most dishes.

Mint Vinegar

Stuff a bottle full of mint leaves. Then fill the bottle with hot vinegar, cap and let set for 6 weeks. Strain and use with meats or in cool drinks.

Meat Flavoring Vinegar

1	large grated onion	1	tablespoon dry mustard
3	red peppers, chopped fine	1	teaspoon turmeric
2	tablespoons brown sugar	1	teaspoon pepper
1	tablespoon celery seed	1/2	teaspoon salt

Stir all ingredients into a quart of vinegar. Let age for 3 weeks. 2 tablespoons of this will flavor and color a stew or gravy.

Vinegar Fish Broth

2	quarts cold water	3	small cut up carrots
1	cup vinegar	2	small sliced onions
1	tablespoon salt	4	thyme leaves

Bring the water to a boil in a large fish kettle. Add the rest of the ingredients and 5 pounds of large pieces of salmon or trout. Simmer gently, until the fish is barely tender. Add a handful of peppercorns and a few sprigs of parsley.

All kinds of fish are easier to scale if they are rubbed with vinegar and allowed to set for 5 minutes before scaling.

Stuffed Peppers
Stuff large green peppers with cabbage slaw and stack in a stone crock. Cover with vinegar and age 4 weeks before using.

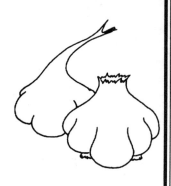

Vinaigrette
1/2 teaspoon salt
1/2 teaspoon paprika
1/8 teaspoon pepper
1/2 cup apple cider vinegar
1/2 cup olive oil
1   tablespoon minced pickles
1   tablespoon grated green pepper
1   tablespoon chopped parsley
1   tablespoon dry mustard
1   tablespoon sugar
1   tablespoon tarragon vinegar

Mix well and chill the vinaigrette. Serve with cold meats or heat it and pour over broccoli, artichokes, or asparagus. A vinegar sauce on vegetables and meats is a nice touch for hot summer days.

If vinaigrettes are made with high quality vinegar, you can use more vinegar and less oil.

Best French Dressing
Soak a split clove of garlic for at least 30 minutes in 1 cup of vinegar. Discard the garlic (or add it to soup). Mix in 1 tablespoon each of dry mustard and sugar; 1 teaspoon each of salt and paprika. Add 1 1/2 cups of salad oil and mix well. Use flavored vinegars to vary the taste.

Spiced Mushrooms
1   pound fresh mushrooms.   1 tablespoon olive oil
1/2 cup apple cider vinegar   1 tablespoon ginger
1   teaspoon soy sauce   3 cloves garlic, peeled
1   teaspoon hot pepper sauce   and chopped

Blanch mushrooms in boiling water for 2 minutes, drain and pat dry. Put all ingredients into a jar with a tight lid and refrigerate overnight. Pile these mushrooms on spinach leaves and serve with hot garlic toast.

Vinegar Salad

1/2 cup salad dressing
1/2 cup apple cider vinegar
1 tablespoon sugar
1 cup raisins

1/2 lb. bacon, cooked crisp and crumbled
1 cup sunflower kernels
2 cups chopped and blanched broccoli
half a head of lettuce

Mix the salad dressing, sugar, and vinegar together and drizzle over torn lettuce, raisins, bacon, sunflower kernels and broccoli.

Cherry-Pineapple Vinegar Cake

1 cup milk
3 tablespoons vinegar
1 teaspoon soda
3/4 lb. flour
3/4 cup butter

3/4 cup brown sugar
1 teaspoon allspice
1/2 lb. candied cherries
1/2 lb. candied pineapple

Stir the vinegar into the milk, add the soda and stir briskly. Cream butter, sugar, and flour together and add the fruit and allspice. Fold in the milk and beat well. Bake in a well greased pan at 350° for 1 hour.

Easiest Vinegar Pie Crust

1 1/3 cup flour
1/2 teaspoon salt
2 tablespoons sugar

1 tablespoon vinegar
1/3 cup oil
2 tablespoons water

Put all ingredients in a pie pan and stir with a fork until the flour is barely moist. Use the fingers to press and smooth the dough onto the sides and bottom of the pie pan, forming a fluted edge along the top. Prick with a fork and bake at 350° until lightly browned. (Or add filling and bake.)

About Vinegars . . . . .

. . . . . All vinegars are not created equal.

Vinegar made from wood shavings cannot be expected to have the same natural balance of healthful vitamins and minerals as vinegar made from apples. And, vinegar made from only cores and peelings cannot be expected to have the nutritional goodness of vinegar made from whole apples. The very best, most wholesome apple cider vinegar is made from apples without pesticide residue on them. These apples will contain an abundance of minerals, because they were grown on rich, fertile soil.

A first class apple cider vinegar is packed full of healthy enzymes, amino acids, vitamins and minerals. This is only true if it has been produced with care, from whole, good quality apples -- that have not been treated with toxic chemicals.

ORGANIC - WHAT DOES IT MEAN?

It seems as if every time we turn around we hear or see something which carries the 'organic' label. Ever wonder, exactly, what it means? Well, somtimes it means a lot. Other times it means very little.

One way to be certain an apple cider vinegar is free of harmful chemicals is to make sure that both the apples it was made from -- and the method of processing it -- are biologically sound. Companies which produce this type of product usually have an outside organization inspect all phases of production and issue an 'organically grown and processed' certificate.

WHAT CAN GO WRONG?

Sometimes, in their haste to market a vinegar, companies process apples with chemicals that speed up the fermentation process. Or, to cut costs, windfalls and apple by-products (such as cores and peels) take the place of whole fruit.

Many vinegars are subjected to excessive heat and have preservatives and clarifying agents added to them. These procedures may make a 'pretty' product, but they can sacrifice some of the healthy goodness which is present in an organically produced vinegar.

WHY IS 'ORGANIC' IMPORTANT?

Everyone experiences the wear and tear of time on their bodies. Scientists tell us that much of what we call aging is damage caused by free radicals. They bounce through our bodies, damaging cells and causing them to mutate. If we eat the right kinds of wholesome foods many free radicals are absorbed. This minimizes the damage. The better job we do of providing our bodies with the building blocks of a healthful being, the better it can retain the vitality and energy of youth.

Apples contain the building blocks for a healthy being. Pure, unfiltered, apple cider vinegar combines the natural goodness of apples with amino acids and enzymes created in the fermentation process. They remain in the vinegar if it is not filtered, overheated, pasteurized, or over-processed.

Good vinegar is good food!

Some apple cider vinegar isn't made from whole, fresh apples.

HOW TO PICK A VINEGAR

Good apple cider vinegar is made by giving meticulous attention to producing a consistent, high quality product. It is not diluted with water, and can take a full four to six weeks to produce.

For a high quality product, check that the apples were organically grown, on soil in an area with a high mineral content (such as the northern area of the U.S.). It should be made of table-grade apples, not merely windfalls, peels or cores. There should be third party monitoring of its organic status.

The best vinegar is aged in wood barrels, not plastic or metal ones. Pectin and apple residues have not been filtered out, so it contains a host of trace nutrients. And, the apples it is made from have been thoroughly washed to remove soil bacteria that could get into the finished product. This kind of vinegar will be full-flavored and have a strong apple aroma. It will not be a washed out, overly bland or puckery concoction.

VINEGAR TEST: SHAKE IT UP!

Check for sediment at the bottom of the vinegar bottle. If there is none, the very best part has probably been filtered out.

FINALLY

If you are sensitive to food additives...
If you don't want possibly toxic chemicals added to your diet....
If you are serious about protecting your health....
If you appreciate the full taste and flavor of a quality product...
Or if you just want to treat yourself to something special that's not fattening -- and is actually good for you -- try a good, organically produced, apple cider vinegar!

Life is a natural process. Your vinegar should be natural, too.

If you expect vinegar to aid health, for goodness sake, use the good stuff!

Chapter Eight

What's New?

Vinegar is a familiar ingredient in all sorts of condiments. Tomato ketchup, alone, uses up 10% of all the vinegar made in North America. Vinegar also adds its zip to salad dressing, mayonnaise, and a variety of sauces. It is used to make pickles and to preserve foods ranging from beets to eggs to fish. But of even more importance is vinegar's medicinal use. It is useful as an antibiotic, an antiseptic, and as a nutritional supplement.

Vinegar is not the only nonprescription health enhancer making news in the 90s. All of alternative medicine is "going mainstream," according to a recent headline in USA TODAY. One third of the population uses some form of alternative medicine. It accounts for 425 million visits, each year, to alternative care providers. That's more than 35 million more visits than all those to family doctors and internists, combined.

The #1 reason for adults to visit the doctor is back pain!

This non-traditional care accounted for $13.7 billion worth of scarce health care dollars. This is particularly significant when taken with the fact that almost all of the cost of alternative medical care must be paid for as an out-of-pocket expense by the consumer. Most insurance does not cover it. Of growing concern to traditional health care professionals is the fact that 72% of those using alternative health care services do not tell their doctors about it.

The National Institutes of Health has responded to this new interest in old medicine. It recently established, for the first time ever, an Office of Alternative Medicine. The new agency's first budget, of $2 million, is almost entirely dedicated to exploring the value of old-time, traditional, low-tech health remedies.

The government's rush to validate traditional remedies is partly driven by a desire to cut skyrocketing costs. After all, old remedies are almost always low-tech, low-cost solutions to the common maladies of mankind.

Devotees of apple cider vinegar are not surprised to hear that improved nutrition is emerging as a major factor in controlling health care costs. It also is a large step forward in increasing the quality of life for many people.

Much new evidence suggests diet supplements may help much more than many doctors have been willing to believe in the past. A recent CBS television special featured the network's resident medical specialist. He guided researchers through a survey of the shelves of health food stores. A laboratory then analyzed the contents of several bottles of popular food supplements.

The lab's results were shocking. Many bottles did not contain the amount of nutrient buyers were led to believe they contained. CBS's conclusion was that consumers cannot count on vitamin and other dietary supplement bottles containing what the labels say they contain.

This report, and others like it, make taking simple, naturally healthy apple cider vinegar look better and better! Some of the newest medical information about vinegar use follows:

DON'T SWIM WITHOUT IT!

Jellyfish stings are no trivial matter. They can easily land a swimmer in the hospital. The Medical Journal of Australia now recommends immediate dousing of fresh stings with vinegar, considering it "...an essential part of the first aid treatment for ... jellyfish stings."

The Massachusetts College of Pharmacy and Allied Health Sciences seconds this approach, noting that without immediate treatment jellyfish and Portuguese man-of-war stings can cause nausea, headache, chills, or even cardiovascular collapse and death. Yet, they add, "Venom can be inactivated with ... vinegar.

Traditionally, vinegar has been the remedy of choice for treating all sorts of stings and bites. Stings of bees, wasps, jellyfish, and many other bothersome critters can be eased by soaking the hurting area in full-strength vinegar. For best results the vinegar should be applied immediately after an encounter with any of these pesky creatures.

DOCTORS RECOMMEND IT FOR EARS

Grandmother said putting diluted vinegar in the ears would ward off infection. Now medical authorities have confirmed her wisdom. The American Academy of Otolaryngology (head and neck surgery) suggests using a mixture of vinegar and alcohol to prevent "swimmer's ear."

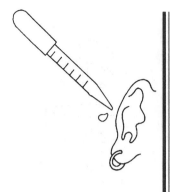

Infections, as well as plain old itchy ears, are a common complaint of swimmers. Doctors specializing in treating these ailments now recommend using vinegar as a preventive. Simply dilute vinegar half and half with boiled water and use to rinse out the ears after each swim. For a more drying solution, mix vinegar half and half with alcohol. This helps to prevent both bacterial and fungus growths.

The Journal of ET Nursing reports vinegar is so good for the skin it is being used to treat some after-urinary-surgery skin complications. When urine, which is often alkaline, leaks onto delicate skin surfaces, it can irritate or even burn sensitive skin. Vinegar's pH balance is very close to that of healthy skin. And so, vinegar compresses, applied to the skin, help restore its natural acid condition, neutralize leaking urine, and promote healing.

MICROBES & PARASITES DESTROYED BY VINEGAR

A recent university test on agents which can kill microbes said: "...(vinegar) was found to be the most effective agent used, which completely inhibited the growth of the test organism..."

Another report addresses vinegar's killer action on bacteria on vegetables intended for eating: "... vinegar solution for 15 minutes exerted pronounced bactericidal effect against this organism."

In Ethiopia, Addis Abba University reports vinegar is being tested as an agent to kill food-borne parasites. Early results show vinegar does a faster job of destroying the parasites than any of the other test mediums!

VINEGAR FOR ARTHRITIS

The Journal of the American Dietetic Association, while remaining extremely conservative in recommending alternative medical solutions, has proposed the possibility that there is room for both approaches to health. An article on arthritis suggested nutrition professionals should be "nonjudgmental" in relating to patients using unconventional therapies (such as apple cider vinegar) for relief of the discomfort of arthritis.

Meanwhile, a national newspaper reports vinegar and fruit juice can beat arthritis pain. Vinegar is sometimes prescribed for those suffering from arthritis or rheumatism, because it is rich in potassium. And potassium, says a University of California doctor, helps relieve arthritis type pain.

According to the Wall Street Journal, vinegar is being combined with apple and grape juices to produce one of the hottest selling sports drinks on the market. This "new" drink is reputed to ease arthritis pain, improve blood circulation, and tackle heart disease. 1 million jugs of this liquid, at $6 a bottle, are expected to be sold this year. Its secret ingredient? Apple cider vinegar!

CANCER DETECTION JUST GOT BETTER

Western Michigan University reports early test results which indicate vinegar can be used to increase the accuracy of conventional tests for cervical cancer. Adding the new vinegar-based test to the standard Pap test allows medical personnel to "...detect women at risk for cervical cancer who would not have been detected by the Pap test alone." The vinegar test is simple for technicians, low-cost, non-invasive, and safe for the patient.

CAN VINEGAR PREVENT ULCERS?

Will new scientific research prove vinegar can prevent stomach ulcers caused by alcohol? Early studies, printed in the Japanese Journal of Pharmacology, indicate vinegar may cause the gastric system to secrete a natural stomach protective. This natural defensive action seems to protect the stomach from alcohol-induced damage. Most surprising of all, a vinegar solution as mild as a 1% concentration appears to offer 95.8% protection from these ulcers.

Much more research work needs to be done before the medical community is ready to recommend using vinegar this way. Results have been noted only in very controlled test situations, so far. Further testing needs to be done to determine exactly how vinegar works to build up the stomach's ability to protect itself from damage that can be done by excess alcohol. But there is a definite possibility this may be a future ulcer preventative!

VINEGAR CAN BE DANGEROUS!

Lead can be a serious health danger. Latest studies indicate vinegar can increase the possibility of foods being contaminated with lead. Many soft plastic bread wrappers have been found to have labels painted on with lead based paints.

If vinegar, or foods drenched in it, are stored in these bags lead could very well leach out into the food. This can happen in as little as 10 minutes. The danger of vinegar leaching lead into food only occurs if the plastic bread wrappers are turned inside out, with the paint side next to the food.

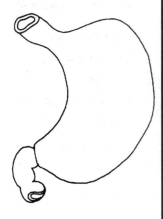

Some individuals report temporary stomach distress when vinegar is taken frequently. This is particularly a problem when vinegar (or vinegar-water) is taken on an empty stomach. Taking vinegar with honey may help to ease this problem.

Dental researchers have reported that excess use of vinegar (and other high acid liquids such as carbonated beverages and fruit juices) can cause loss of tooth enamel. The reports concentrate on damage done to the teeth of relatively young people, but caution should be exercised by anyone using vinegar on a regular basis. You may want to consider drinking your daily vinegar tonic through a straw, to limit its exposure to tooth enamel.

THEN AGAIN, MAYBE ITS NOT SO BAD!

The British Dental Journal carried a study which says vinegary snack foods are among the least harmful to teeth! The study found vinegar crisps (along with peanuts) were less detrimental to teeth than high carbohydrate (sugary) snacks.

VINEGAR CAN BE FUN!

A Louisiana firm now produces some very special pickles. Called Upside-Down Cajun Brand Pickles, they come in rather ordinary looking glass jars. But, the jar labels are applied upside-down. This means, when the label is right-side-up, the lid is at the bottom. Supposedly, keeping pickle jars up-side-down keeps the pickles fresher!

A NEW GENERATION OF VINEGAR

Until recently all vinegar was pretty much the same strength. Now Heinz U.S.A. has introduced a vinegar intended just for cleaning. It is twice as strong as conventional vinegar. This is a white vinegar, not apple cider vinegar. It promises to make cleaning and disinfecting with vinegar easier.

Note: The new Heinz vinegar is meant to be used for cleaning, not for cooking or as a diet supplement.

REFERENCES

ABALAN, F. Med Hypoth 15: 385, 1984.

"ACADEMY Offers Tips to Avoid Swimmers Ear." American Academy of Otolaryngology-Head and Neck Surgery

ALLGEIER, R.J., G.B. Nickol, and H.A. Conner. "Vinegar: History and Development." Part I. [Research Dept. of] U.S. Industrial Chemicals Co. pp. VI-2VI-4.

ALLGEIER, R.J., G.B. Nickol, and H.A. Conner. "Vinegar: History and Development." Part II. [Research Dept. of] U.S. Industrial Chemicals Co.

ANDERSON, J.W., W.J.L. Lin Chen. American Journal of Clinical Nutrition 32(2), 1979. pp. 346-363.

"ASK the Experts." University of California, Berkeley Wellness Letter. Oct. 1990: 8.

"ASSUMING Stomach Atrophy, Elderly Should Take Calcium with Meals." Geriatrics 6 June 1986: 19.

BEADNELL, C.E., T.A. Rider, J.A. Williamson, and P.J. Fender. Medical Journal of Australia 4 May 1992: 655-8.

BELLEME, John. East West Aug 1990: 30(6).

BLOCK, Gladys, Blossom Patterson, and Amy Subar. Nutrition and Cancer 18(1): 1-31.

BLOT, William J., Jun-Yao Li, Phillip R. Taylor, Wande Guo, Sandford Davsey, Guo-Qing Wang,Chung S. Yang Su-Fang Zheng, Mitchell Gail, Guang-Yi Li, Yu Yu, Buo-qi Liu, Joseph Tangrea, Yu-hai Sun, Fusheng Liu, Joseph F. Fraumeni, Jr., You-Hui Zhang, Bing Li. Journal of National Cancer Institute 15 Sept 1993: 1483-1492.

BRAGG, Paul C., ND., Ph.D. [Biochemist], and Patricia Bragg, ND., Ph.D. Apple Cider Vinegar Health System. California: Health Science. pp. 4-5, 26-27.

"Bright Ideas." regarding Michael Brimhall of the Peter Coppola Salon in New York City. Parade Magazine 30 May 1993: 7.

BURKITT, D.P., A.R.P. Walker, and N.S. Painter. Journal of the American Medical Association 229, 1974. pp. 1068-1074.

CANET, Merilyn. British Dental Journal p. 158.

"CIDER." The Encyclopedia Britannica. London: Encyclopedia Britannica Company, Ltd., . p. 700.

DAVIS, A. Let's Cook It Right. New York: New American Library, 1970.

DELANEY, Lisa and Stephanie Ebbert. Prevention Jan 1992: 33(8).

DELHEY, Diane M., MS, RD, Ellen J. Anderson, MS, RD, and Susan H. Laramee, MS, RD. Journal of the American Dietetic Association October 1989: 1448(4).

DE VINCENZI, M., F. Castriotta, S. DiFolco, A. Dracos, M. Magliola, R. Mattei, I. Purificato, A. Stacchini, P. Stacchini, and V. Silano. Food Additives & Containments April-June 1987: 161-218.

"DIETARY Fibre: Effects on Plasma and Biliary Lipids in Men." in Medical Aspects of Dietary Fibre, Spiller, G.A., Kay, R.M., eds., Plenum Press, N.Y. 1980. p. 153.

"DIETARY Supplements Reduce Cancer Deaths in China." Journal of the National Cancer Institute 15 Sept 1993: 1448-1449.

"ELDERLY Are Advised to Take Calcium with Meals." American Family Physician 34 #3: 188.

ERSHOFF, B.H. and W.E. Marshall. Journal of Food Science 40, 1975.

ERSHOFF, B.H. Journal of Food Science 41, 1976. p. 949.

FACKLEMAN, K.A. Science News 25 Sept 1993: 144.

FASANELLA, R.M. Ophthalmic Surgery Feb 1991.

FENNER, P.J., P.F. Fitzpatrick, R.J. Hartwick, and R. Skinner. Medical Journal of Australia 9-23 Dec 1985: 550-1.

GELB, Barbara Levine. The Dictionary of Food And What's in it for You. New York: Paddington Press, 1986. pp. 150, 244.

GHEBREKIDAN, H. " Ethiopian Medical Journal Jan 1992: 23-31.

GRAY, Gregory E., MD, PhD. Journal of American Dietetic Association Dec 1989: 1795-1802.

HAAS, Elson M., M.D. Staying Healthy with Nutrition-The Complete Guide to Diet and Nutritional Medicine. California: Celestial Arts, 1992. p. 299-300, 349.

HADFIELD, L.C., L.P. Beard, and T.K. Leonard-Green. Journal of the American Dietetic Association Dec 1989: 1810-1.

HARDINGE, M.G., M.D., PhD, A.C. Chambers, BA, H. Crooks, BS., and Frederick J. Stare, M.D., PhD. American Journal of Clinical Nutrition 6(5), 1958. pp. 523-525.

HARTLEY, Tom. Business First of Buffalo 4 March 1991: 1,18.

HENDLER, Sheldon Saul, M.D., PhD. The Complete Guide to Anti-Aging Nutrients. New York: Simon & Schuster, 1985. pp. 27, 69-71, 104-106, 144-146, 170, 182-183, l94-195.

HENDLER, Sheldon Saul, M.D., PhD. The Purification Prescription. New York: William Morrison & Co., 1991. p. 56.

HILLS, M. Curring Arthritis-the Drug-Free Way. London: Sheldon, 1985.

"HONEY." Encyclopedia Britannica. 1980 ed.

HUMPHREYS, Dr. Patricia. Countryside & Small Stock Journal May-June 1988: 13-14.

HYLTON, William H., ed. The Rodale Herb Book. Pennsylvania: Rodale Press Book Division, 1974. p. 430-433.

JARVIS, D.C., M.D. Folk Medicine...A Vermont Doctor's Guide to Good Health. New York: Holt, Rinehart and Winston, 1958.

JARVIS, D.C., M.D. Vermont Folk Medicine and Arthritis (Excerpt from D.C. Jarvis, M.D. Arthritis and Folk Medicine. New York: Holt, Rinehart and Winston, 1960.)

JENKINS, D.J.A., A.R. Leeds, C. Newton, and J.H. Cummings. Lancet 1, 1975. pp. 1116-1117.

JONES, J. The High Calcium Diet. Chicago: Nightingale-Conant Corporation, 1986.

KALLAN, Carla. Prevention Oct. 1991: 39-43

KARAPINAR, M. and S.A. Gonul. International Journal of Food Microbiology Aug 1992: 343-7.

KARAPINAR, M. and S.A. Gonul. International Journal of Food Microbiology Jul 1992: 261-4.

KAUFMAN, M.B. Pediatric Emergency Care Feb 1992: 27-8.

KIRK, Ronald S., ed. Pearson's Composition and Analysis of Foods. New York: Wiley, 1991. pp. 458-468.

KORN, Carl, M.D., Assistant Clinical Professor of Dermatology, University of Southern California in Tkac, Debora, et al. The Doctor's Book of Home Remedies. New York: Bantam Books, 1991. p. 629.

KRATZER, Brice L., and Dallas W. Sandt. Nutrition: Where Have All These Labels Been? Nutrition Awareness System. 100-103.

LALANNE, Elaine with Richard Benyo. Total Juicing. Plume, Penguin Group, 1992. pp. 58-59.

LARSON, David. Mayo Clinic Family Health Book. William Morrow and Company, Inc., 1990. pp. 676-677.

LEE, Sally. New Theories on Diet and Nutrition. p. 45.

LEGRO, William, ed. High-Speed Healing...The Fastest, Safest and Most Effective Shortcuts to Lasting Relief. Pennsylvania: Rodale Press, 1991. pp. 57, 275.

LEVEILLE, G.A. and H.E. Sauberlich Journal of Nutrition 88, 1966: 209-217.

LEVIN, B. and D. Horwitz. Medical Clinics of North America 63(5), 1979. pp. 1043-1055.

LI, Jun Yao, Phillip R. Taylor, Bing Li, Sanford Dawsey, Guo-Qing Wang, Abby G. Ershow, Wande Gua, Shu-Fan Liu, Chung S. Yang, Qiong Shen, Wen Wang, Steven D. Mark, Xiao-Nong Zou, Peter Greenwald, Yang-Ping Wu, William J. Blot. Journal of National Cancer Institute 15 Sept 1993: 1492-1498.

LIN, T.M., K.S. Kim, E. Karvinen, and A.C. Ivy. American Journal of Physiology 188 (1), 1957: 66-70.

MARTIN, J.C. and I. Audley. Medical Journal of Australia 6 Aug 1990: 164-6.

MENTER, Marcia. Redbook Jan 1993: 30-32

MINDELL, Earl, R.Ph., Ph.D. Earl Mindell's Herb Bible. New York: Fireside a division of Simon & Schuster, 1992. pp. 42, 79-80.

MODAN, Barich. Lancet 18 July 1992: 162(3).

MORGAN, Brian L.G., Dr. Nutrition Prescription-Strategies for Preventing and Treating 50 Common Diseases. New York: Crown Publishers, Inc. p. 183, 276-279.

MOWREY, Daniel B., Ph.D. The Scientific Validation of Herbal Medicine. Connecticut: Keats Publishing, Inc. pp. 39-46, 89-96.

NAHATA, M.C., D. Hembekides, and K.I. Koranyi. Chemotherapy vol 32, issue 2: 178-82.

JOURNAL of the National Cancer Institute September 15, 1993. Philip R. Taylor, M.D., Sc.D., Jun-Yao Li, M.D., and Bing Li, M.D.

NOTELOVITS, M., and M. Ware. Stand Tall! Gainesville, FL: Triad Publishing Company, 1982.

"NUTRITION Intervention Trials." Journal of the National Cancer Institute 15 Sept 1993: 1445.

OMEGA Nutrition. "Apple Cider Vinegar." Omega Nutrition: Vancouver, B.C. V5X3Y3.

OTHMER, Kirk. Encyclopedia of Chemical Technology New York: Interscience-a division of Wiley, 1963. pp. 254-265.

PEARSON, Durk and Sandy Shaw. Life Extension...A Practical Scientific Approach-Adding Years to Your Life and Life to Your Years. pp. 296-300.

PEARSON, Durk and Sandy Shaw. The Life Extension Weight Loss Program. New York: Doubleday & Co., Inc., 1986. pp. 29-47.

PENNINGTON, Jean A.T., PH.D., R.D., and Helen Nichols Church, B.S. Bowes and Church's Food Values of Portions Commonly Used. New York: Harper & Row Publishers, 1979.

RADER, Lora. Countryside & Small Stock Journal March-April 1993: 14(1).

REDDY, B.S., K. Watanabe, and A. Sheinfil. Journal of Nutrition 110, 1980. pp. 1247-1254.

RODIN, Judith. American Journal of Clinical Nutrition 1990: 51: 428-35.

ROSANOFF, A., AND D.H. CALLOWAY. New England Journal of Medicine 306:239, 1982.

SCOTT, CYRIL. Complete Cider Vinegar. Wellingborough: Thorsons, 1987.

SOLOMON, Caleb. Wall Street Journal 30 Sept. 1992: A1, A4.

SOUTHGATE, D.A.T. American Journal of Clinical Nutrition 31, 1978.

STRAUCH, G., P. Pandos, and H. Bricaire. Journal of Clinical Endocrinology and Metablolism April 1971: 582(3).

STORY, J.A., D. Kritchevsky, and M.A. Eastwood. Dietary Fibers. Chemistry and Nutrition. New York: Academic Press, 1979. p. 49.

"SWIMMER'S Ear." University of California at Berkeley Wellness Letter Aug 1991: 6.

"SWIMMER'S Ear, Itchy Ears and Ear Fungus." American Academy of Otolaryngology-Head and Neck Surgery 1984.

TKAC, Debora, et al. The Doctors Book of Home Remedies. New York: Bantam Books, 1991.

TRENTHAN, David. Science 24 Sept 1993.

TROWELL, H. American Journal of Clinical Nutrition 31(10), 1978. pp. S3-S11.

UNITED States. Department of Agriculture. Nutritive Value of American Foods-In Common Units. Washington, D.C.: GPO, 1975.

UNITED States. Department of Health and Human Sciences. The Surgeon General's Report on Nutrition and Health. Warner Books, 1989.

UNITED States. Department of Health and Human Sciences. The Surgeon General's Report on Nutrition and Health. DHHS (PHS) Publication No. 88-50210. Washington, D.C.: U.S. Government Printing Office. GPO Stock No. 017-001-00465-1.

"VARIETIES of Vinegars Add Taste for Calorie Counters. " The Washington Post.

VISSER, Margaret. Saturday Night June 1992: 42.

WALSH, B.A. Journal of ET Nursing Jul-Aug 1992: 110-3.

"WATER in the Ear." University of California, Berkeley Wellness Letter. August 1987

WILEN, Joan and Lydia Wilen. Chicken Soup and Other Folk Remedies. New York: Fawcett Columbine, 1984. p. 26.

WISE Encyclopedia of Cookery, The. New York: Wm. H. Wise & Co., Inc., 1949. p. 1219.

"WINNING the Fiber Game." University of California, Berkeley Wellness Letter. March 1990: 3.

WOLMAN, Patricia Giblin, Ed.D., R.D. Journal of the American Dietetic Association Sept 1987: 1211-1214.

The
Vinegar
Book II

by

Emily Thacker

Dear Reader,

Thank you so very much for your support of "THE VINEGAR BOOK" - and your ongoing interest in all the other books in the series! You have been a real encouragement to me.

Your letters have shown me your deep and continuing interest in the healthy benefits of vinegar. In reading them I have discovered much wisdom, and found that I had left many questions about vinegar unanswered. This sequel to "THE VINEGAR BOOK" will attempt to answer those questions. And, it brings you a new way to experience vinegar. There is an entry for each day of the year. So now, in addition to the descriptive explanations of vinegar's virtues, you can use this book to learn a bit about its history, how to make it and how use it each day of the year.

Commercially produced apple cider vinegar is one of the best buys in the supermarket. It is inexpensive, low calorie, has no fat and is health promoting. Its content is protected by government standards, so its acid content is constant. Organic vinegars are a bit more expensive, but still a bargain. When cost is not a factor, the superb taste of balsamic vinegar can be a special treat.

Every part of your life affects your health. Doctors are finally recognizing that how we conduct our lives can have a great impact on both how long we live and the quality of that life. I would like to encourage you to explore your healthcare options. Become an aware, cautious consumer of medical care. Ask your doctor about the options that are available to you. Become informed about possible side effects to treatments. And most of all, insist on being a part of all decisions about your medical care!

In this volume, newest medical research is combined with the best of old-time home remedies. The information in this book is intended to help you work with your medical care provider - it can never take the place of proper medical care. But it may, just possibly, help you stay well and heal faster. This collection of vinegar uses also includes ways people in other cultures use vinegar to aid them in the search for better health. One of these complementary health systems, Traditional Chinese Medicine (TCM) contains the ancient wisdom of a people who use vinegar in very much the same ways our grandmothers used it!

Vinegar intensifies the flavor of foods, without dominating their natural goodness and taste sensations. It adds excitement to meals and is an especially effective way to personalize dishes, letting you create your own distinctive hints of flavor. It is a quick way to add a zesty taste to otherwise bland dishes. It can be delicate and subtle or strong and demanding. The choice is yours.

Fortified vinegars, that you make yourself, can have deep, concentrated flavors. Store kinds, by comparison, are apt to be mild and weak. If you enjoy foods with vibrant colors, tantalizing aromas, interesting textures and full, rich flavors - vinegar is for you!

The very best way to ensure good health is with a healthy lifestyle. Vinegar can play an important part in that way of living!

Wishing you all the best,

Emily

And God Said, "Let There Be Vinegar!"

In the Bible, VINEGAR is mentioned 13 times, and it —

— Is "an organic molecule that may have played a role in the formation of life," says the Associated Press.

— Has been "found in a cloud of dust and gas 25,000 light years from earth," reports USA Today.

— Is a "building block for the body," according to Science Digest.

— Is "used by the body to burn fat," says the New York Herold Tribune.

Scientists believe vinegar had an important role in the creation of life. They tell us it was part of the primordial soup which provided a chemical start for life, because when vinegar is combined with ammonia, it makes up the simplest biologically important building block of life! This is why scientists were excited when astronomers at the University of Illinois found vinegar in the cloud of gas and dust called Sagittarius B2 North.

Vinegar (acetic acid) is present in most plant and animal tissues. Even the human body makes some. It is needed to burn both fats and carbohydrates. It also plays a role in how the body stores fat. When vinegar enters the blood stream it is carried to the kidneys and muscles. There, it is either oxidized into pure energy or used to make body tissues, through its ability to make essential amino acids. It even facilitates the process which forms the red blood cells that supply the body's oxygen!

*Vinegar +
Ammonia
= Glycine*

Glycine is an essential to-life amino acid.

NEUTRALIZES POISONS

The acid which we know as vinegar is used by the body as a detoxifying agent. Molecules of this amazing liquid are able to connect themselves to many dangerous substances, including some drugs and poisons. This action creates entirely new compounds, which tend to be biologically inactive. Then, these harmless substances can be safely expelled by the body.

WHAT IS VINEGAR?

Vinegar, with all its life-enhancing qualities, has been used and appreciated since the most ancient of times. Technically, vinegar is formed by the oxidation-fermentation of ethanol, resulting in a brew which contains from 4% to 8% acetic acid. The ethanol (ethyl alcohol) is changed into acetic acid (vinegar) through the growth of an acetobacter*. This is a living substance that eats (oxidizes) the alcohol and produces (excretes) acetic acid.

A good, naturally produced vinegar contains far more than simply acetic acid. The acetobacter's actions load the fluid with newly created enzymes, while retaining particles of the food used to make the vinegar. The final result, that wonderful thing we call vinegar, has some of the goodness of the original food, enhanced with traces of a wide variety of vitamins, minerals and enzymes.

ENZYME POWER

Enzymes have the ability to cause chemical reactions to take place without becoming directly involved in the process themselves. Vinegar's enzymes are made by living bacteria (acetobacter) and because they are catalysts for important biological chemical reactions, they are critical to life.

As foods are turned into vinegar, they often pick up particles of other substances along the way. For example, naturally processed vinegar is often stored for several years in wooden casks. This contributes to its virtues, as can be seen by the way the flavor of the vinegar is changed by the type of wood used to make the barrels**.

A HEALING REMEDY - REDISCOVERED

Vinegar has always been around, but over the past few years sales of this miraculous food have increased dramatically. Flavored and organically pure varieties are now available in most grocery stores. As demand grows, more and more people are becoming aware of both its ability to improve the taste of foods and of its healthfulness.

One of biggest jobs vinegar does in the human body is to promote the growth of beneficial bacteria. They are needed to keep disease-producing germs at bay. For example, human intestines contain millions of good bacteria (such as bifidus and lactobicillus) to keep the gastrointestinal tract healthy and disease free. Helpful bacteria in the intestines also:

*See Chapter Two; **See Chapter Six.*

- Support the immune system.
- Help digest food.
- Make some vitamins.
- Keep the intestines acidic.
- Discourage illness caused by E. coli and clostridia bacteria.

Hundreds of foods make use of the preservative and unique taste qualities of vinegar. It is an important part of naturally formed aged cheeses and wine. It is an essential ingredient in catsup and mayonnaise, and is one of the original preservatives for meats and eggs.

No matter what scientists finally decide about vinegar's role in the formation of life, people have instinctively known, for untold centuries, that vinegar is good for them. It is truly a living substance, capable of bringing health benefits far beyond the ability of today's medical world to fully comprehend.

Throughout the ancient world, cultures depended on the virtues of vinegar to keep them healthy. History tells us the Greeks and Romans often cooked foods in mixtures of honey and vinegar, creating the classic sweet and sour taste celebrated in so many dishes today. They also used vinegar to preserve fruits and vegetables. History reveals a long-standing faith and trust in vinegar-based foods and remedies:

1 Ginger soaked in vinegar has long been used to prevent and relieve motion sickness and digestive upsets. Asians have used it this way for more than 2,000 years.

2 Most meals included a bowl of honey, called oxybaphon, and a bowl of vinegar, called acetabulum. They were used as dips for bread. These common dipping bowls were part of everyday life in Old Testament Bible times, as evidenced by Boaz's invitation to Ruth to share his table and communal vinegar bowl, as well as in New Testament times.

3 Ancient Romans safely ate oysters because they served them in a vinegar sauce.

4 A banquet of that era might feature pork shoulder cooked with vinegar. Tender morsels of this popular meat were served in a sauce of apricots, honey and wine, seasoned with pepper and mint.

5 One of the ways these ancient feasts began was with a dish of chopped olives. They were mixed with vinegar, oil and spices such as coriander, cumin, fennel, rue and mint.

6 The people of old Pompeii preserved onions in vinegar and salt.

7 Others of that era preferred the taste of asparagus in brine and vinegar.

8 For a sweeter treat, elite Romans enjoyed the flavor of endive and vinegar, served with honey. This was especially recommended for wintertime when other greens were less available.

9 Pliny writes of the excellencies of lettuce served with a mustard seed and vinegar sauce.

10 He also recommended cooking the large, coarse leaves of elecampane (we call this sunflower look-alike sneeze weed or horseheal) in vinegar before drying it.

11 Both Greeks and Romans thought vinegar from Egypt was excellent and imported large quantities of it.

12 Ancient Greeks sliced turnips very thin, dusted them with salt, then soaked them in vinegar. These pickled turnips were often flavored with mustard seeds and raisins.

13 Greeks, as well as Asians, considered plums preserved in vinegar to be a special delicacy.

14 Italy of olden times was known for an all-purpose sauce that was used at most meals. The salted entrails of fish were aged in vinegar to make this distinctive, strong smelling, condiment.

15 Purslane was also preserved in a similar manner. It was salted, then covered with vinegar.

16 Romans often flavored their pickled turnips with myrtle berries and honey.

17 Or, they soaked mustard seeds in water until they were softened, pounded them into a paste and mixed them with vinegar. Then this creamy vinegar was used to preserve turnips.

18 They made interesting tasting salads by combining savory, mint, rue, coriander, parsley, chives, lettuce and cheese. These were all seasoned with peppered vinegar and a bit of oil.

19 Stuffed suckling pig, basted with lard and vinegar, was roasted, then eaten with bread crumbs boiled with vinegar, ginger, saffron and cloves.

Pliny -

Roman author + orator.

20 The Roman emperor Tiberius is reputed to have liked the taste of cucumbers with a vinegar and honey dressing. He is said to have eaten this dish with lots of pepper sprinkled over it.

21 Another luxury dish of this era was made by cooking apricots in honey, wine and vinegar. Usually, the liquid was thickened, then flavored with pepper and mint.

22 Olives were preserved by putting them in jars and alternating them with layers of fennel, aromatic resin and vinegar.

23 When Roman soldiers went marching off to war, they took along large supplies of vinegar to mix with the local water. Sometimes they also added dried figs, honey, peaches or even salt to the mixture.

24 A paste of wood ashes and vinegar was used by the Greeks of olden times to treat skin eruptions.

25 Vinegar was sipped to guard against scurvy by soldiers during the U.S. Civil War.

26 French soldiers are reputed to have used it to cool overheated cannons during battles.

27 During the 1500s and 1600s, Europeans cooked thin slices of veal on skews, then served them with vinegar, butter and sugar.

28 And, mutton tongue was often stewed in a mixture of vinegar and orange juice.

29 This was also a time when carrots were frequently cooked with honey and vinegar.

30 Refined Europeans of the 1600s and 1700s carried little boxes, called vinaigrettes, as holders for vinegar soaked sponges. Tiny openings in the tops allowed them to sniff the vinegar to protect themselves from the foul odors and diseases that plagued city life. Often these boxes were made of gold or silver.

31 By the 1700s, people in England used vinegar as a healing gargle, much as we do today.

CHAPTER TWO   FEBRUARY

How Vinegar Is Made

Vinegar's history is as old as that of mankind. The first vinegar probably began as wine which was exposed to air. Wild yeasts fermented it into a wonderful, life-enhancing liquid! For centuries vinegar was thought to be a magically created potion. Those who knew how to oversee and control the making of the wondrous brew guarded the secret carefully, then handed the process down to their children. Because, all vinegar is not created equal. Its aroma and flavor are influenced by the way it is made and aged.

Vinegar is a complex substance, brimming with subtle flavors and aromas and packed with an assortment of nutrients, enzymes and trace elements. The best vinegar is a combination of sweet mellowness from wooden storage barrels and the sharp, sour zing of acetic acid. The flavor, aroma and healthfulness of vinegar are supplied by the food from which it is made, and from the container used for aging it.

MAKING VINEGAR

Vinegar can be made from any plant which contains enough sugar to ferment into the alcohol needed to make acetic acid. That food should have a pleasant flavor and aroma, as these beginning qualities will carry over into the finished product and contribute to the final taste and flavor of the vinegar.

Vinegar production begins when a sugary liquid is changed into an alcoholic one by yeast. Then, this brew is changed into an acetic acid containing solution. The microorganisms which cause the alcohol to change to acetic acid are those of the Acetobacter group.

GOOD BACTERIA - BAD BACTERIA

The action of harmful bacteria causes meat to rot and can cause illness. The action of beneficial bacteria produces cheese, yogurt, tofu and some coffees and teas. Without the action of bacteria, digestion in the colon would not be possible. Good health depends on encouraging beneficial bacteria and discouraging harmful bacteria.

The particular bacteria which produces vinegar is called acetobacter. This gooey glob, called "mother," floats on the surface. These good bacteria feed on oxygen and reproduce rapidly in substances that meet their nutritional needs. Acetobacter tends to continuously change into new forms, so those who want to produce a standardized product use a starter, just as a yeast starter is used in making bread.

Acetic is not the only acid formed during vinegar production. Some newly formed acids react with residual traces of alcohol and form esters. Esters are important to creating the unique, individual aroma of various vinegars. Some facts about making, storing and using vinegar follow:

32 More than 125 million gallons of vinegar are produced in the United States each year. It is so important to food processors that they buy it in huge tank trucks.

33 In the United States, retail sales account for 24% of vinegar use, the manufacture of pickles for 20%. The other 56% is used to make salad dressings, mayonnaise, catsup, mustard and other vinegar-based food products.

34 The oldest commercial production method (named after the French city where it originated in the 1600s) is the Orleans, or slow process. Using this method, a batch of vinegar takes from 4 to 12 weeks to complete.

35 Zoogloea mycoderma, the thick, sticky mass called "mother" aids fermentation. So, bits of it are often transferred from one batch of vinegar to another. Old world vinegar makers guard this valuable starter because it helps retain the uniqueness of each producer's vinegar.

36 Mother is a living substance and will die if it sinks to the bottom of the fermenting liquid and loses its air supply. Jolting the container can cause this.

37 Often a sliver of wood, slice of bread or corn cob serves as a raft to help the mother to remain floating on the surface.

38 The best vinegar is aged in wood, where its ability to react with its container enhances its flavor.

39 Never age vinegar in metal containers. Its acidic nature reacts with metal and can leach out harmful chemicals.

Orleans, France is famous for its vinegar production.

40 Most commercial vinegars are clarified by being filtered, then pasteurized to prevent them from continuing to grow mother after being bottled.

41 A process called "fining" adds chemicals to vinegar to precipitate out any suspended food particles. It makes the product clear and appetizing, but removes nutrients. Bentonite and potassium ferrocyanide casein are used in fining.

42 Large volume, commercial vinegars, are pasteurized by heating them to about 150°F. If heated above 160°F, flavor and aroma deteriorate.

43 At home, preserve vinegar in small bottles, filled to the top, to minimize the amount of air exposure. This will help retain full flavor and strength.

44 It is particularly dangerous to store vinegar in copper, lead or zinc containers.

45 Heating vinegar in an iron pan may cause it to turn very dark, even black.

46 Smell test great vinegar by pouring a few tablespoons into a short, wide glass, swirl the liquid, then delicately sniff the aroma from a few inches above the glass.

TASTE TESTING VINEGAR

47 Vinegar is so acidic that, at the first sip, the taste buds shut down. This makes it very difficult to accurately taste test a second sample. This natural reaction can be minimized by sampling vinegar on a sugar cube. Dip the sugar into the vinegar and taste test the flavored cube.

48 Reactivate the taste buds between tasting different vinegars by sipping a bit of seltzer water.

49 Nibbling on unsalted crackers helps reset the taste buds between taste testing vinegars.

50 Never, never taste test pepper vinegar from a spoon - it can be extremely hot and cause burns to the mouth. Shake a drop or so of this fiery liquid onto a fork full of food to test it.

51 Pepper vinegar may be safely taste tested by adding a drop of it to a tablespoon of soup.

Substances for fining vinegar include ground-up fish bladders!

74

52 Pepper vinegar which is too hot can be moderated by the addition of extra unseasoned vinegar.

STORING & USING VINEGAR

53 Pasteurized vinegar, if the bottle is not opened, lasts for years. Once the bottle has been opened it will begin to lose its zip in about 3 months, even if kept tightly capped.

54 Renew the vitality of old vinegar by adding a dash of fresh vinegar to the bottle.

55 Vinegar is a wonderfully versatile liquid that can absorb both the flavor and healthful characteristics of herbs and spices. When sprinkled on meats, vegetables and fruits it passes on that goodness to them.*

56 Old-timers claim that if you dip your hands in apple cider vinegar before gardening, they will not chill as fast as they otherwise would.

57 In the 1700s and 1800s fruit flavored vinegars were used as drink flavorings, much as lemons are used to make lemonade today.

58 In China, herbs are often processed in vinegar to increase their effectiveness.

59 One of the best ways to use your own homemade vinegars is to put some in a pretty decanter with a shaker top. Keep it on the table to replace the salt shaker.

So Pretty!

LEAP YEAR BONUS:
Make herbal vinegars especially pleasing to the eye by placing a sprig of fresh herb in the bottle. Also a great way to enhance berry vinegars!

* See Chapter Four

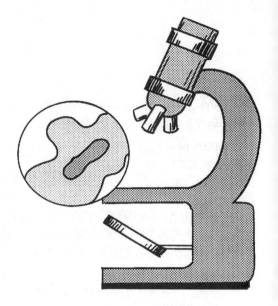

CHAPTER THREE   **MARCH**

Vinegar – It's Good For You!

It is said sharks can detect blood diluted to one tiny particle per billion. Homeopathic medical remedies are often diluted until scientists say there is no measurable trace of the original. Pure, natural vinegar that has not been filtered is a complex mix of tiny traces of nutrients, including enzymes, vitamins and minerals, plus varying amounts of as yet unidentified substances.

Just as sharks rush to tiny traces of blood and homeopathic remedies provide relief of symptoms, vinegar has been credited with having a surprising number of health-promoting qualities. Many believe this is because of its unique combination of ingredients.

Researchers analyzed vinegar using gas chromatography-mass spectrometry. Amazingly, they were able to identify more than 90 compounds, in just its volatile parts! In addition to acetic acid they found three others, as well as an assortment of phenols,* alcohols, esters, carbonyls - and even traces of hydrocarbons in vinegars made from wood products.

Distilled vinegar, usually considered to be the least nutritious of all vinegars, is a surprising storehouse of goodness. It has no fat, less than 30 calories and only 2 milligrams of sodium in an entire cup! Plus, it has a bit of protein, fiber and carbohydrate, plus calcium, phosphorus, iron, potassium, vitamins A and D, folacin, zinc, thiamin (vitamin B-1), riboflavin (vitamin B-2), niacin, magnesium, and ascorbic acid (vitamin C).

The World Health Organization** describes vinegar as a liquid which contains the goodness of its originating food product. These are food particles which are not changed during the production of the vinegar. This means each kind of vinegar has traces of the nutrients found in the originating food. In vinegars which have been filtered, these particles are usually not visible. Organic vinegar may look a bit cloudy and have a layer of sediment in the bottom of the bottle. This is a sign the product has not had precious nutrients filtered or precipitated out.

*See anti-aging antioxidants in Chapter Five; **Of the United Nations.*

The fine particles in cloudy vinegar contain tiny fragments of the original food from which it was made, so each variety has a unique nutritional content. Apples in apple cider vinegar bring amino acids such as tryptophan, threonine, isoleucine, leucine, lysine, methionine, cystine, phenylalanine, tyrosine, valine, arginine, histidine, alanine, aspartic acid, glutamic acid, glycine, proline and serine. And they bring vitamins such as A, B-6, folate, asorbic acid, thiamin, riboflavin, niacin and pantothenic acid. Plus, apples have minerals such as calcium, iron, magnesium, phosphorus, potassium, zinc, copper and manganese. So, while vinegar contains everything found in acetic acid, it also contains much more.

Because vinegar contains traces of the whatever was used to make it, it is extremely important for that food to be free of contaminates. Pesticides such as Alar and Captan are sometimes used on apples. Fruit grown in the United States is inspected for these and other chemicals, but imports from other countries may still contain contaminates. Some good, and some not so good, things that may find their way into vinegar follow:

60 Alar is a chemical which is used to control the time frame in which apples grow and ripen. It is a brand name for daminozide, a chemical which, during processing, changes into UDMH (a substance chemically related to rocket fuel). Scientists feel it is most probably a carcinogen to which children are especially vulnerable.

61 Occasionally, during the commercial production of vinegar, a bit of vitamin C may be added to it.

62 If apples sprayed with Captan are not thoroughly washed before processing, traces can find their way into apple cider vinegar.

63 Researchers have identified eight different esters and more than a dozen and a half alcohols in vinegar. These esters and alcohols are the reason it has such a complex aroma and taste.

64 Japanese researchers have demonstrated that the process of fermentation predigests nutrients. This makes them easier for the body to absorb.

65 Vinegar's carbohydrate is 98% digestible. Enzymes, one of the by-products of vinegar's fermentation process, make other foods more digestible.

66 Enzymes in vinegar influence metabolism, the chemical changes in living cells by which energy is provided to the body. This includes the way fats are burned.

Wheat Bran is only 56% digestible.

67 Vinegar which has not been distilled has more particles of its original food base than vinegar which has been distilled.

68 Apple cider vinegar is the only kind of vinegar which contains malic acid.

69 Over the years, some vinegar makers have added sulphites to extend its shelf life. Others have added salt.

VINEGAR VIRTUES

Some of the reasons researchers have found for vinegar being of use as a germ fighter follow:

70 Vinegar is an antimicrobial agent, effective against yeasts, bacteria and molds.

71 It is effective in killing salmonella and staphylococcus, as well as at least five other germs.

72 Chinese physicians treat hepatitis with a combination of rice vinegar and B-1 supplements.

73 They also have found vaporized vinegar useful against flu germs. This may explain the usefulness of old-time remedies that suggested sniffing vinegar to avoid diseases such as the plague.

74 Vinegar's germ fighting ability can be used externally in compresses to aid in healing stubborn sores and long-lasting skin infections.

75 Asians use good quality vinegar for more than taste. It is an excellent preservative for soy sauce.

76 Spicy foods, horseradish, hot mustard and red pepper encourage decongestion activities in the body. One of the most effective ways to deliver these foods is in a vinegar base.

77 Japanese scientists have shown that vinegar kills germs that can cause colitis, dysentery and some of the most common forms of food poisoning.

OLD TIME REMEDIES

Vinegar's healing ways have long been used to both prevent and fight disease. Some ways it was used follow:

78 In the ancient world, vinegar was considered the treatment of choice for those who had eaten poisonous mushrooms.

79 Many cultures believe fevers will be moderated if the body is wiped down with full strength apple cider vinegar.

80 Romans of long ago treated those considered to have mental problems with watercress soaked in vinegar.

81 One of their philosophers suggests dipping raw cabbage in vinegar to make it as digestible as if it were cooked.

82 Beet leaves in vinegar, with lentils and beans, was recommended for those with strong digestive systems.

83 Egyptians considered vinegar to be an appetite stimulant. Europeans served it before and after a feast to aid digestion.

84 It is said that when the digestive system is stressed by eating too much fruit, relief can be found by sipping a glass of water with 2 tablespoons of ginger vinegar stirred into it.

85 Others suggest one can arouse a sluggish appetite by offering a bit of meat cooked with a dash of vinegar.

86 Ease a toothache, an old adage says, by holding a mix of vinegar and water in the mouth for a minute or so.*

87 In ancient China, vinegar was considered a source of important minerals and vitamins.

88 Traditional Chinese Medicine treated high blood pressure by feeding celery cooked with vinegar.

89 And, awaken one who has fainted by allowing them to breathe the vapors of boiling vinegar. This is especially good for reviving children!

90 A very old remedy for diarrhea says to sprinkle sliced radishes with sugar and allow to set for 10 minutes. Add the radishes and liquid which has formed to apple cider vinegar. Nibble a few slices each day.

See caution in Chapter Five

CHAPTER FOUR   APRIL

How To Make Fruit, Vegetable & Herbal Vinegars

Vinegar producers of the 1800s found they could make acetic acid from wood chips, or even from the residues discarded during paper making. These companies added flavorings and color and called the result apple cider vinegar. This cheap imitation was, of course, deficient in taste and aroma, and did not contain the vast array of natural enzymes and nutrients of the original. Today's labeling laws prevent this kind of product adulteration - if the bottle says apple cider vinegar - it contains vinegar that began life as apples. Nearly every government in the world (as well as the World Health Organization) have strict standards for what can be called vinegar. And most is made from nutritious food.

Through the ages, countries have been known by their premium vinegars. As far back as the 700s, well-to-do Baghdad merchants imported rice vinegar from special provinces in China. Other countries have also become known for the quality of their vinegar. For example, we associate vinegar:

Made of	With	Made of	With
Apples	United States	Dates	Ancient Babylonia
Bananas	Nicaragua	Malt	England
Cane	Philippines	Potatoes	Germany
Rice	China (and Japan)	Coconut	Indonesia

Vinegar can be made of any food with enough sugar content to ferment into the alcohol needed to create it. Some of the many foods which are used to make vinegar include:

Apples	Cranberries	Oats	Plums
Apricots	Dates	Oranges	White potatoes
Barley	Grapes	Papaya	Sweet potatoes
Bananas	Guava	Passion fruit	Raspberries
Beets	Honey	Peaches	Rice
Cane	Mangoes	Pears	Strawberries
Coconut	Maple syrup	Persimmons	Watermelons
Corn	Molasses	Pineapples	Whey

Descriptions of the most popular vinegars, plus when and how to use them follow:

WHITE (DISTILLED) VINEGAR is made from any product leftovers that are cheap and plentiful. It does not have exactly the same components and tantalizing aroma of more expensive specialty vinegars, but can be used for pickling. It is the best choice for preserving the whiteness of foods such as cauliflower and white onions. And, since it has little flavor of its own, it is sometimes used in making vinegars flavored with delicate herbs. This most inexpensive of vinegars is the best choice for cleaning.

APPLE CIDER VINEGAR is the most typically American vinegar. This apple-based product is a good, healthy general purpose product. It is a great choice for most pickling, cooking and skin care. In taste it is similar to, but more tart than, rice vinegar.

To make good apple cider vinegar begin with freshly washed whole apples, chopped or coarsely ground. (Apple cider vinegar can also be made from just cores and peelings.) Include both tart and sweet apples for full flavor and aroma. A few crab apples tossed in will add a bit of zip. Allow the chopped apples to set briefly, so the cut apples begin to react with the air and form the tannins which give it rich color and deep flavor.

Press the juice from the apples, let it ferment to hard cider, then ferment again into vinegar. Adding a dab of mother to the cider will hurry the process along.

WINE VINEGAR, like wine, can begin with either red or white grapes. Red wine vinegar is flavorful and intense, whereas white is apt to be a bit more astringent. Before processing and standardization of acid content it has a higher natural concentration of acetic acid than apple cider vinegar. This is because grapes have a higher sugar content than apples.

Italy's famous balsamic* vinegar is a specially aged wine vinegar. It is very dark, strongly aromatic and sweet. This is considered to be the very best, most concentrated vinegar. Sherry vinegar is a brownish amber color and has the woodsy, nutty taste and fragrance of Spanish sherry. It is not as sweet-tasting as apple cider vinegar. Champagne vinegar is made from grapes picked before they are fully ripe. This vinegar is mild and delicate, which makes it a good choice as a base for flower-scented vinegars.

MALT VINEGAR begins with barley. It is soaked in water, allowed to germinate, then fermented into this dark English favorite. It is a robust, full-flavored vinegar and an essential ingredient of Worcestershire sauce.

See Chapter Six for additional information on balsamic vinegar.

"Lees"
are
sediment.

RICE VINEGAR, at its best, most nutritious, is made from whole rice. Cost conscious producers sometimes make lower grades from the lees left after the manufacture of rice wine. Rice vinegar is one of the mildest kinds and can be clear, red or dark brown in color. It is an integral part of both oriental cooking and Traditional Chinese Medicine (TCM).

ORGANIC VINEGAR indicates a product which is produced without chemical additives, from food which has been grown without the use of pesticides. And, good organic vinegar should contain remnants of the healthful food from which it was made. It is a product which has not had its goodness filtered out, and not been overheated or over-processed. Because organic vinegar can sometimes contain beneficial sediment at the bottom the bottle, it may not be as "pretty" as pasteurized, super-filtered varieties.

A WORD ABOUT HEAT . . .

When using organic products which have not been pasteurized to make specialty vinegars, do not use heat, as it can harm nutrients. Heat can also deplete aromatics. When using supermarket varieties of apple cider vinegar, this care is not needed, as it has already been heated in the pasteurizing process.

FLAVORED VINEGARS

Although vinegar can be made from many fruits and vegetables, the most practical way to enjoy their good taste and health benefits is to add them to standard vinegar. This is a fast, easy way to prepare it in small quantities. Inexpensive supermarket apple cider vinegar is suggested as the base for most of the recipes in this book.

Specialty vinegars can be thick and creamy or clear and sparkling. They can look like ordinary vinegar, or be brightened with leafy sprigs and chunks of colorful food. Ways to make some of the best, most wholesome fruit and vegetable vinegars follow:

91 SWEET RASPBERRY
Bring 2 cups sugar and 1 cup water to a boil. Add 2 cups fresh or frozen raspberries and simmer until the fruit is tender (about 1 minute). Add this to 1 quart vinegar and cap. Refrigerate and allow to sit for 24 hours. Strain, then add a dozen firm, just barely ripe berries to the bottle.

92 TANGY CRANBERRY
Gently simmer 2 cups fresh cranberries and 2 cups sugar in 2 cups water until reduced by half. Strain through a cloth and add to 1 quart vinegar, along with a handful of fresh, whole berries. Great on fruit!

93 RICH BLUEBERRY
Add 2 cups blueberries to 1 cup boiling water. Simmer until the fruit is tender. Add 1 1/2 cup sugar and stir until crystals are dissolved. Strain and add to 1 quart vinegar along with 1 teaspoon allspice and a few fresh, whole berries.

94 GOLDEN PEACH
Cook 2 cups peeled, chopped peaches in 1 cup water and 1 cup sugar. When the peaches are tender add 2 teaspoons vanilla, mix well in a blender and stir into 1 cup vinegar. Especially good diluted and served as a cold soup!

95 THICK STRAWBERRY
Combine in a blender, 2 cups fresh strawberries, 1 cup sugar and 1/2 cup vinegar. Mix well and serve with fruit or sliced cold meats.

96 GREEN ONION
Trim the roots and 1 inch off the top of 3 small green onions. Push them into a quart of vinegar and replace the cap. Let set for 3 weeks and then remove the onions. For stronger taste, repeat the process with new onions.

97 HOT! HOT! PEPPER
Wash and prick a dozen small cayenne peppers. Add to a quart of red wine vinegar and allow to set for a month before using. As the vinegar is used, it can be replaced with fresh vinegar.

98 SWEET PEPPER
Place 1 cup each sweet red and green bell peppers, cut in 1/2 inch strips, in a quart bottle. Cover with vinegar and age for 3 weeks before using.

99 CREAMY GARLIC
Bake 6 garlic bulbs, drizzled with 1/4 cup olive oil and 1/2 cup water, in a covered dish for 35 minutes at 350°F. Squeeze out the soft garlic and discard the skins. Mix this soft garlic and all pan dripping into 1 cup vinegar.

100 MILD, SPARKLING GARLIC
Peel two cloves fresh garlic and add to 1 quart apple cider vinegar. Allow to set for 6 weeks before using. Add more garlic for a stronger vinegar.

Ways to make some of the most healing — and most popular — herb and spice vinegars follow:

101 QUICKEST HERBAL VINEGAR
Heat a quart of apple cider vinegar in a glass pan until it is almost ready to boil. Put an herbal tea bag in a bottle, pour the hot vinegar into the bottle and cap. When cool, remove the tea bag. The vinegar is ready to use immediately.

102 PRETTY PARSLEY
Stuff several large sprigs of parsley into a pint of champagne vinegar and age for 4 weeks before using.

103 CRYSTAL CLEAR PARSLEY
Heat 1 pint of rice vinegar to the boiling point and pour over 1/2 cup dried parsley. Allow to steep for 2 weeks, then strain through a cloth.

104 GARLIC & CHILI
Chop 4 garlic cloves into a bottle. Add 2 tablespoons chili powder and 1/2 teaspoon each of paprika, cumin and cloves. Fill the bottle with vinegar and set aside for 3 weeks. Strain and use sparingly.

105 DRAMATIC DILL
Add 3 large heads of dill to a quart of vinegar. Will be ready to use in about 3 weeks.

106 ONION & CURRY
Add 1 sliced onion and 3 tablespoons curry powder to a pint of vinegar and set aside for 4 weeks. Strain through a cloth before using.

107 FRESH MINT
Pack a pint bottle with freshly bruised mint leaves. Cover with vinegar and age for 3 weeks before using.

108 TANGY TARRAGON
Add 2 sprigs of fresh tarragon to a pint of mild rice vinegar. After 3 weeks replace the tarragon with 1 fresh spring and use immediately.

109 EXOTIC GINGER
Place 1/2 cup chopped ginger in a pint of vinegar and set aside for 4 weeks. Strain, then add a small piece of ginger to the bottle. Use immediately.

CAUTION! Many foods and flowers are sprayed with dangerous insecticides. Anything added to vinegar must be washed and free of poisons.

Dramatic flower vinegars can be made from whatever blossoms are available. Dried flowers have concentrated power, fresh ones the best aromatic qualities and the prettiest petals. Ways to make some old-time scented favorites follow:

110 SPICY NASTURTIUM
Add 1 packed cup of bruised nasturtium leaves and flowers to a quart of white wine vinegar. After 3 weeks, strain and add a dozen fresh flowers before using.

111 SLEEPY LAVENDER
Put 6 sprigs of lavender in a quart bottle and cover with clear vinegar. After 6 weeks it will be ready to use. A mist of this on a pillow is said to induce sound sleep.

112 GOLDEN MARIGOLD
Fill a quart bottle with fully opened marigolds and cover with clear vinegar. Let set for 4 weeks and strain. Add 5 or 6 fresh flowers to the bottle and use this strong infusion as a scented spray.

MORE ABOUT SPECIALTY VINEGARS

113 When vinegar is made from bananas, they are mashed for the first fermentation, then the chunks are filtered out before the second fermentation.

114 Brown rice vinegar is sweeter than white rice vinegar and more expensive. This vinegar is used in soy sauces and is good on stir fried foods, especially noodles.

115 Substitute apple cider vinegar for rice vinegar by adding 1/2 cup water to each pint. This weakened apple cider vinegar will taste and react in recipes very much like the less acidic rice variety.

116 Use lusty red wine vinegar with strong herbs, white wine vinegar with weaker ones. Champagne vinegar is an excellent base for berry or delicate herb mixtures. Sherry goes well with nutty flavors.

117 Vinegar cuts the oily taste of fish, french fries and other fried foods. Keep it in a spray bottle and mist these foods just before serving.

118 The British use straight malt vinegar on deep fried potatoes. Americans are more likely douse fries with apple cider vinegar flavored with tomato sauce (catsup).

119 When tarragon vinegar begins to get old, its flavor oxidizes into a brew that tastes very much like dill.

120 Liquid pepper is the name for vinegar which has had salted hot peppers soaked in it.

CHAPTER FIVE   MAY

Feel Young, Look Good

Much of the body's aging is caused by free radicals. They occur naturally as a by-product of metabolism and are responsible for the degenerative diseases we call aging. Free radicals weaken the immune system, cause the skin to wrinkle and accelerate the development of arthritis. Antioxidants are the body's defense against free radicals. Primary antioxidants are natural (or synthetic) chemicals which contain either a phenol ring, or a chemical equivalent. Secondary antioxidants are usually acids. In addition to esters formed by fermentation, vinegar picks up phenols from wood during its manufacture and while stored in wood barrels. 4% to 6% acetic acid is the basis for all vinegar.

Free radicals are especially devastating to the lipids which form cell membranes. When free radicals attack, cells collapse and the skin forms wrinkles. Beta-carotene, selenium and vitamins C and E are some of the strongest antioxidants. When vinegar is infused with powerful herbs it takes on their qualities, while retaining its own. This kind of antioxidant supplementation has many advantages over pills because when only one chemical is added to the body it can cause an imbalance that destroys or depletes others.

Specialty vinegars taste good and heal the body. They offer a way to add nutrients in a balanced way, by increasing wholesome foods in the diet. Creamy vinegars can add significant amounts of beta-carotene and vegetable flavorids to food. Clear vinegars leach vitamins, minerals and trace elements from herbs soaked in it. These antioxidants help the body repair the damage done by free radicals. The vinegars which follow are especially good to fight aging by strengthening the immune system:

121 Make a creamy, antioxidant fortified vinegar by combining 3/4 cup apple cider vinegar, 5 peeled garlic cloves and 1 cup each of broccoli, spinach and sweet potato in a blender. Serve over fresh greens, pasta or fruits. Vary the ingredients to suit your personal taste and to add other wholesome foods to your diet. Make clear herb vinegars by adding a few fresh sprigs or a tablespoon of dried herb to a bottle of vinegar. Let set for 3 or 4 weeks and strain. Use on salads, boiled pastas or meats.

122 Garlic activates the natural killer cells of the immune system. It also helps to preserve eye function and detoxify pollutants such as lead.

123 Parsley contains the flavonoid, apigenin, a free radical scavenger.

124 Purple coneflower (echinacea) boosts immune system response by improving white blood cell count. It is credited with being able to rouse the body's defenses when threatened by flu symptoms.

125 Purslane is the best plant source of the immune system building Omega 3 acids for which fish oils are known. Purslane is also credited with contributing to the healthy gums needed to retain teeth in old age.

126 Lemon vinegar goes well with many foods and has strong antioxidant properties!

Some other healthy reasons to add fortified vinegars to the diet follow:

127 Researchers in Finland say a diet enhanced with a wide variety of vitamins reduces the side effects of both radiation therapy and chemotherapy.

128 Lung cancer recovery rates are better for those who supplement their diets with vitamins such as those found in fortified vinegars. These include vitamins A, B-6, B-12, C, E and D, beta-carotene, thiamin, riboflavin, niacinamide, calcium, manganese, magnesium, zinc, copper, selenium, chromium and potassium.

129 Adding vitamin C to the diet can lower the body's production of allergy producing histamine by as much as one third.

130 Both migraines and tension headaches increase when magnesium levels are low. Apple cider vinegar supplies this important mineral.

131 Simply inhaling the delightful aroma of vaporized vinegar can kill flu germs. This makes it a good choice when fighting a cold.

132 Resistance to all kinds of infection is greater when the diet contains a wide variety of vitamins.

133 Normal amounts of zinc, such as the kind found in apple cider vinegar, are needed to keep the body feeling truly vigorous and full of life in old age. It is also important to maintaining fertility.

Purslane can be found growing wild!

87

Vinegar which has been made even better by adding other ingredients to it is also good for the outside of the body. Some ways to use vinegar for smooth, young looking skin and bright, shining hair follow:

134   Simmer 2 herbal tea bags in apple cider vinegar. Strain and add to bath water to pamper the skin.

135   Onion juice has antibiotic properties, so pat on this vinegar for a blemish-free complexion.

136   Enzymatic browning of apples energizes natural tannins in apples (this is what gives apple cider vinegar its color). These compounds have astringent qualities that can help control perspiration odor on feet.

137   Use oatmeal soaked in apple cider vinegar for a paste to ease minor burns.

138   Apple cider vinegar kills bacteria, so rub it into the scalp at bedtime to kill germs. Use herbal vinegar as a rinse to rid hair of soap traces, give it a fresh scent and fight dandruff.

139   Neutralize insect bites by dousing them with apple cider vinegar.

140   Help get rid of facial blemishes by applying a paste of corn starch, honey and vinegar.

141   Wintergreen sprigs increase vinegar's ability to ease muscle aches. It is also a skin softener that can be useful on calluses.

142   Honeysuckle vinegar is a complexion aid, reputed to clear away freckles and ease sunburn. Use only the blossoms.

143   Lemon vinegar is a good skin astringent that reduces the redness of sunburn.

144   Soak the blossoms of clove pink in champagne vinegar to make a beautiful, delicate pink brew that has a clove-like aroma. Use it as a facial, to deodorized the home or as a perfume that revitalizes the spirit.

145   For many years apple cider vinegar and corn starch have been used as a paste to ease the pain of shingles.

Honeysuckle berries are poisonous!

Put fresh clove pink flower in vinegar.

146 Simmer fresh willow twigs in apple cider vinegar to make a liquid for wetting poultices for boils and infections. Slippery elm works, too.

147 Apple cider vinegar was once considered a beneficial liquid for cleaning the teeth and strengthening the gums. We now know too frequent use could damage tooth enamel. So, always rinse after using it in the mouth. If you drink an apple cider vinegar tonic every day, try using a straw.

TRADITIONAL CHINESE MEDICINE (TCM)

Traditional Chinese Medicine, the system which has governed the health and long life of millions of Chinese for thousands of years, without modern drugs, recognizes the value of vinegar. TCM says those who regularly inhale the pleasant odor of vinegar have less problems with respiratory infections and more resistance to flu germs. TCM also uses vinegar in the following ways:

148 Those with hepatitis and its jaundice symptoms are given sugar-sweetened vinegar which has had pork bones boiled in it.

149 Allergic itchiness caused by eating fish is treated by sipping on vinegar which has been flavored with ginger and sweetened with brown sugar.

150 Vinegar is also used for food poisoning from contaminated fish, meat or vegetables.

151 Vomiting of blood and nosebleeds are conditions dealt with by giving rice vinegar.

Protect your teeth with a straw.

A Loving Heart, A Sharp Mind

For the past 800 years the Modena region of Italy has produced a most remarkable elixir. Their balsamic vinegar is considered the greatest of all vinegars, and thought by many to have medicinal properties. In Italy, aceto balsamico is known as "the healthful vinegar."

Balsamic vinegar is a wine vinegar that is aged until its vinegary tartness is overlaid with sweetness and flavor it absorbs from a succession of wood storage barrels. The best balsamic vinegars are as expensive and aged as long as good wine. They slowly evaporate and become concentrated, not merely with a higher acidic content, but with richer, more intense flavors. This vinegar begins with grapes that have an extremely high sugar content, making it sweet, rich, thick and brown-colored. The grapes are cooked before processing to concentrate their juice. Then the vinegar is aged in a succession of wooden barrels. The kind of wood influences the ultimate flavor. Many balsamic vinegars are aged 50 years or more.

152 Woods used to age Italian balsamic vinegar can include ash, cherry, juniper, beech, chestnut, locust and mulberry, plus Slovanian, white, red and French oak.

153 Some other countries (and other regions of Italy) use a quick process to make a pseudo balsamic vinegar. Grape juice is heated until it becomes thick and turns brown. Then it is mixed with ordinary vinegar and wood flavoring. This lesser quality product is used as a substitute for true balsamic vinegar.

154 Although some other countries produce a vinegar called balsamic, the original comes from Italy. Balsamic type vinegar made in the United States is usually aged in bald cypress, basswood, beech, black cherry, elm, red gum, sugar maple, sycamore, white ash or yellow birch barrels. Vinegar made in Europe is aged in chestnut, larch, mulberry or pine.

ABOUT BALSAMIC VINEGAR . . .

155 It is dark brown and has more body than other types.

156 Authentic balsamic vinegar comes only from Modena, Italy, and begins with grapes. The label on the bottle may say Aceto Balsamico di Modena or Aceto del Duca. In the aging process it is exposed to the heat of Italian summers and the cool of their winters. It is not unusual for a batch to go through as many as a dozen kegs, each made of a different wood. The procession is always composed of both hard and aromatic woods.

157 Moderately priced balsamic vinegar for export is aged at least 7-10 years. Better grades, for those who love great vinegar, for 50 years or more. The very best balsamic vinegar is aged more than 75 years and is not usually available outside the Modena area of Italy.

158 Age allows the flavor of vinegar to "ripen" and become more mellow. It also develops sophisticated esters and ethers.

159 As vinegar is moved from one wooden barrel to another there is less and less vinegar, because it constantly becomes more concentrated. So, it is not surprising that balsamic vinegar can cost more than a hundred dollars for a small bottle.

160 In Italy, balsamic vinegar can still be found in casks dated in the 1700s.

161 Fresh vinegars are not as smooth as concentrated balsamic types that are mild and mellow enough to use as a complete dressing, without oil or spices. They are often used as a topping for fresh or lightly blanched vegetables.

162 Balsamic vinegar is good on fruit, no sugar or spices needed. In Italy, balsamic vinegar sprinkled on fresh strawberries is considered a special dessert delicacy.

163 Sometimes Modena vinegar is simply sipped as an after dinner treat.

Some good ways to use inexpensive balsamic vinegars include:

164 Soak meats, fish or poultry before cooking on the grill. Baste frequently with leftover marinate.

91

165 Drizzle over baked beets and serve with sour cream.

166 Broil new potatoes, slip off the skins and toss with torn spinach.

167 Bake small onions, covered, in a small amount of water. When tender add a sauce of 2 tablespoons vinegar and 4 tablespoons brown sugar and bake, uncovered, until sugar is caramelized.

168 Clean out seeds and broil hot peppers, then sprinkle with vinegar.

169 Make your own imitation balsamic vinegar by mixing frozen grape juice concentrate and brown sugar with apple cider vinegar.

VINEGAR & LOVE

In Italy, the very best balsamic vinegar is apt to be part of a young lady's dowry. Other vinegars are also associated with love. Scented vinegar can be used to soothe, invigorate or arouse the senses. Add the following to vinegar:

170 Rose petals to inspire love and romance.

171 Lavender to encourage feelings of desire.

172 Licorice to stimulate feelings of love.

173 Garlic to increase passion. This is considered so potent, some religious orders ban it.

174 Onion to excite the libido.

175 Red clover to arouse the senses.

176 Cinnamon to awake warm and loving feelings.

177 Pink monkeyflower to boost confidence.

178 Valerian is one of nature's most well-known sleep aids. Use it to induce relaxation and calmness and as a gentle aid to pleasant dreams.

Many cultures use plants to brighten the memory and sharpen the mind. Add these to vinegar for similar results:

179   In Russia the aroma of bay leaves is used to sharpen the memory. Ancient Romans and Greeks used it this way, too.

180   Eastern medicine uses Gota Kola leaves and their B vitamins to fight stress and to treat mentally handicapped children and the insane. It must aid memory, because elephants eat it!

181   TCM says rue improves mental clarity. European folk medicine calls it an illness preventative. For super healing, mix it with garlic and honey. It is a strong herb, so only add one sprig to a pint of vinegar.

TCM = Traditional Chinese Medicine

Vinegar, Arthritis & Cancer

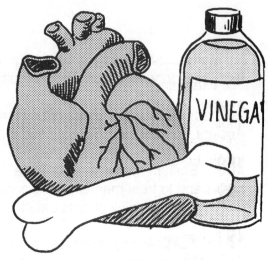

50 years ago a daily apple cider vinegar and honey tonic was recommended to ease arthritis. During the past 30 years, "wonder drugs" have replaced it and other folk remedies. Now, vinegar and many other old-time remedies are finding new followers, including many medical professionals. One reason for vinegar's renewed appeal is that almost everyone has experienced the negative side effects of today's powerful new drugs.

Apple cider vinegar's double fermentation results in an assortment of enzymes and amino acids whose combined actions are not completely understood by researchers. It is very possible this old remedy will, one day soon, be shown to desensitize the body to arthritis causing allergens as it strengthens the immune system.

The immune system and arthritis have very strong ties. It mediates the body's power to heal and repair itself. A weak immune system does not aggressively repair cell damage. And, an undernourished immune system cannot tell the difference between invading germs and healthy body tissue. So, it attacks and destroys cartilage in joints. It also loses the ability to lay down as much new cartilage in joints as is worn away.

THE ARTHRITIS-VINEGAR CONNECTION

The traditional way to take apple cider vinegar for arthritis is to mix a teaspoon of it with a teaspoon of clover honey and stir into a glass of water. Repeat 2 or 3 times a day. One reason this is thought to be of benefit to some people is that many of the elderly have marginal vitamin deficiencies. This is especially true for those taking medications for rheumatoid arthritis. Folic acid stores are especially likely to become depleted. Yet, arthritis' inflammation has been reduced when thiamin, B-6 and B-12 were added to standard medical treatments. Results could be seen in as little as one week!

But, it can be dangerous to take too much of some vitamins and minerals. For example, extra, unbalanced zinc in the body can deplete copper, another mineral long associated with arthritis. It can even bring about a suppression of the immune response. Most doctors agree the best way to add balanced vitamins and minerals to the immune system is with healthy foods. Fortified vinegars can help do this.

182 For a healthy vinegar tonic that can be served over salads, boiled pasta or cold meats, mix in a blender: 1/2 cup apple cider vinegar, 1/2 cup sunflower oil, 1 cup spinach, 1 cup celery, 1 green bell pepper, 1 large carrot and 1 teaspoon basil. This will help you resist these ailments:

183
- Colds because it has vitamin C and zinc.
- Depression because it has thiamin, riboflavin and vitamin B-6.
- Heart disease because it has vitamin E.
- Elevated blood pressure because it has vitamin C.
- High cholesterol because it has niacin.

CANCER & VINEGAR

Phytochemicals are not vitamins. They are substances some researchers believe can actually change cancer cells back into normal ones. The National Cancer Institute is funding research, right now, to study phytochemicals. These seemingly magical chemicals can be frozen and microwaved and still heal. They are plentiful in both garlic and tomatoes, and very complex - there are estimated to be 10,000 different phytochemicals just in tomatoes.

184 Because isolating the action of a specific phytochemical is so difficult, it is best to eat whole vegetables. Pills and extracts will, almost certainly, not contain all the goodness of the complete food. A fortified vinegar that takes advantage of the many benefits of phytochemicals can be made by mixing 1 cup fresh tomato, 6 peeled garlic cloves and 1/2 cup apple cider vinegar in a blender. Some of the reasons to use this fortified vinegar are:

185 It contains compounds to thin the blood, prevent clotting and lower cholesterol and blood pressure.

186 Chemicals in it can stimulate release of the brain's natural tranquilizer, serotonin. It also can slow degeneration of brain cells. Some of these foods are used in China to improve senile dementia.

187 Sulfur based compounds in this vinegar have been shown to prevent the spread of some breast cancers.

188 Substances in it are believed to inhibit the spread of colon cancer.

189 This mix has ingredients that fight esophageal cancer.

190 Skin cancer has been shown to be inhibited by chemicals in these foods.

191 Many scientists believe substances in this fortified vinegar deter the spread of prostate cancers.

192 Some kinds of cancer cells have actually been killed by the chemicals that are so abundant in this mix of foods.

193 Strawberries, too, are being shown to have chemicals in them which fight cancer. They contain a polyphenol, called ellagic acid, that neutralizes carcinogens before they do their damage by invading DNA. And, it is thought strawberries interfere with the formation of nitrosamine in the intestines. (Nitrosamine can be very carcinogenic.) Make a vinegar which is strengthened with strawberries by combining in a blender: 1 cup strawberries, 1/2 cup apple cider vinegar, 1/4 cup honey.

194 Cranberries are another fruit that supplies the health benefits of ellagic acid. Serve them with vinegar and honey, too.

195 Ellagic acid in blackberries is not destroyed when it is cooked, so vinegar made with them can be used on grilled foods.

196 Fruit and honey vinegars fight breast cancer because they have lots of vitamin A.

197 Use sweet fruit-enhanced vinegars with a bit of brewer's yeast added to increase the amount of naturally occurring folate to deter colon cancer.

VINEGAR DOES MORE!

Not only is vinegar a healthy, disease fighting addition to the diet, it is quite useful around the home. Some ways to use white (distilled) vinegar for cleaning dishes and laundry follow:

198 Spray greasy pots and pans with a film of full strength white vinegar, let set a few minutes and wash as usual. The grease will wash off easier, with less soap.

199 Add 1/4 cup white vinegar to the water used to wash greasy dishes and less detergent will be needed.

200 Dampen a sponge with a teaspoon or two of white vinegar and close it in a glass jar that smells musty. In about 30 minutes it will smell fresh again.

201 To freshen stale smelling plastic ware containers, moisten a paper towel with vinegar and leave it sealed in the container overnight.

202 Wool sweaters will be fluffier if rinsed in water with a cup of white vinegar added to it. Cotton blankets will be softer, and smell fresh longer if rinsed this way, too.

203 Many stains can be lifted from permanent press fabrics by wetting the stain with white vinegar, letting it set for a few minutes, then washing with detergent and cool water.

204 Clean carpets by spraying them with a mixture of 1 cup white vinegar to a gallon of water. Wipe off with an absorbent cloth. Colors will seem to glow and musky odors will fade away. (Always test carpet first!)

205 Clean patent leather shoes with a paper towel moistened with white vinegar. Preserve them by applying a thin coating of petroleum jelly, then rubbing it off.

206 Deodorize clothes which have been exposed to cigarette or cigar smoke by hanging them over a tub containing 2 cups of apple cider vinegar and very hot water. This water can be used to freshen and soak ashtrays clean, too.

207   Remove creases from letdown hems by dampening them with white vinegar before ironing. Add creases to fabrics by dampening the fabric with white vinegar before ironing. Works especially well on knit fabrics.

208   Shine stainless steel with full-strength white vinegar and polish dry without rinsing.

209   White vinegar is great for removing wine stains. Simply dab it on and blot the spot away.

210   Lavender vinegar does more than provide a pleasant aroma in the home. It acts as an effective moth repellant.

211   Wring a soft cloth out of a mixture of 1/4 cup vinegar and 1 quart water. Use this to wipe dust from the leaves of house plants.

212   Before setting food out for a picnic, spray the table with bay flavored vinegar. It will make the air pleasant as it chases away flies.

Lose Weight The Tasty Way

Vinegar can be of great value in a weight loss program. Enriched vinegars are especially helpful. Fortified vinegars are a:

- Fat-free way to increase fiber, vitamins and minerals in the diet without multiplying calories.

- Tasty carrier for substances that can actually burn away body fat.

- Healthy way to satisfy cravings by indulging the way mature taste buds function.

Each one of the tongue's nearly 10,000 individual taste buds is made up of a cluster of microscopic cells arranged around a tiny pore that collects saliva. The tongue can only detect substances which are dissolved in saliva. If the mouth is overly dry, the sensation of taste is diminished. And, sensitivity to tastes fades as the body ages. Young adults replace their taste buds about once a week. By about 45 years the tongue begins to lose taste buds, because the replacement rate slows. By recognizing the fainter response of the mature tasting system, vinegar can be used to awaken taste buds and provoke responses that make dieting more acceptable to the senses.

All food flavors are some combination of sweet, sour, salty or bitter. Vinegar's tartness activates sour-receptive taste buds along the sides of the tongue, because they are the ones most sensitive to the hydrogen ions in its acid. When sweet or salty foods are added to vinegar, they activate taste receptors on the tip of the tongue, too. This is why sweet-sour combinations can be exceptionally satisfying. They engage the entire mouth in the tasting process.

Taste buds sense food with hairlike projections called microvilli.

TAKE THIS TONGUE TEST

Try rubbing a pill you know is bitter on just the center of your tongue. There is no sensation of bitterness, because the middle of the tongue has no taste buds. Next, rub the pill across the tip of the tongue and along the edges to sense its true taste.

YES, FOOD CAN REALLY TAKE OFF WEIGHT!

Capsicin (cayenne) peppers probably originated in South America, taking their name from the city that was once the capital of French Guiana. More than 90 kinds of peppers trace their origins to capsicin. These tiny hot peppers have always had a large following that believed they were a healthy food, but new research is showing them to be better than anyone could have imagined! Hot pepper vinegar is a staple in kitchens across the world, one of the simplest ways to add their goodness to the diet. Exciting news about its health benefits have recently been announced by both medical doctors and food researchers. Some of the healthy benefits its use can bring follow:

213 Hot pepper vinegar can boost the body's metabolic rate (the rate at which it burns calories).

214 One-fifth of an ounce of hot pepper vinegar's cayenne can burn away as many as 76 more calories than it contains.

215 Hot pepper vinegar causes blood to come to the surface of the body and stimulates it to sweat. This cools the body in hot weather.

216 The cayenne in pepper vinegar encourages the adrenal glands to produce cortisone, a natural anti-inflammatory.

217 Capsicin, an active compound in hot pepper vinegar, is a naturally occurring chemical that can stimulate the body's ability to turn glucose into energy.

218 Some researchers think hot pepper vinegar's cayenne stimulates the brain's pleasure sensitive endorphins.

219 The cayenne that gives hot pepper vinegar its zing has been shown, even in small amounts, to stabilize blood pressure.

220 Hot pepper vinegar's cayenne has been shown to reduce excessive bleeding - no matter where it occurs in the body. And surprisingly, it does not seem to irritate ulcers.

221 In addition to the alkaloid called capsicin, cayenne peppers add vitamins A and C, flavonoids and carotenoids to vinegar's inventory of nutritious ingredients.

Capsicin is a member of the nightshade family.

OUTSIDE THE BODY, TOO!

Vinegar and hot peppers make up an old-time liniment for relieving the aches and pains of arthritis and rheumatism. Now, the capsicin that makes peppers hot has been proven by researchers to interfere with the way nerve endings in the skin send pain messages to the brain. Put this chemical to work for you to ease:

222 Arthritis and rheumatism aches.

223 Shingles pain.

224 Muscles and tendons that are sore from overexertion.

Hot peppers and vinegar are also combined in Tabasco brand hot sauce and most salsas and curries. Some ways to make and use hot pepper vinegars follow:

> CAUTION: HOT PEPPERS AND HOT PEPPER VINEGAR
> CAN BURN THE TONGUE AND BLISTER SKIN.*

225 To make a clear, super-hot pepper vinegar, pack a jar with tiny cayenne peppers. Leave half of them whole, cut the remaining peppers in half, lengthways. (Include or substitute other hot peppers, such as jalapenos if you wish.) Cover with vinegar and age for 3 weeks. As the liquid is used, add additional vinegar for a continuing supply.

226 To make a fiery hot vinegar, combine a dozen cayennes in a blender with 1 cup apple cider vinegar. Make it even better by adding 5 peeled garlic cloves and 2 medium onions.

A WEIGHT LOSS SECRET - FENNEL SEEDS & VINEGAR

As long ago as the time of the ancient Greeks, fennel seeds were popular as an aid to losing weight. Even today, no one is exactly sure why - or how - they work. Many researchers feel their virtues are linked to substances they contain which react in the body much like estrogen. We do know they contain at least 18 different amino acids, 7 minerals (including generous amounts of potassium and calcium), several vitamins (including lots of vitamin A). In addition, their fatty acids are mostly monounsaturated and polyunsaturated (the good kinds). Three ways to add fennel's flavonoids, vitamins A and C, calcium, phosphorus and potassium to vinegar's goodness follow:

See taste testing guide in Chapter Two

101

227 Add 1/2 cup fennel seeds and 2 fresh sprigs to a quart bottle of champagne vinegar and age for 3 weeks.

228 Loosely pack a bottle with fennel leaves, add 1 tablespoon seeds, fill with white wine vinegar and cap. After 3 weeks replace the cap with a shaker top and sprinkle on salads or meats.

229 Combine in a blender 1 cup tightly packed fennel leaves and 1/2 cup champagne vinegar. When blended, add 1 teaspoon fennel seeds and 6 peppercorns. It is ready to use immediately.

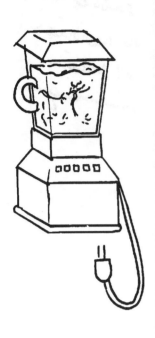

VINAIGRETTES ARE LOW CALORIE

Add oil to vinegar and it becomes a vinaigrette (dressing). Add water or juice and it becomes a milder, low-cal alternative. The traditional ratio for vinaigrettes was one part vinegar to three parts oil. Today's lighter way of eating calls for less oil and lots of herbs for seasoning. Canola, corn, cottonseed, olive, safflower, soybean and sunflower oils are particularly good choices. Some ways to prepare vinaigrettes follow:

230 Mix 1/2 cup apple cider vinegar and 1/2 cup oil with 1/4 teaspoon each of basil, minced garlic, oregano, parsley, tarragon and thyme.

231 Mix 1/4 cup garlic flavored apple cider vinegar with 1/4 cup water and 1/2 teaspoon honey. This gentle vinaigrette softens vinegar's tartness.

232 Add 1 teaspoon coarse salt and 1 tablespoon ground pepper to 1/4 cup red wine vinegar and 3/4 cup oil for a rich, heavy vinaigrette.

233 Prepare a creamy vinaigrette by blending 1/4 cup each of vinegar, oil and yogurt. Use immediately. Can be seasoned with 1 tablespoon parsley or chives (or both).

234 For a super creamy variety, blend 1/4 cup vinegar with an equal amount of yogurt. For variety, season with 1 tablespoon mustard.

235 Blend 1/2 cup apple cider vinegar, 1/2 cup orange juice and 2 tablespoons mustard to make a mild dressing for mixed greens.

236 1/4 cup honey, 1/4 cup apple cider vinegar and 1 tablespoon mustard is a combination that brings together the sweet and sour tastes in which ancient civilizations put so much faith.

237   Serve fennel vinegar over steamed asparagus and celery, garnish with fresh parsley.

238   Fennel vinegar is an excellent topping for broiled fish.

239   Super weight control formula - add 10 peppercorns and 3 tablespoons fennel seeds to a pint of white wine vinegar. Let set for at least 2 weeks, then mix with 1 pint water and use on salads.

240   Replace high calorie gravy with meat juice, sharpened with a splash of vinegar and seasoned with your favorite herbs.

MORE DIET HELP

241   Top steamed vegetables with a low-cal dressing of 1/4 cup of fruit flavored yogurt, thinned with 1 tablespoon herbal vinegar. Also good on fruit salads.

242   Combine 1 tablespoon mustard, 1 tablespoon apple cider vinegar, 1 teaspoon honey and 1/4 teaspoon paprika. This is a nice sweet-sour combination. Give it extra zip and restorative power by substituting hot pepper vinegar.

243   Mustard, like cayenne pepper, burns more calories than it contains. This is because it boosts the metabolic rate. Each quarter of an ounce uses up about 60 extra calories!

Vinegar Is Really Cooking

Vinegar's introduction to the kitchen was simultaneous with the discovery of wine, more than 10,000 years ago. Through the ages it has added desperately needed nutrients to the meager diets of the poor and delighted the taste buds of the rich. Its ability to break down protein makes it a practical way to tenderize; its preservative qualities offer protection against food poisoning and its antibiotic qualities help protect against illness. Vinegar even plays an important part in developing the texture of baked goods!

Fermentation, such as the process which changes fresh, perishable foods into long lasting vinegar, transforms food particles into smaller molecules. For example, yeast ferments the complex sugar, glucose, into less complex substances. This makes food more digestible. Or, as some cultures call it, predigested.

Vinegar denatures or "cooks" protein. This is called cold cooking and is used for some specialty fish dishes. The customary combination is made with half vinegar and half oil. Any favorite seasonings can be used, too. Use this to "precook" fish to be grilled. Do not soak fish too long or they can "overcook" and dry out. (Spices and herbs can make the liquid a more powerful cooking tool.)

244   Vinegar's acid does more than simply add flavor. It softens tough fibers in food. To make an excellent marinade, begin with 1/2 cup vinegar and 1/2 cup oil. Add sliced lemon, bay leaves, thyme, paprika or other spices and herbs. Use this to marinate foods before broiling or grilling to shorten cooking time.

245   Soak tough stewing chicken for an hour in a mixture of 3/4 cup vinegar, 1/2 cup oil and 1 thinly sliced lemon. Drain and cook as a young fryer.

246   A generous splash of vinegar added to pot roast makes it easier to digest. Works well on meat for stews, too.

247   Listeria is a bacteria found on nearly 20% of all hot dogs. The illness it causes is especially dangerous to babies and the elderly. Neutralize this bacteria by boiling hot dogs for a few minutes in water with a couple of tablespoons of apple cider vinegar added to it. Bonus, the hot dogs will taste better than ever!

248   Plain meat drippings, with an equal amount of garlic vinegar whisked in, makes an especially tasty sauce! Dilute with water for a milder taste.

249   Before steaming vegetables, marinate them in this, or use it to baste food for grilling: 1/2 cup rice vinegar, 1/2 cup peanut oil, 1/2 cup soy sauce, 2 cloves minced garlic, 1/4 cup honey.

250   Japanese cooks use rice vinegar to enhance the crispness of vegetables. Soak wilted vegetables in a bowl of cool water with a half cup of rice vinegar added to it.

251   Add a tablespoon or two of apple cider vinegar to a pot of baked beans to make them easier to digest. Also good for green beans.

252   When poaching eggs, add a couple of tablespoons of vinegar to the water. This will encourage the whites to remain firmly formed around the yolks.

253   Vinegar helps keep eggs suspended in sauces, and raises the temperature at which its protein turns into a solid. Plain egg protein coagulates at 160°F, when vinegar is added it rises to 195°F. This makes it easier to prepare cooked sauces without having them curdle.

254   Mustard is a digestive stimulant. Use it and vinegar together for their health benefits, their great taste and for their low-cal way to stimulate the digestive process. Make salt free mustard by blending dry mustard and vinegar together until they are the consistency of thick batter. Then add a few drops of oil. This is a good sauce for rubbing down meats before they are grilled.

255   Bearnaise sauce is a classic topping for broiled fish. Prepare it by gently simmering together for one minute, 1 cup white wine, 2 tablespoons white wine vinegar and 1 tablespoon minced onion. Whisk into this mixture 1/2 cup soft butter and 3 egg yolks. Heat to thicken, do not boil. Season with 1 teaspoon each of tarragon, parsley and chervil. Serve with a sprinkling of cayenne and white peppers. (Leeks or shallots may be used in place of onions.)

VINEGAR + BAKING SODA = LEAVENING

256   Leavening is the process that lightens doughs and batters. Tiny bubbles of moist air form and then expand during cooking to make foods lighter. Vinegar causes this when it reacts with baking soda. During baking carbon dioxide is released in the form of moist air pockets. Then, these tiny bubbles slowly expand, adding to the lightness of the food.

257   Moisture in bubbles of vinegar and baking soda created carbon dioxide has tremendous leavening power. Each droplet of water expands to 1600 times its original size when it becomes steam.

258   Even heavy doughs, such as pie crust, can use the terrific power of carbon dioxide based steam for leavening. The following recipe for vinegar pastry makes enough dough for a double crust pie. Sift together 1 cup flour and 1/2 teaspoon baking powder. Add 1/4 cup oil, 1 egg white, 3 tablespoons vinegar, 3 tablespoons water, 1 tablespoon sugar and 1/2 teaspoon salt (optional).

259   This chocolate-vinegar cake uses vinegar to replace the leavening sometimes supplied by eggs. Combine 1 cup brown sugar, 2 tablespoons cocoa, 1/4 cup oil, 1 teaspoon baking soda, 1 teaspoon vanilla, 1 cup milk, 2 teaspoons vinegar, 1 1/2 cups flour, 1/4 teaspoon baking powder and 1/4 teaspoon salt. Bake at 350°F. for about 30 minutes.

260   Replace sour milk or buttermilk in recipes by putting 1 1/2 teaspoons of vinegar in a glass measuring cup and filling it with milk. Stir after 3 minutes and it will be ready to use.

Vinegar added to the sugar for making taffy helps turn the sucrose of white sugar into glucose and fructose. This inversion process is what makes the length of cooking time critical. If the syrup is not cooked long enough, there will be insufficient invert sugar, and so the candy will be gritty. If the syrup is cooked too long, too much of the sugar will become invert and there will not be enough sucrose left to crystallize and so the candy will be too soft.

261   Make old-fashioned pulled taffy by combining 2 cups sugar, 2/3 cup water and 1 tablespoon vinegar in a good sized saucepan. Stir while the mixture heats, but not after it comes to a boil. Cook to the hard ball stage for a chewy candy, to the soft crack stage for a more brittle candy. Remove from heat, swirl in 1 teaspoon butter and 1/2 teaspoon vanilla and pour onto a cool, buttered (or oiled) surface. As it becomes cool enough to handle, work the mixture until it changes color and begins to set up.

Acid in syrup helps it make invert sugar.

VINEGAR & CALCIUM

Osteoporosis is prevented and fought by adding calcium to the diet. Magnesium is also important, because it boosts bone density. Apple cider vinegar contains both. Vinegar is also very good at conveying nutrients from one food to another. Just as the chemicals in cayenne peppers and fennel seeds end up in vinegar, calcium in chicken bones leaches into vinegar during cooking. Use vinegar in many ways in the kitchen, including as an aid in fighting osteoporosis by leaching calcium from chicken bones.

262 Make a calcium-rich soup stock by beginning with a whole, cutup chicken. Cover it with water, add 1/2 cup herb flavored vinegar and gently simmer for 2 hours. Use this stock for calcium enriched foods.

263 A vinaigrette of hot peppers, garlic, onion and assorted herbs makes an ideal seasoning mix for a nutritious soup. Begin with calcium fortified soup stock and add sliced onions, potatoes, carrots and other vegetables. Add 1/2 cup vinaigrette (or more to taste) and simmer until vegetables are tender.

264 Combine the 10,000 phytochemicals in tomatoes with the super healing powers of hot peppers and vinegar by making salsa. Chop 1/2 cup chilies, 1 cup tomatoes and 1 cup onions and mix together with 1 teaspoon sugar and 1/2 cup vinegar. Let it set overnight, so flavors blend. Use as a dip for corn flour based chips or pile it on rice cakes for an interesting mix of low calorie tastes. (Optional ingredients: salt, black pepper and garlic.)

265 Boiled rice will be snowy white and extra fluffy if a tablespoon of white vinegar is added to the water in which it is cooked.

266 Soak ripe olives in vinegar to make it easier to remove the pits.

267 The unique, zesty tartness of vinegar helps reduce the amount of salt needed to flavor food.

268 Drizzle sweet raspberry vinegar over mixed greens sprinkled with grated hazelnuts.

269 Dribble a teaspoon of fortified fruit vinegar over vanilla ice cream, add slivers of chocolate and top with a sprinkling of raw sugar.

270 Combine 1 cup apple cider vinegar, 2 cups raspberries and 1/2 cup mint leaves in a blender. Use as a dressing for fruit salad.

Vitamin D helps bone absorb calcium.

When you add vinegar you add magnesium

271 Perk up the taste of melon slices by sprinkling them with honey-sweetened thyme vinegar.

272 Intensify ginger flavored dishes with a dash of hot pepper vinegar.

273 Add zip to ginger ale with a spoonful of hot pepper vinegar.

Vinegar is a low-salt, low-cal, no-cholesterol seasoning! It is a way to enhance flavors, and bring new ones to the table, without adding undesirable additives and calories. Almost any bland food can be enlivened with a splash or two of vinegar.

CHAPTER TEN   OCTOBER

Pickled Peppers & More

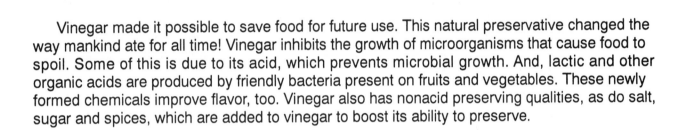

Vinegar made it possible to save food for future use. This natural preservative changed the way mankind ate for all time! Vinegar inhibits the growth of microorganisms that cause food to spoil. Some of this is due to its acid, which prevents microbial growth. And, lactic and other organic acids are produced by friendly bacteria present on fruits and vegetables. These newly formed chemicals improve flavor, too. Vinegar also has nonacid preserving qualities, as do salt, sugar and spices, which are added to vinegar to boost its ability to preserve.

PICKLED FOOD

274 Cinnamon and cloves are two spices that magnify vinegar's power to curb bacterial growth. Nutmeg and allspice are of some help in preservation of food, but are less effective.

275 If preserved pickles are not completely covered with liquid they MUST be disposed of without tasting! Cucumbers not covered with vinegar can cause severe food poisoning, even death.

276 If pickle are too sour, soften the intensity of their taste by stirring in some sugar, 1 hour before serving. Or, drain off 1/2 of the liquid covering them and replace it with water. Allow to set overnight, refrigerated, before serving.

277 Make pickles extra-sour by draining off 3/4 of their liquid and replacing it with new vinegar.

278 Umeboshi plums are a sour, heavily salted food that TCM considers medicinal. These plums are pickled in cedar vats for a few weeks to draw out their juice. Then they are dried in the sun and put back in the juice with plant leaves that turn them a dark pink color. Often, they are aged for a year or more before being served.

279 Make a surprise treat the oriental way. Put a pitted (pickled and salted) plum in the middle of a ball made of rice that has been cooked to a sticky consistency.

109

280 Mash several umeboshi plums and add enough rice vinegar to form a thick puree. Add a small amount of oil and drizzle over steamed vegetables. Replace the oil with yogurt it makes a good topping for rice cakes.

281 TCM practitioners recommend eating one of these extremely tart and salty fruits as a morning wake-up tonic.

EARLY VINEGAR USE

Because vinegar was one of the first ways discovered to protect food from bacterial attack, it developed an early reputation as a wondrous, nearly mystic substance. Even highly perishable foods, such as meats, seafood and eggs were preserved in vinegar. Some ways and places it was used follow:

282 Since the 1500s France has been known for truffles pickled in vinegar. Then, they were soaked in hot water and served with butter. This subterranean fungus was thought to be an aphrodisiac.

283 According to TCM, peanuts soaked overnight in vinegar can lower blood pressure. Chinese practitioners recommend eating several of the nuts each day for 2 weeks.

284 In the 1700s more than 50 kinds of flavored cooking vinegars could be found in Paris street markets. And, more than 90 varieties were to be found for making the outside of the body smell better. The most popular, and least expensive, was pepper vinegar. It was made from wine than had been laced with pepper. Other common vinegar flavors included: clove, carnation, chicory, mustard, fennel, ginger, pistachio, rose and truffle.

285 Early vinegars did not look like the highly filtered ones familiar to today's shopper. Many of these vinegars had lots of sediment and flavorings. They were so thick they could be dehydrated and sold as sticky balls of dried vinegar. Travelers mixed these dehydrated globs with water to make "instant" vinegar.

286 Because vinegar allowed food to be transported over great distances without rotting, sailors in particular benefited from it. They not only ate a lot of pickled foods, they used it to wash down and clean the wooden decks of ships.

287 One of the staple foods of sailors was a hard, all purpose biscuit made of flour and water. To make this hardtack edible they soaked it in vinegar and water to make a gruel they called skilligalee.

Protein came from weevils that infested the biscuits.

VINEGAR IS GOOD TODAY!

288 Because it could be stored for months, pickled cabbage was popular in Poland and Hungary during the 1700s. Today, it is more popular served as a freshly vinegared vegetable. Make a low calorie cole slaw with 3 cups cabbage and 1/2 cup carrots, shredded. Add 1/4 cup sugar and cover with cold water. Set aside for 2 hours, then drain off all liquid. Dress with champagne vinegar mixed half and half with water.

289 Add zest to ordinary mayonnaise by adding a teaspoon of flavored vinegar to each 4 tablespoons of mayonnaise. Use it for hot weather sandwiches to help prevent food poisoning. (Vinegar is the main preservative in catsup, mayonnaise, pickles and most salad dressings.)

290 In Australia, vinegar is regularly sprayed on raw meat to slow the action of the bacteria which causes it to rot.

291 Baked goods which contain vinegar are much slower to produce mold.

292 Pickle boiled beets by submerging them in 1 cup apple cider vinegar mixed with 1/2 cup water and 1/4 cup sugar. Add pepper and mustard to taste.

293 Prepare hard boiled eggs for pickling by pushing 5 or 6 whole cloves into each egg. Cover the eggs with vinegar and refrigerate for several days before eating. Optional seasonings: pepper, mustard or salt.

294 Use white vinegar to pickle onions. This will help them keep their pale, snowy color and unique taste.

295 Deter mold from forming on cheese by wrapping it in a cloth dampened with white vinegar. Put the cloth-wrapped cheese in a plastic bag and store it in the refrigerator.

296 Pickle lovers who need to avoid salt can enjoy a healthy alternative, dill pickle vinegar. Simply add a pre-mixed "pickling spice" packet to a quart of warm apple cider vinegar and age for a couple of weeks. (Mix it yourself by adding all your favorite pickling spices to a bottle of apple cider vinegar.)

297 Vinegar has long been used on butter wrappers to inhibit mold growth.

298 Make a clear garlic vinaigrette by combining 1/2 apple cider vinegar and 1/2 cup oil. This is a simple, uncomplicated dressing that does not overwhelm delicate vegetables like asparagus.

299 For a sweet and creamy garlic and oil dressing, combine 1/2 cup peeled garlic cloves, 1/4 cup oil and 1/2 cup apple cider vinegar in a blender. Add 3 to 6 tablespoons honey (depending on degree of sweetness desired).

300 To preserve garlic cloves, simply cover them with vinegar. CAUTION: Never store garlic in oil - without the addition of vinegar. Garlic preserved in only oil can result in botulism tainted oil. (Botulism cannot be detected by odor or taste.)

STOP UGLY DISCOLORATION

301 Prevent apples for pie from turning brown by slicing them into a bowl of water with 1/4 cup white vinegar added to it. Drain apples before cooking them.

302 When slicing peaches for canning, keep them in a bath of water with a dash of white vinegar added to it and they will not turn brown. (Drain well before canning.)

303 A dash of white vinegar in the cooking water makes for snow-white mashed potatoes.

304 Cauliflower to be used with vegetable dips will stay snowy white longer if it is rinsed in a mixture of 1 quart water and 1/4 cup white vinegar.

Animals Need Vinegar, Too

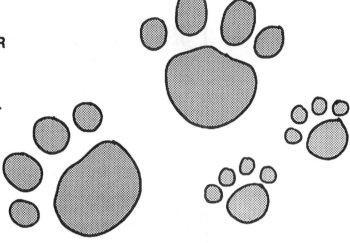

Vinegar can be as important to animals as it is to people. It freshens drinking water, shines coats, discourages parasites and fights infections. Vinegar also has many uses around the home and in the garden.

Some of the remedies - for pets, pests and nuisances - which appear in this chapter have been validated by the latest scientific findings. Others are based on long-standing tradition and folk wisdom. For your safety, and that of your pets and farm animals, ALWAYS CHECK WITH YOUR VETERINARIAN BEFORE TREATING WITH HOME REMEDIES!

PETS

305   Itchy house pets will appreciate a daily vinegar dip. Add 1/4 cup apple cider vinegar to a tub of lukewarm water. It will help normalize the skin's pH balance, reducing the tendency to scratch. When scratching cannot be stopped any other way, try soaking a puppy's paws for 5 minutes a day in 3 cups water with 3 cups apple cider vinegar added to it.

306   To treat a dog's sprained leg muscle, wrap it in a brown paper bag wet with apple cider vinegar.

307   Soak house pets' water dishes for 20 minutes a day in vinegar. This will discourage bacteria from growing on these perpetually wet surfaces. And, it avoids the need to use chlorine disinfectants (such as bleach) that may be harmful to the animal.

308   After bathing a long haired cat, rinse it with 1 quart of water with 3 tablespoons vinegar added to it. This will make the fur shine and tangles will brush out easier.

309   Garden lime and other corrosive alkali based products can cause chemical burns on cats. To neutralize these poisons, rinse the cat with a mixture of 1 quart vinegar and 1 quart water. Repeat as necessary.

310 Fennel flavored vinegar, if used to soak the area where pets spend their time, will discourage fleas from congregating. Rue vinegar will also discourage fleas. Rub it into a dog's hair and use it to wipe down the outside of feeding dishes.

311 Discourage ticks from bothering dogs by wiping down their coats with apple cider vinegar that has had camomile flowers soaked in it. Dab the fur of a cat with it to repel fleas.

312 Jellyfish stings can be deadly to dogs. Pour vinegar over a sting immediately to neutralize the poison.

313 Lift pet urine stains from carpet by blotting up excess liquid, then sprinkling with white vinegar. Blot again, repeat as necessary.

FARM ANIMALS

314 Vinegar compresses can be an effective and safe way to disinfect sores on horses. Also safe for dogs and goats.

315 To make a horse's coat shine, add a splash of apple cider vinegar to its water each day. Will also perk up a sluggish appetite.

316 Peeps will be bigger and healthier if a bit of apple cider vinegar is added to their drinking water. And later, it will strengthen the shells of their eggs.

317 Sprinkle fennel vinegar around the stall of an unruly cow or horse to improve their disposition.

318 Thyme vinegar makes a great pest repellent! Use it on garden paths and on patio stones.

GARDEN

319 Spatter small droplets of a robust sage vinegar on the ground near vegetable vines to keep harmful insects away.

320 Vinegar which has had oregano leaves soaked in it makes a good barricade against insects that gather on cucumbers. Wet the ground around plants once a week. Helps keep bugs from eating the leaves of melon plants, too.

Peeps = baby chickens.

114

321   Steep new leaves of the lavender plant in vinegar for 10 days, then strain and use as a wash for the inside of storage areas for clothes. It will drive away moths.

322   Sprinkle the ground around tomato plants with a creamy, basil fortified vinegar to keep bugs away.

323   Wet a circle of ground around cabbage, Brussels sprouts and cauliflower plants with mint vinegar. Aphids will be reluctant to attack the plants.

HOME & LAWN

324   Mosquitoes will avoid your yard if it is sprinkled occasionally with diluted lavender vinegar.

325   If flies gather around the kitchen, set out dishes of lavender vinegar and they will go away.

326   When grass sprouts in the driveway or in sidewalk cracks, drench it with vinegar to kill it.

327   Sprinkle a strong infusion of rue vinegar around doorways to discourage fleas from entering the house. Basil vinegar also helps keep flies out of the house.

328   Wet the foundation of the home with a very strong infusion of mint vinegar to protect it from rats.

329   Pour full-strength vinegar over fire ant hills. It will drive them away. Spray it in cupboards to discourage ants in the house.

330   White vinegar is the least expensive variety, so is a good choice for cleaning. It is also less likely to stain because it has been filtered so that it contains few trace elements from the originating product.

331   After washing exhaust fans and air conditioner grills, wipe the exposed surfaces with white vinegar to retard future buildup of grease and dust.

332   Deodorize or freshen a room by setting a bowl of hot water with a cup of apple cider vinegar and a dash cinnamon in it on a low table.

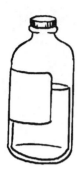

333 A buildup of water-scale on shower heads can be dissolved by soaking the shower head in white vinegar. Simply wrap paper towels (saturated with white vinegar) around the shower head. Cover with a plastic bag, secure with a rubber band and let set overnight. Brush with additional vinegar and the scale will melt away.

334 When varnished wood comes in contact with water it can develop a hazy surface. Prevent this by adding a teaspoon of white vinegar to each cup of water used to wash the wood. Dry immediately. Many kinds of wood paneling can be perked up by wiping them down with a solution made of 1 cup warm water, 1 tablespoon white vinegar and 1 tablespoon olive oil. Mix well, use immediately and dry with a soft, clean cloth.

Better Health With Vinegar

Whatever unpleasantness the body is exposed to, whether it is a harmful virus, deadly poison, infectious bacteria or damaging pollution, flavored acetic acid - that stuff we call vinegar - is involved in neutralizing it. Because it is a building block for living tissue it is needed by plants, animals and humans. This natural by-product of healthy metabolism is used by the body in many ways, including manufacturing essential amino acids. It affects the way energy is released from fats and carbohydrates, and even how fat is manufactured by the body. Without its action the body could not make the life-giving red blood which delivers oxygen to the brain. When scientists examined molecules of glycogen, the body's sugar, they found it there, too.

For many years doctors could find no reason to believe in the arthritis folk remedy that combines apple cider vinegar and honey in a daily tonic. New studies of how foods react in the body in a process called oral toleration may explain why this seems to work for some people. Vinegar's wide assortment of enzymes and amino acids may eventually be shown to desensitize the body to arthritis causing allergens. Perhaps one day soon foods will be considered preventive medicines, or even cures, for most degenerative diseases.

Ways to use this wondrous fluid alone, or combined with other healthful foods follow. They integrate the latest findings of medical food researchers with the wisdom of traditional healing ways.

335   Pectin is a water soluble fiber that is plentiful in apples. It slows the absorption of food in the intestines, allowing it to bind to cholesterol. Make a cholesterol fighting, fortified vinegar by combining 2 cups chopped apples, 1 cup apple cider vinegar and 1/2 cup honey in a blender. Season with 1/2 teaspoon cinnamon and 1/4 teaspoon nutmeg. Serve over fruit salad.

336   Apple fortified vinegar is a good way to fight cancer, because it increases the amount of fiber in the diet. It also adds important amino acids to strengthen the immune system in its battle against all disease.

337   Consider using honey-sweetened vegetable or fruit fortified vinegar as a replacement for the time honored apple cider vinegar and honey arthritis remedy. It contains all the goodness of the original, combined with added nutritional benefits.

338 If oral toleration proves to be an answer to degenerative diseases, fortified vinegars will be an exceptional way to concentrate the benefits of many vegetables into one daily tonic.

339 Even though molds, yeasts and bacteria are essential to life, they cause problems when they attack food. Meat is particularly susceptible to contamination by nasty microorganisms. If vinegar is sprayed on beef, it dramatically reduces the number of germs. And, its action lasts more than a week! This procedure is also effective on pork.

340 Bacteria on meat can cause it to change color. Vinegar sprayed on meat slows color change. This is very important to retailers, because many customers judge meat's freshness and quality by its color.

341 Use vinegar in the kitchen to sanitize cutting boards and other surfaces touched by raw meats.

342 A creamy vinegar fortified with garlic adds vitamins to the diet. Research shows a multivitamin enriched diet can activate the immune system.

343 Garlic, such as that in creamy vinegars, can lower both cholesterol and blood pressure.

344 This marvelous combination contains chemicals researchers have found to improve memory and increase the ability to learn in old age.

345 Sometimes, with age, the stomach does not produce the amount of acid needed for good digestion. Perhaps this is why vinegar has long been considered a digestive aid.

346 Fennel seeds soaked in vinegar also aid digestion. Research indicates they are especially active on fats. In addition, they contain a hormone-like substance. This may explain why they are used by nursing mothers to increase the amount of milk they produce.

347 Use warm fennel vinegar as a facial astringent that cleans pores and conditions the skin. Its hormone-like action fights wrinkles.

348 Flowers in scented vinegars often add natural astringent qualities. Spices and herbs do this too. And, because vinegar's pH is almost the same as that of healthy skin, it soothes and normalizes its surface. Witch hazel adds to its effectiveness.

349   If hot peppers are soaked in vinegar for 3 or 4 hours they will not burn the skin when they are cut up. And, it seems to prevent other some allergic reactions to them, such as dizziness.

350   Without essential fatty acids, cuts would not heal, hair would thin and the immune system would falter. Extra-virgin olive oil, half of the best vinaigrette, contains vitamin E and selenium. These antioxidants promote good health.

351   Vinaigrettes offer a really good way to get polyunsaturated fats (like linolenic acid) from oils into the diet. This is because heat can change them into trans-linoleic acid, a fat that is very unhealthy.

352   A healthy substitute for the popular "sports drinks" can be easily made from vinegar. Simply fill a glass half way with crushed ice and add 4 to 6 drops of a good quality balsamic vinegar. Fill the glass with cold water and swirl. Sip slowly.

When scientific research looks at old-time home remedies, they have often been surprised to find many really work! Grandmother may not have been able to explain chemical reactions, but she knew her remedies worked and food seasoned with vinegar tasted better! For example:

353   A syrup of baked and mashed garlic, honey and apple cider vinegar is the old-time favorite for easing coughs.

354   Add cayenne pepper to the above to ease troubled breathing. Even Hippocrates recognized this old remedy.

355   Prevent water-borne infections from settling in the ears by rinsing them out with a mixture of 1/2 rubbing alcohol and 1/2 vinegar.

356   Zip up the taste of homemade soups with a dash of zesty herbal vinegar.

357   Turn the gravy from the Thanksgiving turkey into an exciting surprise by adding a tablespoon or so of apple cider vinegar to it. Or, use garlic, onion, thyme or celery vinegar.

358   Perk up plain white sauce with 1/2 teaspoon of vinegar for each cup.

359   Soak canned shrimp in equal parts water and vinegar to restore their "fresh" taste.

360   1/4 cup vinegar added to the water when boiling cabbage will keep the kitchen from smelling of cooked cabbage.

Some oils are good!

Hippocrates - the father of modern medicine

TCM

Traditional Chinese Medicine has always recognized vinegar's ability to help the body restore itself to good health. Some healing ways with vinegar from this oldest of organized medical systems follow:

361 For a headache which is caused by elevated blood pressure, TCM recommends eating celery which has been cooked in vinegar. Researchers at the Chinese Academy of Medical Science report that the vapors of boiling vinegar can kill the germs that cause pneumonia and influenza.

362 A teaspoon of fresh ginger root grated into 2 cups of rice vinegar is used for indigestion after eating fish.

363 Vinegar is believed to be able to halt excessive bleeding, no matter the cause. It is also supposed to enhance the health of both the liver and the stomach.

364 Asians also use the ginkgo plant to improve the mind. If the plant is not available for pickling, add its extract to vinegar and flavor with garlic.

VINEGAR FOR SELF DEFENSE!

365 Vinegar can be a self-defense food! The hot pepper vinegar in Chapter Four can be effective for personal protection. A good splash of this fiery liquid on the face or in the eyes should send an attacker running!

REFERENCES

ADAMS, Catherine F. Nutritive Value of American Foods. Washington, DC: United States Department of Agriculture, 1975. Agriculture Handbook, No. 456. pp. 170.

ATLAS, Nava. The Wholefood Catalog... A Complete Guide to Natural Foods. New York: Fawcet Columbine, 1988. pp. 180-181.

BALA, K., W.C. Stringer and H.D. Naumann. Effect of Spray Sanitation Treatment and Gaseous Atmospheres on the Stability of Prepackaged Fresh Beef. J. of Food Science 1977: 42(3): 743-746.

BENNION, Marion. Introductory Foods. 9th ed. New York: Macmillan Publishing Co. 1990. pp. 495-496, 595-600.

BROTHWELL, Don and Patricia. Food in Antiquity. New York: Frederick A. Praeger Publishers, 1969. pp. 66, 109-124, 135-137, 156-159, 191-193.

BROWN, Jo Giese. The Good Food Compendium. New York: Dolphin Books, 1981. pp. 22, 142-143.

CHARLEY, Helen. Food Science. 2nd ed. New York: John Wiley & Sons, 1971. pp. 8-9, 86-87, 169-171, 266.

CHEREMISINOFF, Paul N. and Robert P. Ouellette, eds. Biotechnology Applications and Research. Pennsylvania: Technomic. pp. 88-95.

CONSIDINE, Douglas M., P.E. and Glenn D. Considine. Foods and Food Production Encyclopedia. New York: Van Nostrand Reinhold Co., 1982. pp. 1-10, 50, 2064-2066, 2177.

COOMBS, J. Dictionary of Biotechnology. New York: Elsevier. pp. 120, 322.

FOOD and Nutrition Board. Division of Biological Sciences. Assembly of Life Sciences, National Research Council. Food Chemicals Codex. 3rd ed. Washington, D.C.: National Academy Press, 1981. p.8.

FREYDBERG, Nicholas Ph.D. and Willis A. Gortner, Ph.D. The Food Additives Book. Toronto: Bantam Books. pp. 463-464.

GARLAND, Sarah. The Complete Book of Herbs and Spices. New York: Reader's Digest Association, Inc., 1993. pp. 8-20, 80-115, 135-, 162-169, 247-261.

GEBHARDT, Susan E., Rena Cutrufelli, and Ruth H. Mathews. Composition of Foods - Fruits and Fruit Juices. United States Department of Agriculture. Agriculture Handbook No. 8-9, 1982. p. 23.

GOLDBECK, Nikki and David. The Goldbeck's Guide to Good Food. New York: New American Library, 1987. pp. 509-511.

HEATON, E.K., A.L. Shewfelt and L. Henderson. Effects of Varying Levels of Sucrose, Corn Syrup Solids and Vinegar on the Quality of Sweet Pickled Peaches. J of Science: 1978 43:1015-1018.

HOCHWALD, Lambeth. Special-Interest Supplements. Natural Health Jul-Aug 1996. pp. 103-120+.

KAHN, J.H., G.B. Nichol and H.A. Conner. Identification of Volatile Components in Vinegar's by Gas Chromatography - Mass Spectrometry. J Agri Food Chem 20.

KENT, James A. Ph.D., ed. Riegel's Handbook of Industrial Chemistry. 9th ed. New York: Van Nostrand Reinhold. pp. 937-940.

KINTNER, T.C. and M. Mangel. Variation in Hydrogen Ion Concentration and Total Activity in Vinegar. Food Research 17: 456-459.

KLUGER, Marilyn. The Wild Flavor. California: Jeremy P. Tarcher Inc., 1984. pp. 126-127, 247-250.

KNUTSEN, Karl. Wild Plants You Can Eat. New York: Dolphin Books, 1975. pp. 34-73.

KRATZER, Brice L., and Dallas W. Sandt. Nutrition: Where Have All These Labels Been? Nutrition Awareness System. pp. 100-103.

LANG, Jenifer Harvey. Tastings... The Best from Ketchup to Caviar. New York: Crown Publishers, Inc., 1986. pp. 132-142.

Lu, Henry C. Chinese System of Food Cures Prevention and Remedies. New York: Sterling Publishing Co., Inc., 1986. pp. 86+.

MACRAE, Norma R., R.D. Canning and Preserving Without Sugar. 3rd ed. Connecticut: The Globe Peguot Press, 1993. pp. 6, 17, 186, 234-238.

MARLIN, John Tepper and Domenick M. Bertelli. The Catalogue of Healthy Food. New York: Bantam Books, 1990. pp. 99, 136.

MARSH, Anne C., Mary K. Moss, and Elizabeth W. Murphy, eds. Composition of Foods - Spices and Herbs. Agricultural Research Service. Washington D.C.: United States Dept. of Agriculture, 1977. pp. 02-002 - 02-042.

NEWS and Notes. Eat Your Weeds. Natural Health Jul-Aug 1996. p. 18.

NORMAN, Barbara. Tales of the Table...A History of Western Cuisine. New Jersey: Prentice-Hall, Inc., 1972. pp. 289-321.

O'NEILL, John J. Vinegar - Building Block of the Body. Science Digest Aug 1946. pp. 67-68.

PENNINGTON, Jean A. Ph.D., R.D. and Helen Nichols Church, B.S., Bowes and Church's Food Values of Portions Commonly Used. New York: Harper & Row Publishers, 1985. pp. 124-126, 163.

RALLS, Jack W. and Richard M. Lane. Examination of Cider Vinegar for Patulin Using Mass Spectrometry. J of Food Science: 1977 42(4): 1117-1119.

RALOFF, J. Antibiotics Take a Bite Out of Bad Gums. Science News: 1996 149:308.

RALOFF, J. Radicals Linked to Aging via the Brain. Science News: 1996 149:311.

RECER, Paul. Space Cloud Found to Contain Vinegar. Canton Repository Jun 11 1996. p. A-7.

RINZLER, Carol Ann. The Complete Book of Herbs, Spices and Condiments. New York: Facts on File, 1990. pp. 42-43, 134-135, 164-165, 171-176.

RONSIVALLI, Louis J. and Ernest R. Vieira. Elementary Food Service. 3rd ed. New York: Van Nostrand Reinhold, 1992. pp. 103-105, 175-181, 319-324.

SEVEN Super Foods. Country Livings Healthy Living: Summer 1996. pp. 84-86.

SHIMIZU, Kay. Tsukemono - Japanese Pickled Vegetables. Shufunotomo/Japan Publications, 1993. pp. 7-15, 23.

TANNAHILL, Reay. Food in History. New York: Stein and Day, 1973.

TANNAHILL, Reay. Food in History. New York: Crown Publishers, Inc., 1989. pp. 141, 238-239.

UEHLING, Mark D. Chlorine Alternatives. Popular Science: Jun 1996.

UNITED States. Department of Agriculture-Human Nutrition Information Service. Composition of Foods: Snacks and Sweets. Agriculture Handbook Number 8-19. Washington D.C.: U.S. Government Printing Office: Aug 1991. pp. 186, 319.

WALT, Bernice K. and Annabel L. Merrill, et. al. Handbook of Nutritional Contents of Foods. New York: Dover Publications. pp. 7, 65-66, 147, 158, 160, 165-175.

WEIL, Andrew M.D. Ask Dr. Weil. Natural Health: Jul-Aug 1996. p. 22.

YEPSEN, Roger B. Jr., ed. Home Food Systems. Pennsylvania: Rodale Press, 1981. pp. 254-260.

Dear Reader,

When the original volume of "Home Remedies from the Old South" came out, many kind readers wrote to me expressing interest and enclosing questions on the usefulness of apple cider vinegar. These letters led to "The Vinegar Book."

Now, my mail shows my readers have many unanswered questions about how vinegar cleans, and about how it can be used around the home. So, in an attempt to answer these requests for information, "The Vinegar Home Guide" has come into being.

Over the years, my fascination with all the things vinegar can do encouraged me to gather a collection of cleaning and cooking lore. Many of these hints and tips work wonders — in a particular cleaning situation. In other circumstances they may be ineffective. A lot depends on the cleaning chore. I invite you to enjoy reading the cleaning remedies in this book to see how others have used vinegar. Then, I encourage you to experiment to find what works for you.

Some of my earliest memories are of my Grandfather gathering up apples to take to my Uncle John's apple press. The exact mix of apples was more art than science, and a closely held secret. There were always a few sweet, aromatic apples, some spicy ones to add flavor, and a nice bunch of tart ones to give the mixture body.

The apples were washed and ground up, then pressed in a mill powered by horses walking in a circle. The fresh sweet cider was delicious, but that was just the beginning. When it 'turned' and became hard, it was time to make apple cider vinegar in big old wooden barrels. The vinegar was used for preserving, cleaning and disinfecting. Since then, I've learned that, even today, hospitals use vinegar for killing germs and to fight children's ear infections.

I believe it was the German poet Goethe who wrote, "If everyone would sweep the street in front of their own house, the whole world would be clean." To rephrase that philosophy, I believe that if we each protect our little corner of the earth, the whole planet will be safe. To this end, most of the cleaning tips in this volume recommend using scraps of old cloth for cleaning rather than paper towels. Paper cleaning products are handy things, and wonderful for really nasty cleanups. But please remember, every time you use a paper towel, somewhere, a tree is cut down. Besides, cloth is reusable and so is less expensive, as well as being softer and less likely to scratch fine finishes!

Please remember, this book is an attempt to share information. Many old-time ways are not best for today. And yet, many of the old ways are well worth the trouble to try them. They do not disturb the environment, set off allergic reactions, pollute the air we breathe or deliver harsh chemicals to skin and air. Wishing you all the best,

Emily

Chapter One

What Is Vinegar?

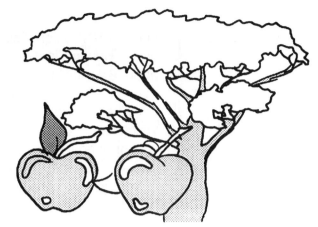

Soon after the first person played a flute in ancient Egypt—

About the time sheep were first domesticated in the Near East—

And Europeans were learning to eat honey and catch fish in nets of hair—

Before the first dogs were domesticated in the British Isles—

—Mankind discovered that a very useful, sour liquid formed when a mildly alcoholic beverage was allowed to set out, exposed to air. Vinegar came into being! And for more than 10,000 years it has been one of the most useful and widely distributed liquids on the planet.

The English word "vinegar" comes from the French word "vinaigre," which accurately describes the origin of this delightful liquid. "Vin" is for the wine the first vinegar was made from — and "aigre" to acknowledge the fact that the wine had turned sour. Vin - gar is, literally, soured wine.

When a sweet liquid, such as apple or grape juice, is sealed up and allowed to ferment (away from air) the sugar in it is changed into alcohol. If this liquid is permitted to ferment for a second time (this time in the presence of air) the alcohol is transformed into acetic acid.

While the very first vinegar came from the natural souring of fermented wine, it soon became such a prized product that mankind learned how to make it intentionally. Since then it has been used as a flavor enhancing condiment, a preservative, and as a cleaning agent for people, pets and objects around the home.

To make vinegar, all that is required is a juice (or sweetened water) with enough sugar content to produce at least a 6% to 10% alcoholic liquid in the first fermentation action. Old-time "slow process" vinegar needs about a 10% alcohol content to get the second fermentation process going. Newer, "fast process" vinegar can be made from a liquid with only about 6% alcohol.

Vinegar is made from many substances. For industrial uses, acetic acid which has been manufactured from wood products is diluted to make a kind of vinegar. At one time this colorless product was colored with caramel and sold as table grade vinegar, although its food value and aroma were inferior to fruit based vinegar. Today, this adulterated vinegar is rarely sold as a food.

Vinegar for table use is made in nearly every country, all across the world. The food product which is used to make vinegar depends, mostly, on where it is made.

In the United States, much of the vinegar intended for table use is made from apples, producing apple cider vinegar. England is famous for its malt vinegar, made from grain. France is noted for its wine vinegar, made from grapes, while Japan and China specialize in vinegar made from rice. Vinegar is made from many natural products, including:

- Apples
- Bananas
- Barley
- Blackberries
- Grapes
- Honey
- Molasses
- Potatoes
- Raspberries
- Rice
- Strawberries
- Wood Shavings

After vinegar is made it is often combined with herbs and spices, or even specially aged in wood kegs. Any kind of vinegar — white, apple cider, wine, malt, etc. — may be enhanced this way.

KINDS OF VINEGAR

Distilled, or "white" vinegar is usually used for cleaning. Because white vinegar is a colorless liquid it is less likely to discolor articles being cleaned. Generally, white vinegar is made from wood or grain, and has a consistent 5% acetic acid content.

White vinegar is often used for pickling, salad dressings, marinating, and for preparing foods when the distinctive flavor of other vinegars is not wanted. It is a reliable, consistent, inexpensive and widely available product.

For most cooking, when special flavor is wanted, or for personal use, other kinds of vinegar are usually used. Apple cider is widely available, inexpensive, has a long history of health uses and has a fresh, distinctive flavor.

Herbal and balsamic vinegars are more expensive and harder to find. Balsamic vinegar is aged in wood, often for several years. It is considered one of the finest flavorings available for many foods. Herbal vinegars can usually be found in health food stores, Or, they can be prepared from white, apple cider, or wine vinegar.*

Vinegars made by old, slower processes are known for their fine aromas and have more subtle flavors than ones made by newer, faster processes. Aromatic vinegars have spices and herbs added to them. They produce a fragrant liquid which is used in the kitchen and in personal care products such as after shave lotions and skin fresheners.

Some of the first 'toilet waters' were aromatic vinegars.

HOW VINEGAR CLEANS

In many parts of the country, water for the home comes from underground sources. When this water runs through underground reservoirs it can dissolve minerals out of rock formations. Limestone, which is mostly calcium carbonate, dissolves especially easily.

This "hard" water carries the dissolved limestone until it finds an object to deposit it on. The inside of plumbing pipes, bathroom and kitchen fixtures, shower walls and curtains, and washer lint traps encourage minerals to precipitate out of water. These minerals show up as a rock-hard coating which can be difficult to clean without scratching metal surfaces.

In a short time these hard water minerals build up into a dirty white scale on bathroom and kitchen surfaces. This is the same stuff that produces stalagmites and stalactites in limestone caves. And it can be just as hard as these natural wonders, but it is not nearly as pretty!

See chapter on cooking with vinegar.

Fortunately, vinegar dissolves calcium carbonate, as well as scale from other minerals. Tradition says Hannibal, a general from Carthage (in North Africa), used the fact that vinegar weakens rock in his march over the Alps from Spain to Italy.

Supposedly, Hannibal's soldiers poured vinegar over heated boulders. This weakened the stones enough that they could be broken up and removed from mountain trails, allowing Hannibal to move his elephants over the narrow mountain trails.

Today, the fact that vinegar wears down and destroys rock formations is important, because this makes it a nearly perfect cleaner for removing mineral accumulations from bathroom and kitchen fixtures. Even though vinegar is good at dissolving minerals, it is non-poisonous and gentle on hands.

VINEGAR ACTS AGAINST GERMS

Vinegar contains a host of germ fighting components. It is has both antibiotic and antiseptic properties. And, it can contain natural tannins which help to preserve foods. Vinegar not only can kill bacteria, its presence slows its ability to grow back.

One of the best things about cleaning with vinegar is its action on mold and mildew. Mold and mildew are not dirt. They are living, plantlike growths. That means cleaning the part that shows is not enough to get rid of them. These fungus growths have to be killed, all the way to their roots, or they will immediately grow back.

And that is why vinegar is such a good cleaning product. It has the ability to actually kill mold and mildew spores that cause new growth.

Vinegar is a completely biodegradable product. Nature can easily break it down into components that feed and nurture plant life. This makes it superior to chemical cleaners that poison the soil today, and remain in it and destroy plant life for many years.

HOW TO CHOOSE A VINEGAR

Most cleaning and laundry chores call for white vinegar. It has a mild odor and does not have anything in it to leave a stain on fabrics. Apple cider vinegar is a good choice for cleaning that calls for giving the air a

Mushrooms & truffles are in the mold & mildew family!

pleasant, apple-fresh scent. Either one leaves a room smelling as if it has just been cleaned.

Throughout this book, whenever a cleaning tip does not specify the kind of vinegar to be used, white vinegar is usually the best one to use. But, it is always possible to do the cleaning chore with any kind of vinegar. The choice is always yours!

WHEN TO CLEAN WITH VINEGAR

Vinegar is the cleaner of choice for those with allergies, asthma or a sensitivity to harsh chemicals. It also appeals to those who are interested in protecting the environment from pollution, and is the cleaning product of choice for the thrifty consumer.

Vinegar's acid character makes it especially useful for neutralizing the effect of alkaline-based cleaning products. This includes most soaps and detergents. Vinegar also has the ability to dissolve the dulling film these products can leave behind.

Copper (and compounds which contain copper) can be cleaned with vinegar. When metal develops a green tarnish it usually means there is copper in it. This green coating can be seen on objects that are 100% copper, as well as on copper compounds such as brass and bronze.

Brass can develop a dull, greenish discoloration because it is mostly copper, with some zinc mixed into it. Bronze also has a copper base. The copper in bronze is mixed with tin (and sometimes a bit of zinc, too).

WHEN NOT TO CLEAN WITH VINEGAR

Just as important as when to use vinegar, is when not to use it. Because, like all good things, vinegar should not be used on some things.

Vinegar will tarnish silver, so never expose it to vinegar, unless you want it to instantly look old and dirty. And, never soak pearls in vinegar, as it will dissolve them!

If you reuse plastic bags, such as bread wrappers, never turn the bag inside-out, so that a food with vinegar in it touches the colored ink of the bag label design. Many have dyes that release lead into food when soaked in vinegar.

HOW TO CLEAN WITH VINEGAR

Vinegar is a cost efficient cleaner, so be generous with it. In general, begin cleaning by removing loose dirt with a sweeper, brush, dust cloth, or just shake it off. Then scrape or peel off any lumps or globs of dirt. Remove what remains with detergent, water and white vinegar.

For best results, keep your cleaning equipment clean. The best cleaning machine in the house is usually that old toothbrush that reaches all the places nothing else will. Rinse it out once in a while in full strength vinegar, shake it partly dry, and then allow it to dry in the sun.

CAUTIONS

ALWAYS test a small, inconspicuous area of fabrics, wall coverings, flooring, etc. before using any cleaning product — including vinegar.

No product, even one as safe and gentle as vinegar, is safe for every person or every situation. While vinegar has been safely used for thousands of years, it is possible for certain individuals to be sensitive to it. If there is any possibility that you may be sensitive or allergic to vinegar, consult a medical professional before exposing your skin to it.

When cleaning copper, always dispose of all cleaning cloths or paper towels as soon as the job is finished — that green tarnish on copper is poisonous!

Chapter Two

General Cleaning

Vinegar is an acid based cleaner. This makes it especially good for taking out stains made by coffee and tea, lifting rust and lime deposits, cleaning stains made by condiments such as mustard or catsup, and removing wine or stains made by alcohol based liquids. Used this way, white vinegar acts as a very mild bleach.

And, because vinegar is acid, it is a good final, neutralizing rinse after using alkaline cleaning solutions such as detergents and soaps (including dishwasher soaps), wax strippers, drain and oven cleaners. A final vinegar rinse in the washing machine helps colored clothing stay bright, because vinegar helps remove lingering traces of detergents and the film left by soaps.

In addition, vinegar helps water sheet off glassware, so it helps prevent water spots on dishes and streaks on windows. Some more specific ways people have suggested using vinegar in general cleaning follow:

Vinegar Wet Wipes
Mix 3 tablespoons white vinegar and 1 teaspoon liquid detergent in a bowl with 2 cups of water. Wet small pieces of clean, soft cloth (6 to 10 inch squares) in the vinegar mixture, then wring them out. Place the cloths in a tightly capped container. Whenever there is a need for a quick cleanup, use one of these wet wipes.

Vinegar wet wipes are good for touch-ups on windows, spots on mirrors, and cleaning faucets, door knobs, sinks, counter tops, appliances and light switches.

Dirty Ashtrays
Spray full strength vinegar on ashtrays with heavy stains or encrusted dirt and allow them to set for 5 minutes. Wipe the dirt out and spray again to remove lingering odors.

Sweeter Smelling Ashtrays

Reduce ashtray odor by spraying clean, polished ashtrays with apple cider vinegar. Begin by wiping the inside of a clean ashtray with a wax-based furniture polish. (This will help to keep odors from penetrating.) When the wax is dry, spray the ashtray with apple cider vinegar and allow it to dry without wiping.

Mild Brass Cleaner

1/4 cup vinegar	2 cups water
1/4 cup liquid detergent	
1/8 cup salt	

Put all the ingredients together and stir until the salt is dissolved. Wipe the liquid on tarnished brass, then immediately wipe it off. Polish with a soft cloth until completely dry. Apply a coating of creamy car wax and buff to keep brass clean longer.

Water-Stained Carpet

When jute-backed carpet gets wet, the brown coloring in the backing is released. It runs into the fibers in the front of the carpet, where it shows up as a brown or yellow stain. Neutralize jute stains by dampening the stains with a mixture of 1/4 cup white vinegar and 1 cup water. Immediately blot the carpet dry. One or two applications should remove the stain.

Gentle All-Purpose Cleaner

Fill a spray bottle almost full of water, then add 1/4 cup white vinegar and 3 tablespoons liquid detergent (the kind used to wash dishes by hand). Use a few squirts of this gentle liquid to clean away light dust and dirt before moisture in the air turns them into a sticky film that is more difficult to remove. Use this gentle all-purpose cleaner on chair railings, window frames, baseboards, anywhere dust or dirt accumulate.

Doorknobs

Some of the dirtiest places in the home (and most forgotten hiding places for germs) are the doorknobs. Most will benefit from an occasional cleaning with a cloth dampened in vinegar. It will kill germs and wipe away dirt. Glass doorknobs will sparkle like new!

Glass or Plastic Beads

Dip strands of beads in a quart of warm water to which 1 teaspoon liquid detergent has been mixed. Rinse in another quart of water to which 1 tablespoon white vinegar has been added. Blot dry with a towel, then finish drying with a hair dryer, set to low heat.

Sanitize The Telephone

Germs that cause colds and flu live on surfaces which are handled by many members of the household. Wipe the telephone receiver down with full strength vinegar to kill any bacteria which may be breeding on it.

Air Freshener

Pure white vinegar makes a great freshener for stale air. Simply use a pump spray to deliver a fine mist to musty areas or to remove cooking or smoking odors. For a fresher scent, use apple cider vinegar.

Scented Air Freshener

Fill a pump spray bottle with well-strained herbal vinegar and use to both cleanse the air and to add refreshing, natural scents. Often these scented air fresheners do not cause the allergic sniffles and sneezes some people experience when using commercial fresheners.

Broom Revitalizer

Old plastic brooms (and cornstalk ones, too) can be reshaped and deodorized by soaking them in a bucket of very hot water, to which a cup of apple cider vinegar has been added. Let the bristles soak for at least 10 minutes, then shake the broom to remove most of the water. Wrap two or three large rubber bands around the bristles and set the broom in the sun for several hours. When the rubber bands are removed the broom will retain its new, neat shape. And best of all, it will smell fresh and clean!

'New' Stubby Broom

When a broom is finally ready to be discarded, try cutting about half the length of the bristles off. Angle the cut so that the bristles on the short side are about 1 inch in length and the ones on the long side about are about 5 inches in length. Soak the broom as above, shake it out and set in the sun until dry. This 'new' stubby broom will do a great job in corners and other places that are hard to reach with a regular broom. And, the long handle will save the bending and crawling that using a regular whisk broom requires.

One-Pass Sweeping

A broom will pick up more dust if it is sprayed with vinegar water. Just put a cup of warm water in a pump spray bottle and add 1 cup vinegar. Spray the broom before using, and occasionally during use.

Louvered Doors and Shutters

Remove dirt, dust and musty odors from louvered surfaces with vinegar and a paint stirring stick (available, free, at most paint stores). Simply wrap a soft cloth over the end of the flat stick, spray it with vinegar, then run it over and under each louver.

Revitalize and Deodorize Drapes

Remove musty or smoky odors from drapes — and take out fine wrinkles at the same time! Mix 1 tablespoon white vinegar with 2 cups warm water and place the mixture in a pump spray bottle. Set to 'fine mist' and spritz each drapery panel lightly, without removing the drapes from the windows. As they dry, most wrinkles will disappear, along with stale odors.

Fiberglass Drapes

Fiberglass is, in many ways, a wonderful material. But when it comes time to wash drapes, fiberglass requires great care. These drapes must never be washed in the washing machine, or put in the dryer! The agitation of the washer, and the tumbling of the dryer, will break, crack and pulverize the glass fibers.

Not only will washing machines and dryers weaken (and eventually destroy) the drapes, tiny fiberglass particles will be deposited in the appliances. These little pieces of glass will cause great itching and irritation for anyone who wears clothes exposed to them.

Wash fiberglass drapes by hanging them on a clothes line and spraying them, gently, with a hose. Follow with a spray of vinegar and water from a pump spray bottle (1 tablespoon of vinegar to each 2 cups of water). This will keep them smelling fresh and clean.

If it is inconvenient to hang fiberglass drapes outside, they may be dipped in a laundry tub of sudsy water, rinsed in clear water, then dipped in a mild vinegar and water solution. Remember to THOROUGHLY rinse out the laundry tub after washing fiberglass drapes!

Fireplace Ashes

A vinegar spray can keep fireplace ashes from flying all over the house when they are cleaned out. Simply spray the ashes with vinegar and water before beginning (1 tablespoon vinegar to 2 cups water). Shovel ashes onto newspapers which have also been dampened with water and vinegar. Continue to spray the ashes every so often and flying dust particles will be prevented.

Putting vinegar on the ashes also helps to neutralize this strong alkali. Prevent alkali burns on hands by rinsing in water and vinegar as soon as the job is finished. Rinse any tools used, too.

Brighten Lights

Get the most from your lighting dollars by keeping light bulbs clean and free of dust and dirt. Wipe cool bulbs with a cloth dampened in vinegar water (1 tablespoon vinegar to a quart of water). Always clean bulbs with current turned OFF!

Grandmother got lye by soaking wood ashes in water.

134

Light fixtures, chimneys, reflectors, and diffusers also need to be cleaned regularly. Dip them in sudsy water, then rinse in water with some white vinegar added to it. As with light bulbs, always clean AFTER they have completely cooled!

Use a mild vinegar and water solution for plastic parts, a strong one for glass items.

Mop Magic

For stay-shiny-longer floors, make this special glossy surface cleaning solution. To a bucket of warm water, add 1/2 cup fabric softener and 1/4 cup vinegar. Mop as usual and watch the magic shine appear. This works best for lightly soiled floors.

Waxing Floors

Make your floor wax go on smoother, last longer, and shine better by rinsing the floor with a strong solution of water and white vinegar before applying the wax. A cup of vinegar to a half bucket of warm water is about right.

Quick Pick-Up For No-Wax Floors

Mix white vinegar and water, half and half, in a pump spray bottle. Mist the traffic areas of no-wax flooring and immediately buff dry with an old towel. This quick pickup will have the floor looking shiny clean in about two minutes!

Cleaning Waxed Floors

Ammonia and heat both remove wax. Preserve wax surfaces when cleaning by using cool water and a vinegar rinse. This will make the shine last longer.

Really Dirty Vinyl Floors

Pre-treating really dirty vinyl floors can make the job of cleaning them easier. Spray full strength vinegar on spots, globs and sticky areas. Let set for 5 minutes, then mop as usual.

Ballpoint Ink

Pen marks on painted walls and woodwork can often be lifted by soaking them in white vinegar. Dribble full strength vinegar on marks and allow to soak for 10 to 15 minutes. Marks on vertical surfaces can be soaked by draping a vinegar-damped cloth over them.

Walls

Wash painted walls with a gentle detergent and then rinse in warm water and white vinegar. Add 1/2 cup vinegar to half a bucket of water.

Ceilings

Lightly soiled ceilings can be washed and rinsed in one operation. To half a bucket of water, add 1 tablespoon liquid dish detergent and 1/2 cup white vinegar. Wipe a 3 foot square of ceiling clean, then dry with a soft cloth to prevent streaking.

Glass and Ceramic Candlesticks

Soak glass and ceramic candlesticks in very warm water with plenty of detergent in it. Wipe wax residue off with a soft cloth or sponge. Then, rinse in hot water with a bit of white vinegar in it. Put a coating of oil in the candle-holding well to make it easier to remove old candles.

Lamp Shades

Before throwing a hopelessly stained or misshapen lamp shade away, you might want to give it a chance to redeem itself. Make a sudsy solution of white vinegar, liquid detergent, and lukewarm water in a laundry tub. Immerse the end of the shade with the heaviest soil buildup first. Swish it around a little, then turn the lamp shade over, with the opposite end submerged in the water. Turn the shade over and repeat the process. Swish it around again and drain the water out of the laundry tub. Fill the tub with cool water, add 1 cup white vinegar, and rinse the shade thoroughly. Blot most of the water from the lamp shade and finish drying out of the sun, and without heat.

Old Windows

When window glass seems dull and 'old' looking, it is usually because soap scum and hard water minerals have been allowed to build up on it. Vinegar is very good at cutting through the haze and restoring the shine to such window glass. Use a strong vinegar and water solution, or even full strength vinegar, to remove soap scum and hard water minerals.

Streaky Windows

Streaks are often caused by the sun heating the glass, making the cleaning solution dry too fast. Wash windows on a cloudy day to minimize sun streaking. Or, wash windows on the shady side of the house, then wait for the sun to move. Using a squeegee to remove the cleaning solution will also minimize streaking.

stretched out areas can be shrunk with hair dryer heat

Mildewy Windows

Windows that are frequently damp can grow mildew and mold in their corners and on their frames. Use full strength white vinegar to remove all traces of mildew and mold. Any spores that are missed will encourage its fast return.

Good Window Cleaner

1	tablespoon white vinegar	2	drops liquid detergent
1	tablespoon ammonia	1	cup water

Mix all ingredients together and store in a pump spray bottle. Spray onto windows and wipe off with wadded up newspaper or a soft cloth.

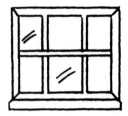

Sparkling Window Cleaner

1	tablespoon white vinegar	1	teaspoon cornstarch
1	tablespoon ammonia	2	drops liquid detergent

Add 1 cup water and store in a pump spray bottle. Shake before spraying onto windows, then wipe off with wadded up newspaper or a soft cloth.

Film-Free Window Washing

Outside windows that have their frames painted with latex paint, and windows in homes where the siding is painted with latex paint, often pick up a cloudy film. This is because of the natural sloughing-off process of this kind of paint.

Soaps and detergents do not dissolve this fine coating of latex. Rinsing windows in water with lots of white vinegar in it neutralizes the film and helps to keep the glass clear and clean.

Mirrors

Clean mirrors by spraying a white vinegar and water solution onto a cloth and wiping the mirror with the cloth. Never spray ANY liquid onto a mirror. Dampness can get to the silvering on the mirror's back and cause it to flake or peel away.

Glass Spots

Splatters, spots and isolated fingerprints on windows and mirrors can be removed by wiping them down with vinegar wet wipes. (See the first page of this chapter.)

Chapter Three

In The Kitchen

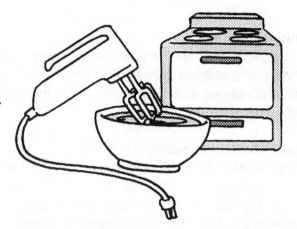

Grandmother knew the value of vinegar in the kitchen, and she used it for more than cooking! All sorts of viruses, bacteria and fungus can grow on kitchen surfaces. Keeping everything clean and dry helps to eliminate them and the sickness they can bring. Vinegar can be big a help in doing this.

Use white vinegar for its antibiotic and antiseptic qualities —

Use apple cider vinegar to add the fresh aroma of ripe fall apples to vinegar's power —

— Or, for a very special effect, clean with your own homemade herbal vinegar!* Herbal vinegar can add a very special aroma to your kitchen, a hint of the best of the foods prepared in your kitchen.

Waxed Surfaces
Clean waxed surfaces with vinegar, instead of ammonia-based products, because ammonia dissolves wax. Also, use cool water to keep the wax hard. Hot water softens wax and makes it easier for tiny particles of dirt to become embedded in it, rather than being washed off.

Miscellaneous Glassware
When soap scum and hard water minerals build up on drinking glasses, vases, mixing bowls, cups, etc., it makes them look old and dull. A good soaking in full strength white vinegar will dissolve the hazy film and bring back their natural, clear beauty.

To clean dull glassware, immerse pieces in a container filled with white vinegar. Let soak for 30 minutes, then scrub with a soft brush dipped in warm, sudsy water. Rinse in clear water, then rinse again in a sink full of very warm water with 1/2 cup white vinegar added to it. Dry with a soft cloth and see how your glassware sparkles!

*See chapter on cooking with vinegar for herbal vinegars.

Lead Crystal

Fine crystal should always be washed and dried by hand. A bit of white vinegar in the rinse water will help keep them from developing a scummy buildup of dulling minerals. To wash: place a rubber mat (or a dish towel) in the bottom of the sink. Add enough hot water and detergent to make enough nice sudsy water to allow you to completely submerge each piece. Wash thoroughly and rinse in hot water with several tablespoons of white vinegar added to it. Dry with a very absorbent cotton towel.

Fine China

When hand washing good dishes, a splash of white vinegar in the last rinse will help prevent streaks and spots - but only use it on china that does not have gold or silver trim. Vinegar can cause metal trims on china to discolor. After drying plates, slip an inexpensive paper plate between each piece of china and you will reduce the chance of dishes being chipped.

Ceramic Dishes, Bowls & Casseroles

Clean encrusted foods from ceramic cookware by scouring them with a nylon scrubber dipped in white vinegar.

Vase Cleaning

Small vases often have tiny openings that make cleaning difficult. Use a small brush dipped in full strength white vinegar to scrub them clean.

Better Vase Cleaning

If you do not have exactly the right size brush for scrubbing the inside of a small vase, use vinegar, water and rice to scour it. Put a handful of rice in the vase and fill it 1/3 of the way full with a half and half mixture of white vinegar and cold water. Shake well, let set for 30 seconds, shake again. Empty out the rice and liquid, rinse in water and vinegar, and set the vase upside down to dry.

Even Better Vase Cleaning

For really tough cleaning jobs, put a few tablespoons of fine sand in a dirty vase. Fill to 1/3 full with a mixture of half white vinegar and half hot water. Shake until deposits are removed, empty and rinse well before drying.

Enamel Ware

Bleach stains from enamel cookware by boiling a few cups of white vinegar in them.

'Silver' trim on china is almost always made of platinum!

Sanitize Cutting Boards

Disinfect wood cutting boards at least once a week (and after each time they are used to cut meat) by applying a liberal coating of salt. Let the salt set for 5 minutes, then wash with 1/2 cup vinegar. This keeps cutting boards sweet-smelling and sanitary. Traditional wood boards should be wiped down with vegetable oil once in a while, too.

Black Appliances

Black (and dark colored) appliances are a special challenge to keep clean, as they reflect every smudge and fingerprint. And, every bit of cleaning solution residue will show up as a streak or hazy film. The secret to keeping these appliances shiny is to clean them often - and to use vinegar as a rinse to remove the film of soapy residue. After washing the appliance, spray full strength white vinegar onto a soft, lint-free cloth. Wipe the appliance surface with the vinegar dampened cloth, then buff with a dry cloth.

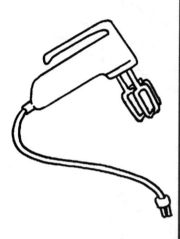

Appliance Cords

Keep electric cords, especially white ones, clean and free of food smears by wiping them frequently with a cloth dampened with white vinegar. (Always unplug electric cords before cleaning them!)

Small Appliances

Can openers, toasters, mixers, blenders and such can be wiped down with a cloth wrung out of white vinegar, then buffed dry. They will stay nice looking longer, and work better, if kept clean.

Always spray vinegar on a cloth (or use a cloth wrung out of vinegar), never spray the appliance directly. Liquid could enter the air vents over motors and damage internal parts. (ALWAYS unplug appliances before cleaning.)

Blender Buttons

White vinegar, on a cotton swab, does a good job of cleaning push buttons and control knobs on blenders and food processors. Rub the vinegar into the small spaces around and between buttons, too.

Mixers

One of the hardest cleaning jobs in the kitchen is getting food splashes off of the underside of mixers. Make this chore easier by wrapping a vinegar dampened cloth around the mixer for a few minutes. Wipe off loose dirt, repeat if necessary.

Can Opener Cleaning

Can opener blades often harbor dried-on food and bits of unidentified gunk, even in the most spotless of kitchens. Soak removable blades in white vinegar until the encrusted food is soft enough to scrub off.

Use a vinegar dampened cotton swab to clean the air vents over the motor, being careful not to push dried food into the motor housing.

Microwave Cleaning Magic

Soften cooked-on food particles by placing a heat safe bowl containing 1/2 cup water and 1/2 cup vinegar in the oven. Heat until the solution begins to boil, then run the microwave, on its highest setting, for 30 seconds. Spills and caked-on foods will wipe off with ease.

Microwave Odor Remover

Place a cup of water to which 2 tablespoons apple cider vinegar have been added in the microwave. Bring the mixture to a boil and then let it set for 3 minutes. The oven will smell fresh and clean again. This is especially good for removing odors from the air after cooking fish or popcorn.

Electric Knives

Wipe all surfaces with a cloth wrung out of a solution of sudsy water and vinegar. Give special attention to crevices around blade mounting areas. Finish by wiping the electric cord and wall plug.

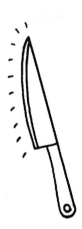

Sharpen Knives

Need to sharpen a knife in a hurry? Spray vinegar onto the bottom of a clay flower pot. Then use the edge of the pot as a whetstone.

Self-Defrosting Refrigerators

The water collecting tray under self-defrosting refrigerators and freezers should be washed occasionally in soapy water. Any buildup of minerals should be dissolved with white vinegar. A teaspoon or two of vinegar in the tray will retard the growth of bacteria and help prevent moldy smells.

Really Dirty Refrigerators

The top of tall appliances such as refrigerators and some freezers can collect a layer of gummy dirt. Dust settles up there, gets mixed with grease in the air and then steam from cooking cements it together into a cleaning challenge.

Vacuum as much of the gunk up as possible. Then spray a damp sponge with full strength vinegar and drizzle liquid for hand washing dishes over the vinegar. Pat the sponge over the entire refrigerator top and let it soak for 15 minutes. Use the sponge to wipe the stuck-on dirt off. (It will come off easily now.) Rinse with a solution of hot water and a dash of white vinegar, then buff dry.

A light coating of wax or polish on the top of the refrigerator will help to keep greasy dust from sticking to it.

Gas Stove Grates

Boil iron burner grates from gas stoves, for about 10 minutes, in water with a cup of vinegar added to it. They will be much easier to clean.

Stove Tops

Wipe spatters and grease from stove tops with a cloth wrung out of a solution made from 1/2 cup white vinegar, 1/2 cup water, and 1 teaspoon liquid detergent.

Oven Cleaner

Put 3 cups of water into a shallow baking dish and heat oven to 300°. Turn the oven off and let set for 20 minutes. Replace the water with 2 cups of ammonia and allow to set overnight. To 1/2 cup of the ammonia, add 1/2 cup white vinegar and 2 cups baking soda. Smooth this mixture over oven surfaces and allow to set for 20 minutes. Wipe away the cleaner and rinse with clear water.

Oven Racks

Spray oven racks with vinegar and let set until they dry naturally. Then place them in a tub of very hot water with 1 cup of vinegar and a tablespoon of dishwasher detergent added to it. Let the racks soak until the water has cooled. Repeat soaking process and then wipe the racks down with a sponge.

Dishwashers

Dishwashers, especially those used in hard water areas, often attract an unsightly buildup of lime and other minerals. In addition to discoloring the inside of the dishwasher, minerals can damage its working parts. These deposits can be dissolved by running the dishwasher for a complete washing cycle, with no detergent in it. Instead, put 2 cups white vinegar in the bottom of the dishwasher. Stop the machine before the drying cycle begins and wipe the top and sides down with a soft cloth.

Never dry the bottom of the dishwasher, as many brands rely on a small amount of water remaining in the bottom to protect seals from drying out and being ruined.

Quick Kitchen Deodorizing Treatment
Dampen a sponge or cloth with full strength apple cider vinegar and place it over a heat or air conditioning register. Allow air to circulate through the vinegar-wet cloth for 15 to 20 minutes and the air will feel fresh and pure.

Emily's Favorite Kitchen Deodorizer
Keep a small pump spray bottle of water, with 2 tablespoons of white vinegar added to it, handy in the kitchen. Whenever odor is a problem, a few puffs into the air will neutralize it. An old pump hair spray bottle works well, because it puts out a fine, easily diffused mist. Use when cooking fish, cabbage, after boilovers, or anytime the air needs a quick freshening.

Coffee Pots
Coffee oils are very thick and sticky, so they tend to collect on the inside of pots and on percolator parts. When they become old, these oils decompose. This releases the acids that give coffee a sour taste and rancid smell.

An occasional touch of vinegar will dissolve coffee oils and so keep coffee pots from developing rancid odors. Just add 1 tablespoon of vinegar to a full pot of hot water and let it set for 10 minutes. Rinse well and the pot will make excellent coffee again.

For heavy buildups, make this special pot of 'coffee' - replace coffee grounds with 1 teaspoon liquid detergent and 1 tablespoon vinegar. When the full brewing cycle has finished, rinse the pot several times with hot water.

Coffee Pot Cleaner
Mix together equal parts water and white vinegar and use only this for a complete cycle of an automatic coffee pot. It will freshen the pot, help to loosen and remove mineral deposits, and prevent build-up of rancid coffee oils. Great for soaking teapots, too!

Thermos Cleaner
Fill a stained vacuum bottle with a mixture made of 2 parts white vinegar to 1 part cold water. Let stand for an hour, then add a tablespoon of uncooked rice and shake for several minutes. Rinse several times and wipe dry.

Teapots need cleaned, too!

Kitchen Counter Tops

To preserve glossy surfaces, use vinegar and water to wipe down lightly soiled counter tops. Use detergent, soap or ammonia based products only when really needed, as they break down wax-based polishes. Laminated plastic counter tops (such as Formica) need to be kept covered with a layer of wax to protect them from tiny cuts and scratches which will eventually make the surface look dull.

Counter Top Scrubber

Make a great, disposable, counter top scrubber by dipping a piece of old nylon hose in vinegar and using it to scrub globs of stuck-on goo off laminated plastic counter tops. This combination has enough cleaning power to remove the mess, yet will not scratch the surface. (Really hard globs can be allowed to soak for a few minutes.)

Very Dirty Counter Tops

When counter tops have really hard globs of foods or other materials on them, use a vinegar compress to loosen the dirt. Soaking the material loose will save the work of scrubbing and scraping and, more importantly, save wear and tear on the counter top.

Wet a cloth, paper towel or sponge with full strength white vinegar. Lay it on the material to be loosened and let it soak for at least an hour. Wipe off as much of the dirt as possible and repeat as necessary.

Crumb Catcher

A cloth dampened with a light spray of vinegar will catch a whole counter top of crumbs, without spreading them all over.

Counter and Appliance Stain Remover

Mix a solution of equal parts white vinegar and water. Use a cloth or sponge wrung out of this fresh smelling mixture to wipe down appliances and counter tops. It will not leave streaks, and they will shine.

Copper Cleaner

1	cup white vinegar	1/4	cup flour
1/2	cup water	1/2	cup salt
1/2	cup powdered detergent		

Whisk all ingredients together, then slowly heat in a double boiler until the detergent is dissolved and the mixture begins to thicken. Set aside until cool. To use, wipe onto copper with a small cloth, let set for 30 seconds, then wipe off with a clean cloth.

Drain Cleaner

Slow-running drains can often be improved by treating them with baking soda and vinegar. Begin by sprinkling 1/4 cup soda into the drain. Immediately pour 1/2 cup vinegar into the drain. Allow it to foam and sizzle for a few minutes. When the action has stopped, pour at least 2 quarts of boiling water down the drain.

Drain & Septic Treatment

Plumbing lines which empty into septic systems can benefit from an occasional bacteria boosting treatment. Begin by using a vinegar and baking soda drain cleaner (see above) in all drains. When the drains are clean and free-running, pour 1 package dry yeast and 2/3 cup brown sugar into the toilet and flush twice. Do this about once a month and the system will work efficiently for years.

Drain Deodorizer

Pour 1/2 cup vinegar down each drain, every week. The vinegar will keep the drains smelling sweet (and discourage clogs, too)!

Magic Garbage Disposer Freshener

Mix equal parts apple cider vinegar and water and freeze the mixture in an ice cube tray. Store the frozen cubes in a plastic bag. Then, grind a few of these special freshener cubes in the disposer each week for instant cleaning that will also leave it smelling fresh.

Vinegar Magic For Aluminum Pots and Pans

Aluminum pans become discolored if they get a lot of exposure to salty foods, ammonia or cleaning products that contain ammonia. If 1/2 cup white vinegar, with a couple of cups of water added to it, is occasionally boiled in such pans, staining will be kept to a minimum.

For lightly stained cookware: make a paste of white vinegar and baking soda. Spread over stained aluminum cooking utensils. Remove with fine superfine steel wool.

For medium stains: mix the baking soda with an equal amount of cream of tartar, then stir in the vinegar.

For badly stained pans: use baking soda and cream of tartar (as for medium stains) and mix with vinegar which has been mixed half and half with liquid detergent.

Iron forms rust; copper forms verdigris.

Copper Pans

When copper pans oxidize, a green film forms. This is called verdigris and, while it is a bit unsightly on the outside of pans, it helps them do a better job of absorbing heat.

On the inside of pans this green oxide is a bigger problem - it is poisonous. This is why most pans only use copper on the outside, or sandwiched between two other metals. If a copper pan develops these patches of green on the inside, consider throwing it away. To clean verdigris from the inside of copper pans: fill with water, add 1/3 cup vinegar and 1/3 cup salt. Boil for 10 minutes and scrub vigorously. Rinse well.

No-Stick Pans

Mineral salts from hard water can build up on the surfaces of pans coated with fluorocarbon compounds. These no-stick coatings should not be scrubbed with harsh chemicals or steel wool pads. Whitish mineral stains can be removed by boiling 2 cups of water and 1/3 cup white vinegar in the pan for a few minutes, then wiping the pan dry with a soft cloth.

Foil & Vinegar Scrubbers

Make your own scrubber for removing cooked on food from pans and baking dishes. Simply crumple up a wad of aluminum foil (new or used), dip it in vinegar, and rub the cooked on food away. Extra hard spots can be soaked in vinegar for a few minutes before scrubbing.

Vinegar & Apple Cleaner

Remove stains from the inside of aluminum cookware by boiling 1 quart of water, 1 /2 cup white vinegar and 1 cup apple peels for 15 minutes. (Also very good for removing the smell of cooking fish from the kitchen.)

Rust Stains From Metal

Rust stains on stainless steel sinks can be wiped away by scouring with salt, dampened with vinegar.

Never use an ammonia containing solution with one which contains bleach (or chlorine-based cleaners).

'Teflon' & 'Silver-stone' are two brand names for no-stick cookware.

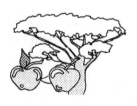

Chapter Four

In The Bathroom, Bedroom & Office

Bathrooms are always a special cleaning challenge. They sprout mildew and mold, attract odors and breed tub and shower slime. Bedrooms are a haven for dust balls, stale air and musty smelling closets. Offices present their own problems with assorted chemical stains and paper bits. Vinegar can help solve all these problems.

BATHROOM

Better Wet Wipes

Mix 1 cup vinegar, 1 cup water and 1 tablespoon liquid detergent in a bowl. Wet small pieces of clean, soft cloth in the vinegar mixture, then wring them out. Place the cloths in a tightly capped container.

Use wet wipes for cleaning and moving spots on faucets and fixture handles, drains, around tub enclosures and sinks, and even on the outside surfaces of toilets. They also do a good job cleaning windows, walls and floors.

Disposable Wet Wipes

Make disposable wet wipes by substituting sheets of extra heavy paper towels for pieces of cloth. They are great for wiping up unpleasant bathroom messes.

Mildew

That slimy growth in showers, around tubs and in other damp places is really a plant. It is a soft, spongy fungus, and can be white as well as black or purplish in color. Mildew grows best where it is dark and the air is warm and wet and stagnant. It thrives in showers and tubs, where it lives on body oil, dirt particles and soap scum.

Vinegar helps to remove the dirt, oil and soap that provide its food. It also leaves behind an acid environment to slow the future growth of mildew.

Dryrot and corn smut are also fungus.

147

So, the cure for any area attacked by mildew, mold or other fungus is to keep it dry, give it lots of sunshine, and regularly rinse it with vinegar!

Mildew And Mold Removal

The metal edges of shower and tub surrounds are especially attractive to mold and mildew. Scrub them down with a piece of crumbled up foil which has been dipped in full strength vinegar. Use a toothbrush dipped in vinegar for crevices and corners. Rinse with clear water, then with water and vinegar and buff dry.

Use white vinegar to dissolve soap film and kill mold and mildew. It will leave the bathroom smelling fresh and clean. Use apple cider vinegar for the same cleaning power, but with a stronger, fresher, longer lasting fragrance.

Soap Film Remover

Shower walls, in particular, seem to attract scummy soap film. Vinegar and baking soda can eat right through it! Simply take 1 cup baking soda and add enough white vinegar to make a thick, frothy cream. Spread it over areas where soap film has built up and let set for 5 minutes. Wipe off with a soft brush or sponge, rinse in water with some white vinegar added to it and buff dry.

Extra Power Soap Film Treatment

Mix together 1/4 cup white vinegar and 1/4 cup ammonia.* Add enough baking soda to make a thick paste. Spread this mixture over the area that has a coating of soap film. Let set for 10 minutes, then remove with a medium-bristled brush. Follow with a rinse of cool water, with a little vinegar in it.

Soap Film Preventive

Prevent soap film buildup by rinsing all exposed surfaces, every week, with a solution of vinegar and water. A cup of white vinegar to a quart of water is about right for hard water areas, a cup to a gallon of water for soft water areas.

Bathroom Odors

Instead of using an aerosol air freshener to fight bathroom odors, keep a pump spray bottle of vinegar water handy. Just fill the bottle with water and 1 tablespoon white vinegar. Whenever odor relief is needed, a few sprays will release a fine mist that neutralizes odors.

For best results, use a pump sprayer of the type hair spray comes in. It will release a very fine mist, spreading the vinegar into the air rapidly.

A mist with vinegar in it, instead of a floral scent, is especially good for households where someone has hay fever or is allergic to flowers and grasses. Vinegar neutralizes odors without adding a fragrance that can trigger allergies and add to indoor pollution.

Hair In The Sink
Cleaning pesky hair clippings from the sink can be a messy, frustrating job. Make it easy with a dash of vinegar. Simply spray vinegar on a piece of bathroom tissue and use it to wipe out the sink. Fold the tissue over the hair, wipe again, discard the tissue and hair.

Denture Cleaner and Freshener
A quick brushing with white vinegar will help to brighten dentures. It will also remove lingering odors. If dentures are set overnight in water, adding 1/2 teaspoon vinegar will help keep them odor free.

Using apple cider vinegar will add a refreshing flavor to the mouth. Herbal vinegars, such as thyme or mint, also act as breath fresheners.

Ceramic Tile
Floors, back splashes, shower walls and such will shine their best if rinsed in a mild vinegar and water solution, then buffed dry. Keep ceramic tile showers free of soap scum and hard water salts buildup by drying after each use.

A synthetic chamois cloth does a wonderful job of wiping down tile because it absorbs water so well. Keep the cloth fresh and clean by washing it occasionally in a mild liquid detergent, then rinsing it in vinegar to neutralize the soap and minerals it will be constantly wiping up.

Hair Rollers, Brushes & Combs

Over time, hair rollers, brushes and combs pick up a coating of hair spray, mousse and setting gels. This buildup attracts dirt and dust, turning it into a dark, sticky coating. Remove this coating by soaking rollers, brushes and combs for an hour in a quart of warm water with a cup of white vinegar added to it. Then scrub with an old toothbrush which has been dipped in liquid detergent. The buildup will now come off easily. Follow with a clear water rinse, then a rinse in warm water with a dash of white vinegar. Blot most of the water off and air dry, in the sun if possible.

Shower Heads

When heavy mineral deposits are visible on the shower head, it usually means these salts have been deposited inside, too. Unscrew the fixture and soak it in full strength white vinegar. The vinegar will dissolve and soften the buildup. If the small openings are clogged, use a toothpick or small nail to remove the minerals which have been deposited on them. Then scrub with an old toothbrush and rinse well.

Keep shower heads sparkling bright by wiping them down once a week with white vinegar. Give the tiny nozzle openings special attention, so that mineral precipitations do not develop. A thin coating of wax can help prevent hard water deposits from sticking to the metal.

Shower Curtains

A shower curtain that is stained with mildew or mold can be revived by soaking it in a laundry tub of warm water with 2 cups of white vinegar added to it. Let it soak for a couple of hours (or over night) and then wash in warm, sudsy water and dry in the sun.

Wipe down the shower curtain on a regular basis with white vinegar and it will be less likely to develop mildew or mold stains. Just spray the bottom fourth of the curtain with white vinegar and wipe it off with a soft cloth.

Keep It Shiny

After wiping chrome, brass or other metal bathroom fixtures with vinegar and water, dry completely and apply two light coats of wax. They will look bright and shiny longer, clean up easier next time, and will resist the buildup of hard water mineral salts.

BEDROOM

Urine Stained Mattresses

Spray stains with white vinegar and blot dry. The process may need to be repeated several times, but it will lift stains and remove unpleasant odors.

Freshen Bedding

Musty, stale smelling blankets and bedspreads can be freshened, often without actually having to clean or wash them. Simply put the bedding in a clothes dryer with a cloth wrung out of full strength apple cider vinegar. With the dryer set to 'air,' let it fluff for 5 minutes. Most odors and dust will disappear, and the apple cider vinegar will leave a clean, outdoorsy smell behind. Dusty drapes can be refreshed in the same manner.

150

OFFICE

Taking The White Out

White correction fluid is wonderful stuff, until it shows up where it is not needed! Usually, a quick dab of white vinegar will melt it away. (For stubborn spots, reapply or soak for a few minutes.)

Super-Glued Fingers

When an errant drop of one of those new fast drying contact glues gets on skin, fingers can end up cemented together. For a skin saving remedy, soak in full strength vinegar.

Colored Paper Stains

Vivid shades of construction paper can brighten up office projects, but a little dampness can cause bright colors to transfer onto clothing. Lift these stains by dampening with a solution of half white vinegar, half water, then blot dry. Repeat until all trace of color is gone.

Books

After awhile, even the nicest books can develop a musty smell. Keep them spotlessly clean by running a vacuum cleaner over them frequently. If individual volumes need to be hand dusted, try wiping the covers with a soft cloth which has been very lightly sprayed with a weak vinegar and water solution. (You only want enough vinegar to kill the musty smell and to deter mold and fungus growth.)

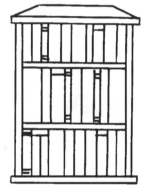

Bookshelves

Use a strong solution of vinegar and sudsy water to wipe off bookshelves, then rinse in clear water and dry. Make shelf cleaning less exhausting by only removing 4 or 5 books from a shelf. Wash and dry the exposed part of the shelf, then slide the next 4 or 5 books over this clean spot and wash the part now exposed.

Repeat the process to the end of the shelf. When the entire shelf has been washed and dried, slide the books back to their original positions and replace the few books which were removed at the beginning. This way, lifting of heavy books is minimized for the one doing the cleaning, shelf order is maintained, and the books do not suffer unnecessary handling.

Chapter Five

Vinegar Goes Outside

Vinegar is exceptionally useful in the garden, yard and garage. For cleaning and polishing, or for deterring insects, it is difficult to find a better, more environmentally safe substance.

Vinegar is a gentle, inexpensive cleaner, yet it is surprisingly effective. It is safe for children and pets, yet it attacks germs and harmful bacteria. Whether shining and polishing the car or washing the dog, there is usually a good a reason to keep the vinegar bottle handy!

GARDEN

Gardener's Friend
Keep ants away from plants by making a circle around them with vinegar. Just dribble a generous stream around each plant. It will act as a barrier to wandering ants.

Home Ant Repellant
Sprinkle apple cider vinegar on windowsills, around doors and other openings to prevent ants from entering the home.

Flowerpots

After a very short time, clay flowerpots develop a buildup of mineral salts. This whitish buildup not only looks ugly, it interferes with the way the pot should breathe and absorb water. Remove mineral salts by rubbing with a scrub brush dipped in full strength vinegar. Finish with a clear water rinse.

Soil Ph Balancer
Many plants need an acid soil environment to thrive. To acidify alkaline ground, pour 1 cup vinegar into a bucket of water and dribble it in a circle around acid loving plants such as azaleas, blueberries, marigolds, and radishes.

YARD & GARAGE

Barbecue Grills

Place soiled racks from barbecue grills in a large black plastic bag. Use 2 cups vinegar to wet them down, then tie a loose knot in the bag to seal in the moisture. Lay the plastic bag in the sun for 3 to 4 hours, then add 2 tablespoons dishwasher detergent and 2 quarts hot water to it. Re-tie the bag and allow it to soak in the sun for another 2 hours. Burnt food and stains will now wipe off easily.

Cement Garage Floors

Sweeping cement can produce a fine dust that is very corrosive. Reduce dust with newspapers and vinegar water. To a gallon of water, add 1 cup vinegar. Sprinkle this liberally over a pile of shredded newspapers. Toss the shredded newspapers over the floor, then sweep as usual. Dust will cling to the damp newspaper and the vinegar will help neutralize odors.

Green Sweep For Cement Floors

Cut down on dust when sweeping cement floors by spreading grass clippings over the floor (the fresher the better). Dampen the clippings by sprinkling with water that has had a little apple cider vinegar added to it. The sweeping will not generate dust, and when the job is done, the area will smell fresh and clean!

CAR & BOAT

Odor-Eater For Car Ashtrays

Wipe ashtrays out with a wadded up newspaper or paper towel moistened with full strength vinegar. Allow to air dry. The vinegar will neutralize ashtray odor, and as it drys it will remove stale smells from the entire car.

No-Freeze, No-Streak Windshield Washer Liquid

1/2 cup white vinegar
2 cups rubbing alcohol
2 teaspoons liquid detergent
6 cups water

Stir the detergent in the water and when it is well mixed, add the vinegar and alcohol. This liquid will also help remove ice and snow from a cold car's windshield. Simply spray a good coating on before trying to clear the windshield of ice. It will make the job much easier.

153

Car Chrome Cleaner

Remove small spots of rust from car chrome by rubbing them out with a piece of aluminum foil dipped in vinegar. Rinse, and then finish up with a coat of wax to discourage new spots from forming.

Decal Remover

Soak bumper decals in full strength white vinegar and they will come off easily. Just wrap a cloth around the bumper, wet it thoroughly with vinegar, then allow it to set for 45 minutes. The glue holding the decal to the bumper should begin to break down, making removal much easier!

Boat Cleaning

Aluminum boats, in particular, are very sensitive to alkalines in water. These salts can etch aluminum and cause it to discolor. Vinegar neutralizes alkalines, so it can be used to scrub off discoloration. Use full strength white vinegar to scrub stains, but always follow with a clear water rinse, then immediately wipe dry.

ESPECIALLY FOR CAMPERS

No-Scrub Laundry

Do laundry while on the road by placing soiled clothes in a watertight container with a tiny bit of detergent and some white vinegar. After a few hours on the road the laundry will be ready to rinse and hang out to dry!

Vacation Skin

Always tuck a bottle of vinegar into the camping pack. It is great for soothing skin that has been subjected to sun and wind. It is also good for softening hard water.

Iron Pans And Kettles

Half the fun of camp cooking is using a big old iron frying pan or kettle. A dash of vinegar added to the cooking pot will help transfer iron from these utensils to food.

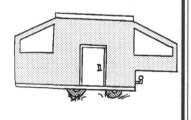

Fiberglass Campers

Because it is light in weight, many camping trailers use fiberglass for both exterior and interior surfaces. This material tends to pickup hard water stains and soap scum film. White vinegar helps dissolve this whitish discoloration. Use it on fiberglass sinks, wall panels, tubs and showers.

Plastic Picnic Coolers

Spray a strong vinegar and detergent solution over the inside of the cooler. Close it up to soak while you wash the outside of the cooler with vinegar and water. By the time you get to the inside, odors and food remains will wipe right off.

PETS

Itch Control For Dogs

Help to control itching by following the dog's bath with a vinegar and water rinse. Add 1/3 cup apple cider vinegar to 2 quarts water and pour over a well shampooed and rinsed dog. Do not rinse out. Dry as usual and the coat should be soft and shiny, and there should be much less itching and scratching.

Odor Control

Control odor from any furry pet by spraying its coat daily with mild vinegar water. 1 tablespoon to a cup of water is about right for eliminating odors.

Behavior Control

Train cats and dogs to respect furniture with a squirt gun filled with water which has a teaspoon of vinegar added to it. Whenever the pet approaches a forbidden area, tell them 'No' and reinforce it with a quick liquid reminder. Soon, simply picking up the squirt gun will ensure good behavior.

Carpet Spots

Use a solution made of 1 cup white vinegar to a gallon of lukewarm water to neutralize urine stains in carpet. Sprinkle it on, then immediately blot it up. Repeat as needed.

Pet Hair

Turn an old tube sock inside out and slip in onto your hand. Spray it, lightly, with white vinegar and use it to wipe down your pet. Loose hair will stick to the damp sock. Great for cats, dogs, hampsters, rabbits and other furry creatures. It also deodorizes their fur. A vinegar dampened sock is also good for removing pet hairs from furniture, carpets and clothing.

Vinegar Is For Birds, Too!

Keep birdbaths clean by rinsing them out regularly. A few drops of vinegar added to birdbath water will help control the growth of fungus and bacteria.

Chapter Six

Vinegar Is
For People

Over the years vinegar has been credited with to power to act as a soothing skin tonic, add shining highlights to hair and, when combined with herbs, bring calming comfort or energizing zest to the bath.

What follows is a collection of old-fashioned remedies which use vinegar to make people feel better. Please remember, these old-time remedies are not medically proven. They are simply ways many people have used vinegar mixtures for relief of discomfort and for its fresh, pleasing aroma.

EVERYONE

Instantly Soft Hands

Pour 1/2 cup water, with 1 teaspoon vinegar stirred in, over the hands. Sprinkle the water and vinegar dampened hands with 1/2 teaspoon white sugar, then with 1 teaspoon baby oil. Work this mixture into the hands for 2 minutes, then wash with a gentle soap. Hands will be almost magically smooth and velvety feeling!

Silky Smooth Hands

Make hands silky smooth, and keep them that way, by moisturizing them in warm water and vinegar, then sealing the moisture in with petroleum jelly. For best results, treat hands just before retiring for the night.

Add 1 tablespoon apple cider vinegar to 2 cups warm water. Soak hands in this mixture for 5 minutes, then pat them dry. Smooth 1/2 teaspoon petroleum jelly over the hands and pull on a pair of cotton gloves. By morning the hands will be unbelievably soft and smooth, no matter how much hard work they do during the day.

Soft Feet

Rough skin on the feet can be softened by soaking them in water and vinegar, then applying body lotion. Use lukewarm water, with a tablespoon of apple cider vinegar added for each quart of water. Pat the feet completely dry, gently apply body lotion, then cover with cotton socks.

Softer Feet

Hard, dry calluses and coarse skin can make feet feel uncomfortable, and contribute to pain when walking. Soften feet by soaking for 5 minutes in warm water with a little vinegar in it, then rubbing granulated white sugar over rough spots. Follow with a quick baby oil massage, then wash thoroughly with a gentle soap before covering with cotton socks. (Baby oil makes feet VERY slippery! Always wash it all off BEFORE standing or walking.)

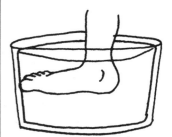

One way to prevent slipping is to soak feet in vinegar and water, in the bathtub. Then, fill the tub for a regular bath (let the vinegar do double duty as a soothing, full body conditioner). Use the sugar and baby oil while sitting in the tub. This way there is no mess, and no chance of falling!

Soften Corns & Calluses

To soften skin made rough and scaly by corns and callouses, soak the feet every day in a pan of warm soapy water, to which a cup of vinegar has been added.

Easier Nail Trimming

If tough toenails make trimming them a chore, soak the feet in warm water with a couple of tablespoons of vinegar added to it. After about 10 minutes, nails will be much softer and easier to trim.

Dandruff Remedy

Shampoo and rinse the hair as usual, then work a solution made of equal parts apple cider vinegar and water through the hair. Do not rinse this out.

Grandmother's Dandruff Treatment

After washing and rinsing the hair as usual, treat it to 5 minutes of conditioning with a mixture of 1/2 cup apple cider vinegar to which 2 aspirins have been added. Rinse well, then follow with a final conditioning rinse of a quart of warm water to which 1/2 cup apple cider vinegar has been added.

Herbal Baths

Homemade scented vinegars are the essential component of great herbal baths. Use 1/4 to 1/2 cup vinegar to a tub of warm water. For a relaxing soak, use herbal vinegars such as catnip, lemon balm, lavender, borage, chamomile or slippery elm. For an invigorating soak, use herbal vinegars such as ginger, peppermint, sage, or tarragon.

Steamy Vinegar Facials

Heat 1 cup herbal vinegar to the boiling point and pour it into a large bowl. Lean over the bowl and drape a towel over your head and the bowl. Allow the warm, moist steam to soften facial skin. When the vinegar has cooled, pat it onto the face as a cleansing astringent. Strawberry vinegar is especially good for the skin.

An herbal vinegar steam treatment is a wonderful way to soften the skin before applying a moisturizer, or to soothe the skin after a cleansing facial.

ESPECIALLY FOR WOMEN

Vinegar Facial Mask
    1/4   cup oatmeal
    1   tablespoon honey
    1   tablespoon apple cider vinegar

Combine ingredients and pat the mixture onto wet skin. Let set until dry. Wash off with cool water and apply moisturizer.

Bubble Bath

Put 1 cup vegetable oil in a bottle and add 1/4 cup apple cider vinegar and 2 tablespoons liquid hand soap. Shake well before adding a few cupfuls to bath water. A few drops of perfume may be added, if desired. Or, replace the apple cider vinegar with lavender, rosemary or woodruff herbal vinegar.

Hair Moisturizer.
    1   egg yolk
    1   teaspoon honey
    1/4   cup olive oil
    1/4   cup apple cider vinegar

Beat all ingredients together for several minutes, or combine in a blender to produce a thick, smooth cream. Rub the mixture into the hair and onto the scalp and let set for about 10 minutes. Shampoo out and rinse in lukewarm water with a splash of apple cider vinegar added to it.

Skin Lightening Solution

1/4	cup white vinegar
1/4	cup lemon juice
1	cup white wine
1	tablespoon honey

Put all ingredients into a jar and shake until will mixed. Pat onto the skin morning and evening.

Shiny Hair Spray

Combine 1 cup water and 1/4 cup apple cider vinegar in a pump-spray bottle. A light spritz will add sparkling highlights and a bit of body to dull, limp hair. It works even better with a drop or two of perfume added to it, or if the apple cider vinegar is replaced with herbal vinegar.

Oil & Vinegar Hair Treatment

Restore the health of dry, sun damaged hair with oil and vinegar! Heat 1/4 cup olive oil until it is comfortably warm, then massage it into the scalp and hair. Make sure ends get a good coating, using extra oil for long hair.

Next, add 1/2 cup apple cider vinegar to a sink full of very hot water. Soak a towel in the hot vinegar water and then wring it out. Wrap the warm, wet towel around the olive oil treated hair and cover with a second, dry towel. After 15 minutes, remove both towels and wash the hair with a gentle shampoo.

Soft Skin - Forever

Keep the skin on your face soft and youthful looking by moisturizing it before applying makeup. Just wring a washcloth out of warm water with a dash of vinegar in it. Hold the warm, wet washcloth over the face for 15 - 20 seconds, pat the skin barely dry, then apply moisturizer, followed by makeup. Skin will remain soft and youthful looking, and will be less likely to develop blemishes.

ESPECIALLY FOR MEN

Men's Scented Splash-On

Vinegar with spices and herbs added to it was the original skin tonic for men. Some of the best ones for tightening and conditioning the skin are made with spearmint, bee balm, chamomile or blackberry leaves.*

See chapter on cooking with vinegar for herbal vinegars.

Skin Bracer

For a healing, refreshing facial tonic, mix 1/2 teaspoon cream of tartar and two tablespoons vinegar into a half cup of warm water. Pat onto the face after washing.

Begin by mixing together a basic aftershave lotion of 1 cup white vinegar and 2 tablespoons sweet clover honey. Add 1 tablespoon of an aromatic herb. Let the preparation set for a week, strain out the herb leaves, and the aftershave lotion is ready to use!

Some especially fragrant herbs for aftershave lotions are sage, thyme, cloves, bay and coriander. Combine a couple of herbs to make your own distinctive scent.

Another Aftershave

Combine 1/2 cup white vinegar, 1/2 cup vodka and 2 tablespoons honey. Variations:

• Spice it up by soaking 1 teaspoon aromatic herbs in the mixture for about a month, then strain and use.

• Apple cider vinegar, substituted for the white vinegar, makes a more robust aftershave

• Rubbing alcohol may be substituted for the vodka for a less expensive version.

• A teaspoon of glycerin added to the aftershave mixture will soothe and moisturize a dry face.

Refrigerated Aftershave

This is a cooling aftershave for warm weather use. Puree a small cucumber in the blender (do not peel) with several fresh mint leaves. Add this mixture to a basic aftershave and set in the refrigerator overnight. Strain and it is ready to use. (Must be kept refrigerated.)

BABY, TOO!

Baby Bottle Nipples

When boiling nipples to sterilize them, add a teaspoon of vinegar to each 2 cups of water. It will help prevent them developing an 'off' taste. (For fast sterilizing, try boiling the nipples and vinegar water in the microwave.)

Diaper Rash

Discourage rashes on baby's bottom by adding 3/4 cup white vinegar to the last rinse water for diapers. (Diapers should always be rinsed twice.) Skip the fabric softener when drying diapers. Chemicals in softeners may irritate baby's delicate skin, and softeners make diapers less able to soak up liquids quickly!

Easy Highchair Cleaning

Wash baby's highchair quickly and easily in the shower. Simply set the chair in the shower, spray with full strength white vinegar and let set for 3 minutes. Then turn the shower on for another 3 minutes. A quick buffing with a brush will now loosen any dried on food, then another quick rinse will complete the job. The chair will be shiny clean, with no hard scrubbing or scraping.

Baby Odors

Save on utilities, neutralize odors, humidify, and safety-proof baby's room with one simple trick! Take a damp towel, direct from the washing machine, and spray it with white vinegar. Hang the towel over the top of the door to baby's room. As the towel dries it will control odors, add moisture to the air, and prevent the door from closing all the way, so the little one cannot accidently lock his or her self in the room.

Sanitizing Toys

Wipe down plastic dolls, blocks, cars and other toys with a cloth wrung out of a solution made of 1 part vinegar and 4 parts water. Or, spray full strength white vinegar onto a damp cloth and use it to wipe dirt and germs from toys.

Do not soak wooden chairs!

Chapter Seven
Vinegar & Laundry

3000 B.C. — Cotton fabric is first made in the Indus valley.

400 B.C. — Generally, laundry is washed in a stream.

1625 — Soap is made at home by boiling grease, fat and wood ashes.

1837 — Procter & Gamble starts selling soap.

1907 — Thor, the first completely self-contained electric washing machine is introduced by Hurley Machine Company of Chicago.

1907 — Persil, the first dishwashing detergent, comes on the market. (Unfortunately, it is not suitable for heavy duty laundry use.)

1922 — Maytag's Gyrofoam washing machine is a market star.

1934 — The first Washeteria (laundromat) opens in Fort Worth, Texas with four washing machines.

1946 — Tide, the first detergent strong enough for washing clothes is introduced by Procter & Gamble.

A popular homemaker's advice book of 1849 admonished the housekeeper: "Remove soil spots with equal parts vinegar, turpentine and linseed oil." And, "Boil soiled laundry for 20 minutes in water with soap, lye, sal soda, and turpentine."

Wash day has changed! Today's fabrics are often delicate, and require gentle cleaning. As the washing of clothes left river banks and soap gave way to detergent, standards of cleanliness changed, too. Now, laundry is expected to be more than clean. Whites must gleam and colors need to sparkle.

Fabrics which come through the laundry room may be synthetic or natural, delicate or sturdy, drab or iridescent, easily faded or colorfast. This parade of materials, textures, fibers and dyes presents difficult cleaning choices — does one use soap or detergent? Bleach, an alkaline washing booster or vinegar?

Understanding how laundry cleaning substances do their jobs can help you decide when to use soap, when to use detergent and when to use vinegar as a cleaning agent.

SOAP OR DETERGENT?

Soaps clean by encouraging tiny bits dirt to become solid curds that can be rinsed out by water. Soap leaves a light, oily film behind that protects wood, but attracts more dirt to fabrics.

Detergents include an ingredient to make water 'wet' better, by breaking its surface tension. This lets it do a better job of dissolving dirt out of fabrics. Detergents also contain emulsifiers, which help to keep the bits of dirt suspended in water. Rinsing in lots of water helps get rid of this dirt, too.

Surface tension is what lets a water spider 'walk on water!'

Most soaps and detergents are alkaline. Vinegar's acid nature makes it a good neutralizing rinse for laundry washed in either soap or detergent.

USE VINEGAR WITH CARE

Vinegar has been considered, throughout history, to be an indispensable part of cleaning laundry. This is because it is often the best product for rinsing natural fibers. It is not always as compatible with synthetic fibers.

There are some fabrics for which vinegar is not appropriate. For example, in some situations vinegar acts as a mild bleaching agent. So, before applying it to dark or bright colors, test it on small, hidden areas. And, because vinegar is an acid, it can intensify the actions of other acids, making it a poor choice for treating some man-made fibers.

Generally, silk and wool can take a dash of full strength white vinegar. For fine cottons and linens, use vinegar which has been diluted with an equal amount of water, as it can weaken these fibers.

Acetate and triacetate are cellulose based and should not be exposed to vinegar at all. Triacetate is the material which is often used for lightweight, finely pleated skirts. Ramie, a plant fiber based material, is not helped by vinegar either. (When cellulose products decompose they turn into something much like vinegar!)

163

USE VINEGAR TO NEUTRALIZE ALKALINES

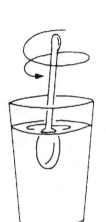

Vinegar is particularly good at neutralizing alkaline stains. So, use vinegar to neutralize the effects of caustic products, such as dishwasher detergents, and solutions containing lye, such as oven cleaners.

This means vinegar can be very helpful as a neutralizing rinse for hands exposed to caustic alkaline cleaners. And, use vinegar on stains made by:

Syrup	Food Dye	Apples	Blueberries
Jelly	Hair Colorings	Pears	Grapefruit
Honey	Spaghetti	Cherries	Blackberries
Oranges	Perfume	Grapes	Raspberries

Vinegar is useful for removing many of the discolorations caused by medicines, inks and fabric dyes. It is also good for lifting traces of beer, wine, grass, soft drinks, coffee, tea and tobacco.

Ammonia is very alkaline, and can alter the color of some dyes. Stop this change in color by neutralizing the action of ammonia with vinegar. When fabric begins to bleed color because it has been exposed to ammonia, rinse it in cool water. Follow with a strong vinegar and water solution, then finish with a clear water rinse.

One of the few stains vinegar should not be used on, is one caused by blood. Vinegar can set it and make it nearly impossible to get out. (See Spit & Polish, near the end of this chapter, for vinegar's contribution to removing blood stains.) Do not use vinegar on stains made by: blood, vomit, eggs, butter, milk or grease.

LAUNDRY HINTS

Pre-Treating Solution

   4 Tablespoons white vinegar   2 Tablespoons baking soda
   3 Tablespoons ammonia   Cool water
   1 Tablespoon liquid detergent

Many laundry stains many be removed by pre-treating clothes with a few spritzes of this stain remover. To make, put the vinegar, ammonia, and liquid detergent in a quart-size pump spray bottle. Mix together, then add the baking soda. When it stops foaming, fill the bottle with cool water and use immediately. (If the mixture is stored in this container, the pump spray may be damaged.)

General Perspiration Stains

White vinegar is the traditional remedy for removing perspiration stains from clothes. Sturdy fabrics can be treated with a full strength application of vinegar, rubbed in as they are put in the washing machine. Delicate fabrics should be soaked in vinegar diluted half and half with water.

Stubborn Perspiration Stains

White fabric that has been stained by perspiration can sometimes be cleaned with white vinegar, salt and lots of sunlight. Begin by wringing the entire garment out in cool water. Then soak the stains with full strength white vinegar. Spread the clothing out in direct sunlight and then sprinkle the stain with salt. When the garment is completely dry, repeat the process. Most perspiration stains will eventually come out this way.

Perspiration and Silks

Delicate silk garments are notorious for attracting perspiration stains. White vinegar is the safest, surest way to pre-treat this kind of discoloration. Many silks can tolerate a brief splash of full strength white vinegar to underarm areas without harm. (As always, test on an inconspicuous area before using any stain treatment!)

To begin, wet the entire garment, then apply white vinegar to discolored underarm stains. Let set for 3 minutes (longer on sturdy, colorfast fabrics and some whites). Wash as usual, being sure to add a dash of white vinegar to the final rinse water.

Keep Silks Shiny

To help silk garments keep their soft shine, always include a dash of white vinegar in their last rinse water. It helps them retain their glossy sheen.

Easy White Vinegar Rinse

An easy way to add vinegar to the last rinse water is to soak several white washcloths in full strength white vinegar and store them in a closed container. Then, just toss one of these prepared cloths into the rinse water when the washer tub has filled. It saves measuring and eliminates the possibility of splashing vinegar directly onto delicate fabrics.

Static Cling Solution

Make your own dryer sheets by preparing several small cloths wrung out of full strength white vinegar (as above). Then, simply toss a damp cloth into the dryer with each load of laundry. (This is also a good way to freshen and soften clothes if you forget to add vinegar to the last rinse cycle!)

Tumble until just barely dry.

Static Cling

Fight static cling in the dryer with nylon fabric and vinegar. Simply spray a 2 foot square of nylon net with a half and half solution of white vinegar and water and add it to a dryer load of clothes. The nylon net square will not only help reduce static cling, it will collect lint.

Warmer Blankets

The fluff on the blanket is what makes it keep you warm. The softer and fluffier the blanket, the better job it will do of keeping you warm. Spray lots of white vinegar on blankets before drying them. It will help to make them soft and fluffy. (Or, add the vinegar to the rinse water.)

Ink Stains

Ink stains can often be lifted by soaking them in white vinegar. Put full strength vinegar on ink stains, allow to set for 15 seconds, then blot. Repeat several times for dark stains, then wash as usual.

Coffee Stains

Blot coffee splatters until as much as possible of the liquid is removed. Immediately rinse in cool water. Follow with a rinse of white vinegar, then wash in lukewarm, soapy water.

Tea Stains

Fresh stains can be treated as coffee stains. Dried tea (and coffee) stains should be soaked for 30 minutes in white vinegar before washing in warm, soapy water.

Stubborn Coffee and Tea Stains

Coffee or tea stains that are very dark, or those that have been allowed to set, require extra treatment. Dampen the stain with white vinegar and sprinkle it with salt. Then, expose the stain to bright sunlight for at least an hour. Follow this by washing the material as usual. Repeat the process as necessary.

Red Wine Stains

Blot spills thoroughly, then immediately rinse the area with white wine. Blot again, until nearly dry, then rinse several times with white vinegar. Wash with mild suds and check to see if any discoloration remains. If further treatment is needed, soak in vinegar, then wash again in soapy water before drying.

Alternate Red Wine Remover

Blot as much of the liquid up as possible, then saturate the stain with a solution made of 1 tablespoon white vinegar and 3 tablespoons water. Rub the discoloration with salt, set in the sun until dry. Repeat if needed.

Rust Stains

Rust marks on cloth can usually be lifted with white vinegar and salt. Simply wet the rust stain with vinegar and then cover it with salt. Let it dry, preferably in the sun. Rinse the salt out and reapply until the stain is gone.

Basic Fabric Softener

Add 1/3 cup white vinegar to the final rinse water for softer, scent-free laundry. This inexpensive laundry treatment is safe for the gentlest fabrics and is great for those who are allergic to harsh chemicals and strong scents.

Amazing Fabric Softener

Combine 1/3 cup white vinegar and 1/3 cup baking soda and add the mixture to the final rinse water for even softer laundry. This combination is scent-free and irritation-free, good for the most delicate skin and fabrics.

Softener Hint: Keep vinegar-based fabric softeners in a pump spray bottle, such as liquid hand soap comes in. Then just add a few squirts to laundry water. No muss, no fuss!

Scented Fabric Softener

To add a very faint hint of clean, outdoorsy smell to laundry, use apple cider in any of the previous fabric softeners. For stronger scents, use herbal vinegars.

Lint Trap

Hard water can cause a buildup of minerals on the lint trap of the washing machine. Soak it in full strength vinegar for a couple of hours, then use a brush to remove the deposits.

Panty Hose Revitalizer

Soak stretched out, shapeless panty hose in 1 quart of warm water, with 1/4 cup white vinegar added to it. Let them set for 5 minutes, then squeeze gently and blot with a bath towel. (Never wring or stretch wet hose.) Allow the panty hose to dry, spread out flat on a towel.

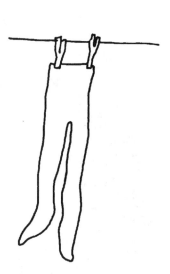

Brightener For Synthetics

When polyester or nylon fabrics have become dull and drab looking, they can sometimes be revitalized by boiling them in 2 quarts of water, with 3/4 cup white vinegar added to it.

Protecting Wool

Good wools, as well as silks, can be easily damaged by harsh alkaline laundry products. For many hundreds of years white vinegar has been the cleaning fluid of choice for these fabrics. It helps to keep them soft, while lifting odors and stains.

Help keep the fibers of wool garments springy and resilient by including a couple of tablespoons of white vinegar in the last rinse water. This will also protect colors by preventing a buildup of soap or detergent residues.

Renewing Wool Apparel

Add new life to wool garments whose cuffs, bottoms or necklines have become stretched out and have lost their ability to snap back into their original shape. Combine vinegar and heat to recondition these wool clothes.

Wool revitalizer: Add 2 tablespoons of white vinegar to a small bucket of very hot water. Carefully dip only the stretched out edge of the garment into the hot water. Immediately blot with a towel, then blow dry with a hair dryer set on its highest setting.

Alpaca

Alpaca is a wool-like fiber from llamas. This material will hold its shape and remain soft and springy for many years if rinsed in water with a tablespoon of white vinegar in it.

Camel Hair Wool

This is an exceptional soft and silky kind of wool. Wash it in gentle suds, rinse in a dilute water and vinegar solution, and dry on a flat surface.

Angora

Angora has a texture much like that of fine lamb's wool. It can be made from the fur of angora rabbits or goats. It responds well to a gentle washing, followed by a rinse in cool water with a couple of tablespoons of white vinegar mixed in.

Cashmere

This wool is named after the goat whose undercoat provides the hair it is made of. Originally found in Kashmir, Tibet, these goats are now raised in many other areas. Treat cashmere as any good wool.

Wool Mixes

Wool is animal hair, and sometimes it is almost as fine as fur. Most wool comes from sheep, but mixed wool can contain hair from goats, rabbits, llamas, etc. The finest wool is made from the light downy underfur of the animals. These short hairs produce an extra soft wool.

Mohair is another name for angora.

Fresh Smelling Linens

Remove stale odors from linens by spraying them, lightly, with vinegar water, then fluffing them in the dryer for 5 or 10 minutes. (To a 1 quart pump spray bottle of water, add 1 or 2 tablespoons of white vinegar.) Or, put the dry linens in the dryer with a vinegar and water dampened bath towel.

Easy Creases For Pants

'No-iron" cotton pants will hold a sharp crease if treated with wax and vinegar. Begin by turning the pants inside out. Then run the bottom of a wax candle down the crease line (on the wrong side of the fabric).

Next, turn the pants right side out and cover the crease line with a cloth wrung out of half water, half white vinegar. Press with a very hot iron until dry. The crease will be sharp, and it will stay that way for a long time!

Wrinkle Remover

Remove wrinkles from stored clothes by hanging them up in the bathroom. Put 1 cup vinegar in the bath tub and turn the hot water in the shower on. When the tub is 1/2 full, turn off the water and allow the clothes to hang in the steamy room for 20 minutes. Most wrinkles will be removed and any stale odors will be gone, too.

Scorched Ironing

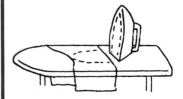

When a too-hot iron leaves an ugly spot of scorched fabric behind, a cloth damped with white vinegar will often remove the mark and save the day. Begin by wetting a clean, soft cloth with full strength white vinegar. Pat the vinegar onto the scorched spot, and let it set for a few minutes. If the scorch remains, wet it with vinegar once again. (Add a dash of salt for stubborn marks.)

Reviving Straw Hats

Stained and misshapen straw hats can be revived with a vinegar and salt treatment. Stir 1/2 cup salt into a large bucket or laundry tub of warm water. When the salt has dissolved, submerge the hat in the water.

When the straw is soft, gently wipe away any stains, using a little liquid soap if necessary. Remove the hat from the water and allow to drain for a few minutes. Gently push it into the desired shape, then spray the hat with a fine mist of vinegar water. (Add 1 teaspoon white vinegar to 1 cup water.) Allow to dry, away from the sun.

Crystal Clear Leather Cleaner
1/4 cup white vinegar   1 cup water
1/4 cup rubbing alcohol

Gently wipe leather with a cloth dampened in clear leather cleaner, then dry at once with another cloth. This cleaner also works well on leather look-alike fabrics.

Curtains and Sheer Panels
Revitalize delicate fabric window coverings by using this vinegar based treatment in the final rinse. To a quart of hot water, add 1 tablespoon white vinegar and 2 envelopes of plain (unsweetened, unflavored) gelatin. Add this mixture to the final rinse water and dry as usual. Limp fabrics will be instantly revitalized!

Removing Gum
Break up sticky gum residue by soaking it in white vinegar. Begin by scraping away as much of the gum as possible. Then pat white vinegar onto what remains and let set for 20 minutes. Blot the vinegar away, taking as much of the gum with it as possible. Repeat until all the gum is gone.

Spit & Polish
For one of the best ways vinegar can help remove stains, it does not even need to touch the stain! Stains made by dairy products such as milk, eggs and cream are best dissolved by special digestive enzymes — the kind of enzymes found in human spit.

To lift these stains, place a few tablespoons of apple cider vinegar in a small bowl and breathe the vapor that rises from it. This will encourage digestive juices to flow, ensuring plenty of spit for soaking away stains. Small drops of blood or wine that have left spots on cloth can often be removed this way, and some kinds of grease, too.

Something Good Just Got Better
Ordinary white vinegar contains a 5% solution of acetic acid. A special just-for-cleaning white vinegar can contain a 10% solution of acetic acid. This 'super vinegar' will lift some stains faster, and it can make cleaning with vinegar better than ever!

PLEASE REMEMBER!

Always test fabrics and surfaces before using even a gentle cleaner like vinegar. No one cleaner is perfect for every laundry chore. Vinegar's antibacterial, antiseptic, and mild bleaching actions, as well as its acid nature may not be perfectly safe for every fabric. As with all cleaning substances, your own test on fabrics is the only sure test of safety.

The Heinz company makes just for cleaning white vinegar.

Chapter Eight

Cooking With Vinegar

Vinegar does more than just clean, it is one of the most ancient and useful foods. One reason vinegar is a safe basic ingredient for pickling, marinating and preserving is because it prevents the growth of botulism bacteria. And, at only two calories per tablespoon, it is the ideal topping for salads and vegetables.

Vinegar is well-known for its ability to tenderize meat and vegetables and to give foods robust flavor without added salt. It is an inexpensive way to turn dull vegetables into pickled delights and to pep up salads, sauces and dressings. A few ways to cook with vinegar follow:

Chef's Fish
After deep frying fish, spray each piece, while hot, with a mist of apple cider vinegar. It makes a tangy difference everyone will love and moderates fishy odors. Make strongly flavored fish taste milder by presoaking raw fish in 1 cup of water which has had 1/2 cup white vinegar added to it.

Better Hot Dogs
Improve the flavor of hot dogs by boiling them a few minutes in water with a tablespoon of vinegar added to it. They will taste better, and if you pierce them before boiling, they will be have less fat (and calories)!

Tangy Chinese Vegetable Dip
1/3	cup plum jelly	1/3	cup apple cider vinegar
1/3	cup applesauce	1/2	teaspoon brown sugar

Mix well, double the plum jelly for a more zesty sauce. Also good drizzled over fried noodles.

Salad Dressing
Personalize salad dressings by adding 1/4 cup herb flavored vinegar to commercial mayonnaise, or make oil and vinegar salad dressings with your own herbal vinegars.

Chicken Soup

Boil a cutup chicken in 2 quarts of water and 1/4 cup vinegar until the meat begins to fall off the bones. Strain the liquid and return 1 cup of chopped chicken to the soup pot. Add 1 minced onion, 2 tablespoons parsley, 5 cloves of garlic, 2 chopped stalks of celery, and 1 diced green pepper. Season with 1 teaspoon dill seeds, 1/4 teaspoon pepper and 1 tablespoon parsley. Simmer for 45 minutes and serve.

Fruit & Vinegar

Wash and mash fresh, well ripened fruit, using 2 cups of vinegar for each cup of fruit. Set in the refrigerator for 4 or 5 days. Strain off the flavored vinegar and heat it to the boiling point. Add 1/2 cup sugar for each cup of vinegar and simmer until the sugar is dissolved. Store in a glass jar.

Good fruits for making vinegar are: raspberries, blueberries, blackberries, strawberries and peaches. Combine several fruits for even better flavor. (Lemon and orange go well with most berries.) Plum is an exceptionally good vinegar. Drizzle it over a fresh fruit platter for a low calorie taste delight.

Vinegar Marinate

Begin with equal parts white vinegar and water. Add about 3 tablespoons of sugar and a dash of salt for each cup of vinegar. Use marinate to tenderize meats and vegetables, or to preserve beans, eggplant, broccoli and other vegetables. (Some examples of preserving vegetables follow.)

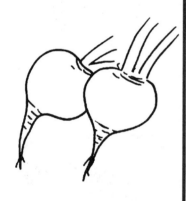

Vinegar & Onions

Wash tiny onions, peel, blanch, and cover with a layer of salt. Sit overnight and rinse the salt off. Add to enough Vinegar Marinate to cover and boil with spices until the onions are just barely tender (about 10 minutes). For a pound of onions use 1 tablespoon pickling spice, 4 cloves and 4 peppercorns.

Vinegar & Beets

Heat vinegar, water, sugar, and salt (as in Vinegar Marinate) to the boiling point, pour over sliced, fresh-cooked or canned beets. Marinate for at least 24 hours before serving.

Spicy Vegetables & Vinegar

Wash and cut vegetables into bite-sized pieces and blanch with a solution made of equal parts vinegar and water. Add your favorite herbs and spices and cover tightly. Refrigerate for at least 3 days before using.

Vinegar-Pepper Sauce Supreme

Place an assortment of small whole red and green peppers (or sliced large ones) in a decorative bottle. Use sweet peppers for a mild sauce, hot peppers for a tangy one. Add a couple green onions and a small leek. Fill the jar with apple cider vinegar which has been heated to the boiling point. Cap the jar and set aside for at least a month.

Use vinegar-pepper sauce on salads (especially pasta salads), to add zing to vegetable dishes, and to enliven meats. Add a Mediterranean flavor to the pepper sauce by adding a few cloves of garlic to the basic pepper and onion recipe.

Herbs & Vinegar
Make herbal vinegar by adding 1/4 to 1/2 cup fresh (or 1 to 2 tablespoons dried) herbs to a small bottle of vinegar. Use apple cider or white vinegar, depending on the flavor wanted. Let the herbs soak in the vinegar for a month, shaking the jar every few days. Strain before using, or not. For a special look, strain out the bits of herb, then put a sprig of fresh herb in the finished vinegar. It will add to the flavor, and it looks great for vinegar which is used for gifts.

Herbal Vinegars
Herbal vinegars can be prepared easily by simply adding fresh or dried herbs to white, wine or apple cider vinegar. Let the herbs steep in the vinegar for 2 to 4 weeks before using. Herbs may be strained out, or left in.

Many different herbs can be used for making vinegars. Use a single herb, or combine several to create your own special blend. Choose herbs for their flavor and compatibility with other foods. Some herbs to try, and the special qualities they bring to herbal vinegars follow:

Anise
This relative of fennel has a sweet, licorice-like taste and pretty fernlike leaves.

Bay
Leaves of the sweet bay tree are shiny and dark green. Their flavor goes well with meats.

Use this to make bay - rum after shave.

Ginger
A small piece of ginger adds a lot of flavor. Use this unusual tasting condiment in Oriental dishes.

Horseradish
Slivers of horseradish root produce a vinegar with an especially zippy flavor.

Sweet Marjoram

This Old World herb is very strong and makes a vinegar that can pep up a bland stew or soup.

Other herbs for making vinegars are dill, basil, rosemary, mint, catnip, lemon balm, sage, tarragon, caraway and thyme. Combine several herbs to create your own special flavors. Then add a dash of cloves, allspice, nutmeg or cinnamon.

Herbal Vinegar Shortcut

A quick and easy way to prepare herbal vinegar is to add a herbal tea bag to a bottle of vinegar. Let it age, just as you would fresh or dried herbs, then remove the tea bag before using. (Or leave it in if you do not mind the way it looks.)

Garlic Flavored Vinegar

2	garlic cloves	2	cups vinegar

Place peeled cloves in apple cider vinegar and let set for at least a week. For a more robust vinegar, use additional garlic cloves.

Puckery Pickles

For truly tart and sour pickles, give them an extra helping of vinegar. Begin with a jar of whole dill pickles. Drain off the pickling juice and discard it. Next, cut the pickles into thin slices and put them back into the jar. Fill the jar with white vinegar and refrigerate for 5 days before eating. Pure puckery pleasure!

Tasty Pimientos

Pimientos are merely pickled sweet peppers! Make your own by thinly slicing sweet red peppers, blanching them to soften, and soaking in vinegar.

3/4	cup vinegar	dash of salt	
3/4	cup water	4	garlic cloves
1/4	cup sugar	2	red peppers
1	teaspoon olive oil		

Simmer everything for the pimientos except the garlic and peppers for 10 minutes. Put the garlic and thinly sliced peppers into a glass jar, pour the hot liquid over them and marinate for 3 weeks. Enjoy! For an interesting change, use green peppers, or mix red and green half and half for a bright holiday look.

Chutney

Chutney is made by combining chopped vegetables, fruits and spices in a sweet pickling liquid. Originally, it came from India, where it was made with mangoes, raisins, tamarinds, ginger, spices. In the United States and England it is more likely to be made with tomatoes, apples, gooseberries, peaches, or bananas. Serve chutneys with cold meats.

Vinegar-Nut Pie Crust

1/2	cup butter	1/2	cup ground nuts
3/4	cup flour	2	tablespoons sugar
3/4	cup oatmeal	1	tablespoon white vinegar

Melt the butter in a pie pan and then add all the other ingredients. Mix with a fork, then pat the dough into shape. Bake for 15 - 20 minutes at 350°, fill with fresh fruit and a cornstarch based sauce.

Easiest Vinegar Pie Crust

1 1/3	cup flour	1	tablespoon vinegar
1/2	teaspoon salt	1/3	cup oil
2	tablespoons sugar	2	tablespoons water

Put all ingredients in a pie pan and stir with a fork until the flour is barely moist. Use the fingers to press and smooth the dough onto the sides and bottom of the pie pan, forming a fluted edge along the top. Prick with a fork and bake at 350° until lightly browned. (Or add filling and bake.)

White Vinegar Taffy

2	cups sugar	1	tablespoon butter
3	tablespoons white vinegar	1	teaspoon vanilla extract
1/2	cup water		

Combine sugar, vinegar and water and boil to the hard ball stage. Add butter and vanilla an stir just to mix. Pour onto a greased plate or counter top. When cool enough to touch (but still hot) begin to knead with buttered hands. When the taffy lightens and begins to firm up, cut ropes into small pieces. Wrap in waxed paper to keep it from becoming sticky.

Make honey taffy by replacing half of the sugar with honey. Make butterscotch taffy by replacing half of the sugar with brown sugar, increase the butter to 2 tablespoons.

Teresa's Peanut Butter-Vinegar Fudge

1	cup chocolate chips	1/4 cup corn syrup
3 1/2	cups sugar	1	tablespoon white vinegar
1 1/2	cups evaporated milk	3	cups peanut butter
1/2	cup butter	1	cup marshmallow cream

In a large saucepan, combine sugar, milk, butter, corn syrup and vinegar. Cook over medium heat, stirring constantly until mixture comes to a full boil. Boil and stir for 5 minutes, then remove from heat. Add the peanut butter and marshmallow cream and stir until smooth. Pour half of the hot mixture into a bowl with the chocolate chips and stir until smooth. Pour it into a wax paper lined pan. Top with the remaining hot mixture, allow to cool, then cut into squares.

1½ cup milk is a 12 oz. can.

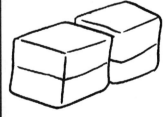

Chapter Nine

Odds & Ends

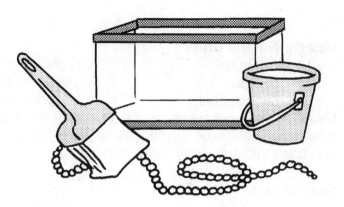

Vinegar —

Weed   An herb in the same family as peppermint.

Tree   A source of acid berries that can be used to make vinegar.

Eel   A harmless, threadlike worm that sometimes be found vinegar.

Bible The result of a 1717 misprint in Oxford, England by Clarendon Press.

Vinegar is a weed, a tree, an eel and a Bible! Vinegar also has terrific versatility as a cleaner and neutralizer of caustic substances. On the pages which follow, you will see its usefulness on shoes, furniture, floors, luggage and much more!

Renew Suede Shoes
Put 2 cups water and 1/4 cup white vinegar in a pan and heat to the boiling point. Set heat to simmer and, while holding each shoe in the steam, gently brush up the nap. Set the shoes aside until completely dry before wearing.

Stay-Tied Trick For Leather Shoelaces
Leather shoestrings are notorious for their inability to hold a knot. The next time you want leather shoelaces to stay tied, put 3 drops of apple cider vinegar on the knot and give it an extra tug. The laces will stay tied until you untie them.

Setting Dye
After cloth has been treated with a commercial dye, soak it for an hour or two in a gallon of water, which has had a cup of white vinegar and a tablespoon of salt added to it. Rinse in cool water.

Red Dye

1/2   cup vinegar
1   pound beets
1   quart water

Wash a pound of fresh beets and place them, with their skins on, in a sauce pan and cover with cool water. Simmer until the beets are tender, then remove skins. Chop the beets and return them to the same water in which they were cooked. Let them set for 2 hours, then strain off the liquid and add the vinegar. Use this liquid to turn cloth a warm, rose color.

End Squeaky Floors

Quiet noisy wooden floors by forcing a mixture of vinegar and liquid soap into the cracks between boards. To each cup of liquid soap, add 2 tablespoons vinegar and mix well.

Old-Fashioned Wallpaper Paste

1/2   cup cornstarch   6   cups boiling water
3/4   cup cold water   1/4 cup white vinegar

Mix cornstarch and cold water and stir, all at once, into boiling water. When the mixture boils again remove from heat, pour through a strainer and stir in the vinegar. (This also makes a great laundry starch!)

Peel-No-More Painting

Concrete walls and floors will take a coat of paint without troublesome peeling if the surface is first painted with vinegar. Brush on the vinegar, let the concrete dry, then paint as usual. This works on metal, too!

Paint Brush Renewal

Old, stiff paint brushes can be restored to their former softness by removing dried-in paint. Simply put paint stiffened brushes in a small saucepan and cover them with full strength vinegar. Bring to a boil and simmer for 15 minutes. When cool enough to touch, work the softened paint out of the bristles under hot running water. Repeat as necessary. (Wood handled brushes are better candidates then plastic handled ones which may distort when heated.)

Dry paint brushes by shaking them or spinning them between your palms. Do not stand brushes on their bristles, as that will ruin their shape.

Painted Windows

Make removing paint from window glass easier with this trick. Mix a good, thick liquid detergent half and half with white vinegar. Spread this over the paint and allow to almost dry. Then remove the paint with a plastic scraper or a razor blade. The thick detergent helps keep the vinegar from running off, and together they soften the paint so that it comes off easier.

Tape Remover

A compress of vinegar will loosen the sticky glue on adhesive bandages, making removal less painful. Vinegar also softens the adhesives on masking, duct, strapping and other tapes.

Glue Removal

Most glues can be softened by soaking them in full strength vinegar. Add a drop of liquid detergent to help vinegar penetrate faster.

Better Humidifying

Add a couple of tablespoons of white vinegar to the water in a humidifier to eliminate odors in the home. Vinegar will also discourage the growth of germs in the humidifier's water reservoir.

Cleaning the Humidifier

At least once a week, soak the water reservoir for 10 minutes in a solution of 1 part white vinegar to 10 parts water. The vinegar will help to dissolve minerals salts, allowing them to be washed out so there is no buildup on the inside of the humidifier.

Instant Humidifying

Keep a 12 oz. pump spray bottle (the kind hair spray comes in) filled with water and 2 teaspoons white vinegar. These pump sprays deliver a very fine mist which is ideal for putting moisture into the air. Whenever a room is too dry, several pumps of the sprayer will provide an instant improvement in the humidity level.

Flavorful Humidifying

Any time vinegar is added to water to moisturize the air, you have the choice of using white, apple cider, or even an aromatic herbal vinegar. White is best if it is being used where there is some possibility of it settling on anything that could be stained.

If this is not a consideration, consider using a vinegar with a bit more 'spirit.' Apple cider vinegar adds a fresh, apple scent. Or, experiment with the many aromatic herbs that can add their unique fragrances to the moisture being put into the air.

Cleaning the Dehumidifier

Clean the water collecting tray with a brush dipped in full strength vinegar. If it is cleaned regularly, minerals will not build up in the tray and clog the outlet.

Better Dehumidifying

Put a splash of white vinegar in the dehumidifier's water collecting tray to discourage the growth of germs. This will keep the water from smelling stale and mildewy. (It will make cleaning easier, too!)

Air Cleaners

Air cleaners collect dust and other allergens. A cotton swab, dipped in water and vinegar, is good for cleaning hard to reach crevices and contact points. Fan blades need to be carefully wiped off, too.

Aquariums

A mild vinegar and water solution is the ideal substance for cleaning the outside of glass aquariums. Spray a soft cloth with a weak vinegar and water mixture (1 cup water, 1 teaspoon vinegar) and wipe surfaces until completely dry.

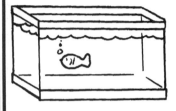

Very dirty aquarium glass can be scrubbed with a cloth wrung out of full strength vinegar. Rub dry with a soft cloth. Never spray aquarium glass, because fine droplets of mist can settle into the water and disrupt its the delicate ph balance.

Carpet Cleaner

    1   cup white vinegar
    1/4 cup rubbing alcohol
    1   teaspoon liquid detergent

Mix well, then pat gently onto soiled spots. Blot off and rinse with clear water. Repeat as necessary.

Wallpaper Stripper

To each cup of vinegar, add 1 tablespoon liquid detergent. Spray or wipe this solution onto walls and allow to set a few minutes. Most papers will scrape off easily.

Wood Scratches

Repair scratches in wood furniture with vinegar and a fresh walnut! Wipe the scratched area with a cloth dampened in full strength vinegar. Crack open a walnut and immediately rub the scratch with a piece of the kernel.

Water Resistant Furniture Polish

To encourage wood furniture to resist water spills and spatters, polish it with a mixture made of 1/2 cup lemon oil and 1 tablespoon white vinegar. Wipe the oil and vinegar on, then buff it off with a clean cloth.

Wet-Dry Vac

Half fill a pail with warm water and a cup of vinegar. Suck this solution up into the shop vac to clean and deodorize it. Let the warm liquid set for 3 minutes, then dump the water out and wipe the inside of the vac clean. Allow to air dry before putting it back together. Keeping the unit clean will extend the life of filters and prevent foul odors.

Plastic Wall Tile

Plastic tile scratches easily and attracts hard water mineral buildup. Clean it with non-abrasive white vinegar.

Plastic Food Containers

These storage containers pick up and hold food odors very easily. Keep them odor-free by soaking them in sudsy warm water, with a generous splash of white vinegar added to it.

Refrigerator and Freezer Gaskets

Wipe the gaskets around refrigerator and freezer doors with a mild detergent solution to keep them free of dirt and grease. If mold begins to form on the gaskets, remove it with white vinegar, then rinse with clear water before drying.

Window Shades and Blinds

Keep shades and blinds clean and free of smudges by wiping them down regularly with a cloth dampened in a mild vinegar and sudsy water solution.

Molded Plastic Luggage

Hard-sided suitcases can be cleaned with a solution made of half gentle liquid detergent and half white vinegar. Follow with a clear water rinse before buffing dry. Remember, handles need cleaning, too.

Play-Clay

1	cup flour	1	teaspoon vinegar
1/2	cup salt	1	tablespoon oil
1	cup water		

Combine all ingredients in a saucepan and heat. Stir continually, until it forms a ball. Remove from heat, allow to cool, then knead until smooth. A few drops of food coloring may be worked into it while kneading. Store between uses in a tightly sealed container in the refrigerator.

Flavorful Mouthwashes

A glass of water with a couple of teaspoons of vinegar in it is a traditional mouthwash and gargle liquid. Use white vinegar for a neutral taste, apple cider vinegar for its healing reputation, or herbal for breath enhancing flavor. Some good herbal vinegars for mouthwashes are sage, raspberry, peppermint and lavender.

DEAR READER,

Thank you for your interest in this book and others in the series. Your response to my previous books has been phenomenal. THE VINEGAR BOOK has more than 3,000,000 copies in print, in many languages, and in more than a dozen countries!

Your many letters are a continuing encouragement. They are filled with kind words and examples of ways you, too, use vinegar and natural home remedies. My mail also contains many requests for information on how to use vinegar as a regular part of the diet and as an aid in controlling weight. And so, I have put this collection of special diet information, weight loss tips and nutritional guidelines together for you. My sources include both antidotal accounts from regular vinegar users and scientific studies from major medical centers.

THE VINEGAR DIET is a common sense approach to life, health and eating for optimum health. It is an attempt to share with you what others are doing and how you can combine research findings and folk wisdom. And so, it should come as no surprise to you that researchers now say a super-low-calorie diet is usually nutrient deficient and is particularly dangerous for the mature adult.

Gradual changes in the way you eat improve your health with the most lasting results. THE VINEGAR DIET does not encourage you to suddenly drop 5 - 15 pounds in a single week. This approach to weight usually results in regaining any weight lost because, when you lose weight too fast, you send your body into famine mode. It begins to conserve fat and can actually make you gain weight by increasing your hunger!

THE VINEGAR DIET encourages you to eat the food you want. You do not need to deprive yourself. You can eat the same number of calories you now eat, lower your risk of developing diseases linked to poor nutrition, and still lose weight. The secret is using a complex biological process called "thermogensis" to burn away unwanted fat. THE VINEGAR DIET is as easy as filling your plate and as simple as increasing your body's metabolic rate. And, you will keep the weight you lose off because you will be eating more wisely and moving more.

THE VINEGAR DIET is not intended as medical advice; it has not been prepared or reviewed by a medical practitioner. Moderation, common sense and old-time remedies have always been the key to successful living. But they cannot take the place of medical advice so, when you are sick, you should seek the guidance of a competent medical practitioner. For everyday healthy living you may want to try THE VINEGAR DIET. It is designed to help you gradually, permanently, normalize weight, optimize energy and be vital at any age. This plan works because "dieting," as the term is commonly used, is not the way to regulate weight. A good diet is!

All diets have side effects. Some can leave you exhausted and hungry. Because THE VINEGAR DIET features generous amounts of vegetables and fruits its side effects can include extra energy, healthier bones, lower cholesterol, less risk of cancer or high blood pressure, less depression and a newly invigorated immune system!

Healthy eating offers you the opportunity to regain a more vibrant, vital body, a clear mind and the true joy of living. Promise yourself you will begin today!

Emily

The Wonder of Vinegar – What Others Are Saying

"I went down to 183 from 280 .... I wouldn't trade what I did for all the money in this entire country. I feel and look different, and I'm 78 .... I just wanted you to know what apple cider vinegar did for me."   VS., Meridian, Mississippi

"I went on .... apple cider vinegar and honey in water 3 times a day. I dropped 30 pounds so fast it scared me!"   J.G., Sibley, Illinois

"My husband and I drink apple cider vinegar with apple juice, grape juice and water every day (for stabilizing blood pressure and cholesterol)."   J. G., Sibley, Illinois

"Enjoyed your book very much. I read the whole thing in one afternoon!"   G. S., Jamestown, New York

"I just finished reading your vinegar book. I bought 4, 3 for gifts. I know and believe much of what you wrote. "   F.H., Hayes, Virginia

"2 teaspoons vinegar in a glass of water and drink with each meal — this will help you to lose weight."   B. N., Willmar, Minnesota

"I am 70 years old and have used these recipes all my life and they work. .... To lose weight, a teaspoon honey and a teaspoon apple cider vinegar in a cup of tea or decaffeinated coffee."   M.B., Sissonville, West Virginia

"Just a note to thank you for this great book. I am taking vinegar and water before meals for weight control.... also its settled the diarrhea caused by irritable bowel syndrome. I'm really pleased as I've suffered quite a few years...."   K.T., Victoria, Australia

"I have used the honey and vinegar recipe for weight loss .... Thanks a lot."   M.T., Sauk City, Wisconsin

"I thoroughly enjoyed the book .... being of Creek Indian heritage, my grandmother used many of your cures. I have read it five times already and have started using the honey and vinegar morning and night to already lose one and a half inches in my waist in one and a half weeks."   Z.L., Pensacola, Florida

"My nephew told me that his cholesterol was 282. .... I told him to take one ounce vinegar and one tablespoon honey and six ounces of water, twice a day. In two months his doctor checked his cholesterol, it was 201. I ordered the vinegar book for (him)."   J.S., Cleveland, Ohio

"In 1959 .... I started using a tablespoon of vinegar and a tablespoon of honey in two ounces of water every day. .... I'm still with the daily use. My hair still hasn't turned gray and I'm now past 80. Still bowling three times a week and have a 153 average .... Love that vinegar!"   V.C., Seattle, Washington

Chapter One

Why Vinegar? Because It Works!

FOOD —

"Anything that sustains, nourishes and augments."

"Must contain in some form the actual chemical constituents of the new tissues which are being laid down."

DIET —

"A manner of living; food and drink habitually taken."

"Food prescribed for the prevention or cure of disease, or for attaining a certain physical condition."

VINEGAR IS PART OF A HEALTHY DIET! Vinegar has been used for centuries to aid health. Scientists tell us vinegar was probably part of the primordial soup of life. It is needed to burn fats and carbohydrates. The acid we know as vinegar is also used by the body as an aid in neutralizing poisons.

Emily Says

Vinegar is good food!

Often vinegar is combined with honey in a tonic that brings together the exceptional nutritional qualities of these two very special foods. Millions learned of this age-old tonic when its virtues were chronicled by physician D. C. Jarvis of Vermont. In Dr. Jarvis' book, FOLK MEDICINE, he praised the virtues of taking a daily tonic of apple cider vinegar and honey. His strong belief in the ability of apple cider vinegar to maintain an acid balance in the body was a large part of his faith in the tonic. His book stressed the common sense approach to food the Vermont country folk of his generation practiced. His "prescription" for maintaining health was to take, at least once a day:

2 Teaspoons apple cider vinegar
2 Teaspoons honey
Full glass of water

For those suffering from the pain of arthritis, rheumatism and other degenerative diseases he suggested the vinegar and honey combination be taken two to three times a day, with or before meals. Many people find a milder dose more palatable:

1 Teaspoon apple cider vinegar
1 Teaspoon honey
Full glass of water

DIET VS. DIETING

In recent times there has been an explosion of medical information. New ways of treating disease with drugs has driven food-based treatments into obscurity. The result, over the years, has been that much time-proven wisdom has been lost, forgotten or pushed aside. The notion that a well balanced diet was necessary for good health, as well as for weight control, was lost.

And so, The Vinegar Diet came into being! It is built around the fact that conventional "dieting" is not the best way to regulate weight and health. "Dieting" can be a dangerous health concept. It has come to mean a special, temporary way of relating to food that some how turns a flabby, prematurely aged, malnourished body into a slim, trim, youthful one.

THIS IS BOTH UNTRUE AND UNFORTUNATE!

UNTRUE because it suggests a temporary change in eating can correct a lifetime of poor habits.

UNFORTUNATE because it leads to impossible expectations and almost ensures failure.

Throughout this volume the word diet will mean a lifelong way of nourishing a healthy body. It will not mean a temporary attempt to alter weight. Changes in body mass which come about by following the guidelines of The Vinegar Diet should be lasting, as well as promoting better health. It is a way to look better, feel better, be better!

DO YOU NEED THE VINEGAR DIET?

Does your present diet supply everything you need for optimum health? Ask yourself:

Emily Says

RDA = Minimum amounts of vitamins and minerals, not optimal amounts!

- Are you as healthy as you want to be?
- Are you as healthy as you ought be?
- Are you as healthy as you can be?

MOST DIETS ARE NUTRITIONALLY INADEQUATE! The typical diet does not supply enough of the nutrients needed for optimum health. It is estimated that less than 10% of the population follows the U.S. Agriculture Department's dietary guidelines. This means many do not get the Recommended Dietary Allowance (RDA) of important vitamins and minerals. And, the RDA gives only dietary minimums, the very smallest amount needed to prevent major diseases known to be caused by shortages. These amounts are not usually enough for maximum health.

Studies show more than half of those admitted to a hospital have a nutritional deficiency. The elderly are particularly at risk because, as the body ages it does not process foods as efficiently as it once did. And, the elderly tend to take more nutrient-depleting medications.

To extend the good years as long as possible means fighting the effects of degenerative diseases. Extra amounts of many nutrients can increase vitality and vigor, even in old age. But this can only be done by getting much more than the RDA of vitamins and minerals. The most frequently found nutrient shortages include:

Calcium	Magnesium	Thiamine
Chromium	Niacin	Vitamin A
Copper	Potassium	Vitamin B-12
Folic acid	Riboflavin	Vitamins C & D
Iron	Selenium	Zinc

DEFICIENCY SYMPTOMS

A low level of CALCIUM has been linked to depression and loss of bone mass. Foods high in phosphorus, such as meat and carbonated drinks, increase calcium loss, as do salt and caffeine.

Even marginally low levels of CHROMIUM can increase the risk of developing clogged arteries.

A body low on COPPER is more likely to get infections and some arthritis has been linked to unusual copper levels.

The likelihood of FOLIC ACID deficiency increases with age and can cause fatigue and increased susceptibility to infection.

Too little IRON is the most frequent cause of anemia and is associated with depression. It has even been linked to increased numbers of cold sores.

As many as 80% of senior citizens have at least marginally low levels of MAGNESIUM, which can cause diminished heart function and can be part of the cycle involved in angina pain.

The elderly, particularly those in institutions, frequently have lowered levels of NIACIN.

A low level of POTASSIUM is associated with depression, muscle weakness and fatigue.

Insufficient RIBOFLAVIN is associated with depression and increased susceptibility to infection, perhaps because it is needed to metabolize protein.

Too little SELENIUM has been linked to an increased risk of cancer and clogged arteries.

Slow healing of cuts and scrapes can be a sign of a shortage of THIAMINE, as can depression.

Those who do not get enough VITAMIN A are more likely to get infections.

Shortages of VITAMIN B-12 are linked to depression and excessive tiredness.

It is estimated that 40% of the women in the United States do not get enough VITAMIN C. Low vitamin C is associated with depression, tiredness and insufficient synthesis of collagen (which may encourage the advance of arthritis).

A shortage of VITAMIN D has been linked to bone loss and can result in arthritis doing damage to cartilage at a faster rate than it would otherwise.

Slow healing of cuts and scrapes and susceptibility to infection can be a sign of a shortage of ZINC. Its levels can be hurt by substances in eggs, milk and grains.

Emily Says

Low iron is the most common nutritional deficiency.

IS THERE A QUICK FIX?

Can taking mega-doses of vitamins and minerals head off or cure health problems? Not usually. Good nutrition is not that simple, because supplements can be risky. For example, everyone knows about the discomfort associated with too much acid in the stomach. But those with too little stomach acid are more susceptible to infections and parasites and are unable to properly absorb minerals such as calcium and iron. Only the proper balance aids digestion.

Individual metabolism determines the amount of a nutrient which can cause dangerous side effects. Anything which is a bit unusual about the way a body processes food can change a supplemental nutrient into a possibly life-threatening poison. Nutrients also need to be taken in proper proportion to each other because they interact in ways that are not yet fully understood. Researchers do know:

VITAMINS AND MINERALS CAN BE DANGEROUS IF TAKEN IMPROPERLY!

Emily Says

Add supplements only with medical supervision.

Too much CALCIUM can interfere with the body's supply of vitamin K or its absorption of zinc.

If the body's level of COPPER is too high, it is more likely to get infections. Zinc levels can be lowered by copper, too.

Vitamin B-12 and zinc are compromised by too much FOLIC ACID.

Overdoses of IRON can result in liver damage, nausea and lowered levels of zinc and vitamin E.

Retaining too much MAGNESIUM is associated with depression. This mineral is depleted by a diet high in alcohol, caffeine, calcium and fat.

Flushing and itching are frequently associated with NIACIN supplementation.

Too much POTASSIUM interferes with the absorption of vitamin B-12.

Excess SELENIUM can cause diarrhea, hair loss, easily broken fingernails and garlicy smelling breath. Supplements are linked to a decrease in the risk of prostate, colorectal and lung cancer. But over supplementing can be fatal. It is hard to judge the amount of selenium in the diet because the natural content in food varies widely, depending on the soil where it was grown.

Itching and shortness of breath can be symptoms of excess THIAMINE.

Too much VITAMIN A increases fatigue symptoms, the risk of getting infections, headaches, brittle nails, and yellow tinted skin. The body needs plenty of vitamin A to repair cells and make strong scar tissue.

Extra VITAMIN B-12 can decrease feelings of tiredness and ease some allergic reactions of the skin, including itching. Too much can cause itching, too!

The body needs plenty of VITAMIN C to make strong scar tissue and to reduce the likelihood of getting infections. Some allergic reactions are dampened by extra vitamin C. Too much can cause diarrhea.

VITAMIN D helps the body use bone-building calcium. Too much can result in reduced kidney function as well as calcium deposits in joints and lungs.

When ZINC is elevated the immune response is dampened and copper absorption can be blocked. Extra zinc can decrease feelings of tiredness.

Emily Says

Suceptibility to infection rises with too much or too little zinc.

CAUTION: If you are taking mega-doses of nutrients — do not suddenly stop taking them. A body which has adjusted itself to a high level of a particular vitamin or mineral may react to an abrupt change by developing deficiency symptoms. ALWAYS consult with a medical professional before making changes to your normal routine!

POPPING PILLS IS NOT THE ANSWER

A good diet provides a generous supply of all the substances the body needs to maintain health and fight disease. There can be hundreds of important nutrients in a single serving of wholesome food. A good diet will also keep weight within normal limits. The next chapter tells how to get balanced nutrients from food. And that is what The Vinegar Diet is about! It is a lifelong system of eating — a way of living — and a philosophy of health! Its principles can be the beginning of a new tomorrow of personal health for you.

Chapter Two

Vinegar Magic

Good food contains more than the popular vitamins and minerals listed in most nutrient charts. In depth analysis of an ordinary apple reveals it contains more than 400 different substances! A single stalk of celery has nearly 450 identifiable components! Doctors do not yet know how the many substances in food work together in the body. They do know, when the body does not get everything it needs the result is sickness and wasting away of both tissue and bone. Even a marginal deficiency of a trace element or an essential nutrient can result in the body being unable to rebuild tissue and maintain the immune system.

THE MAGIC OF VINEGAR & HONEY

Since the most ancient of times people believed certain foods can have dramatic — even supernatural or miraculous — effects on health and well being. Vinegar and honey have been among these marvels, perhaps because they supply so many different nutrients.

APPLE CIDER VINEGAR A good, naturally produced vinegar contains far more than acetic acid. As apple juice ferments it produces a liquid laced with newly created alcohols, phenols and enzymes, while retaining tiny particles of apples with their storehouse of vitamins and minerals. Vinegar's enzymes are made by living bacteria. These enzymes are catalysts for biological reactions that are critical to life.

Along the way, vinegar picks up particles of other substances, too. Naturally processed vinegar is traditionally stored in wooden casks. This contributes to its virtues, as can be seen by the way its flavor is changed by the wooden barrels. The final result, that wonderful thing we call vinegar, has the goodness of the original food, plus much more!

HONEY Often, the concentrated flower power of honey is included in vinegar tonics. This rich sweetness is an ideal companion to vinegar's puckery tartness. Honey is nature's original sweetener. It contains an assortment of dissolved sugars such as sucrose, glucose and fructose. It also contains nearly 200 other substances, including minerals, vitamins, pigments, enzymes and amino acids.

Together, apple cider vinegar and honey provide a unique combination of health-promoting nutrients, many of them minute amounts of trace elements. Biochemists have now identified and measured hundreds of substances in the foods we eat. (Most nutrient charts list only the most plentiful and the most well known ones.) For a long time trace elements were ignored by most doctors and their importance to good health was underestimated.

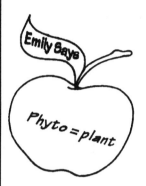

Supplements are not the same as eating foods. The complex mix of phytochemicals in plants can not be duplicated chemically. And so, multivitamin and mineral pills include only a very few of the substances known to be necessary for life. And, if too much of a vitamin or mineral is taken it can be stored in the body and end up as a poison. Extra nutrients that are not stored in the body must be filtered out by the kidneys, causing them to work harder than they otherwise would have to. The safest way to get the goodness of food is through healthy eating habits.

FORTIFIED VINEGARS

Fortified vinegars offer a way to combine the tremendous nutritional benefits of fruits and vegetables with the goodness of vinegar. Whole fruits and vegetables are used, so all their vitamins, minerals, enzymes and the hundreds of other components are preserved. They are an easy way to get a daily dose of vinegar. Fortified vinegars also perk up bland foods and — most of all — they are just plain good tasting!

Fortified vinegars begin with fruits and vegetables that are pureed in a blender with good, wholesome vinegar. Herbs and spices may be added, too. To prepare the recipes which follow, simply blend all ingredients until they are smooth and free of chunks. The intensity of flavor which is best for you may vary from that of others. So, some optional seasonings are listed. Feel free to experiment with these recipes to produce your own personal variations. They make great dips, dressings for salads or marinades.

FORTIFIED APPLE CIDER VINEGAR & HONEY TONIC

2   Medium apples
1/2   Cup apple cider vinegar
1/4   Cup honey
    If you, like thousands of others, take a daily tonic of apple cider vinegar and honey, 1 tablespoon of this dressing is an especially appetizing way to do it! Optional ingredients: 1/2 teaspoon cinnamon, 1/4 teaspoon nutmeg

and an additional 1/4 cup honey (if cinnamon is added). In addition to all the nutrients in apple cider vinegar and honey this combination adds the goodness of fresh apples. Included in the nearly 400 substances that have been identified in apples are:

- Calcium, beta carotene, carotenoids, chlorophyll, fiber, folacin, fructose, glucose, clycine, lecithin, lysine, pectin, niacin, selenium, sorbitol, sucrose, thiamin, tryptophan and zinc.

CUCUMBER-CELERY

1 Large cucumber
2 Cups celery
1 Cup red wine vinegar
1 Cup water

Good for seasoning steamed vegetables, boiled potatoes or pasta. Optional ingredient: 1/2 teaspoon salt. In addition to all the nutrients in vinegar this combination adds the goodness of fresh cucumbers and celery. Included in the nearly 450 substances that have been identified in celery and the more than 175 substances that have been identified in cucumbers are:

- Calcium, beta carotene, carotenes, choline, copper, coumarin, beta elemene, glycine, histidine, iron, lysine, riboflavin, tryptophan and tyrosine. (Celery)

- Beta amyrin, calcium, beta carotene, fluorine, folacin, iron, lysine, riboflavin, selenium, beta sitosterol, thiamin, tryptophan and tyrosine. (Cucumbers)

GARLIC

8 Garlic bulbs
1 Cup apple cider vinegar

Bake fresh, whole garlic bulbs until tender. Peel away the outer skin and squeeze the soft garlic paste into a blender. Blend in the apple cider vinegar. Optional ingredients: 1/2 to 1 cup oil, 1/2 to 1 teaspoon salt, 2 teaspoons sugar, 2 teaspoons dry mustard. In addition to all the nutrients in vinegar this combination adds the goodness of fresh garlic. Included in the more than 275 substances that have been identified in garlic are:

- Ascorbic acid, calcium, beta carotene, copper, fiber, clycine, lysine, niacin, riboflavin, selenium and thiamin.

RASPBERRY

1 Cup raspberries
3 Tablespoons red wine vinegar

Raspberries may be fresh or frozen, sweetened or unsweetened. Great over ice cream, peaches, melon slices or fruit salad. In addition to all the nutrients in vinegar this combination adds the goodness of red raspberries. Included in the more than 100 substances that have been identified in red raspberries are:

- Acetic acid, ascorbic acid, boron, calcium, beta carotene, chromium, fiber, lactic acid, pectin, riboflavin, salicylic acid, selenium, tannin and thiamin.

CUCUMBER-ONION
1   Large cucumber
1/2 Cup red wine vinegar
1/4 Cup onion

No need to peel the cucumber or remove the seeds. Optional ingredients: 1/4 to 1/2 cup oil or replace the red wine with champagne vinegar. In addition to all the nutrients in vinegar and cucumbers, this recipe adds the goodness of onions. Included in the nearly 350 substances that have been identified in onions are:

- Ascorbic acid, calcium, beta carotene, choline, fiber, lysine, niacin, pectin, riboflavin, selenium and sulfur.

CARROT
1   Cup carrots
1/2 Cup apple cider vinegar
1/2 Cup water
3 to 4 Tablespoons honey (optional)

Use raw carrots for a cool vegetable dip, cooked ones for a smoother sauce to top cooked foods or add to soups. In addition to all the nutrients in vinegar this recipe adds the goodness of carrots. Included in the more than 400 substances that have been identified in carrots are:

- Ascorbic acid, boron, calcium, citric acid, copper, glycine, lecithin, lysine, niacin, riboflavin, selenium, thiamin, tryptophan, vitamin B-6, vitamin D and vitamin E. Plus, carrots contain alpha, beta, epsilon and gamma carotenes.

Recipes for some other fortified vinegars which are packed with healthy phytochemicals follow:

STRAWBERRY
1   Cup strawberries
1/4 Cup champagne vinegar

This is a mildly tart vinegar that is high in vitamin C. Optional ingredients: 1/2 cup yogurt or 2 tablespoons honey.

HONEYDEW
2   Cups honeydew melon
1/4   Cup champagne vinegar
1/4   Cup water
   Excellent topping for fruits and ices. Optional ingredients: 1 tablespoon honey or 1/4 teaspoon ginger.

BLUEBERRY
2   Cups blueberries
3/4   Cup red wine vinegar
3/4   Cup water
   Use fresh or frozen berries. Optional ingredient: 2 tablespoons honey.

LEMON
1   Lemon
2   Tablespoons champagne vinegar
1/2   Cup water
   Use the entire lemon, both pulp and peeling. Excellent splashed on sea food. Optional ingredient: 1 cup cabbage.

PARSLEY
2   Cups fresh parsley
1/2   Cup red wine vinegar
1/2   Cup water
   This bright green vinegar goes well with meats and steamed vegetables.

KALE-MUSTARD
2   Cups kale
1/4   Cup apple cider vinegar
1/4   Cup water
2   Tablespoons dry mustard
   This is a thick and healthy dip or a topping for vegetables. Optional ingredient: 15 peppercorns.

MINT SAUCE
2 Cups fresh mint leaves
1 Cup apple cider vinegar
2 Tablespoons honey
   Malt or red wine vinegar may be substituted.

ARE YOU OVERFED & UNDERNOURISHED?

Once it was thought good nutrition was only important for babies and growing children. Now scientists realize the adult body needs adequate amounts of protein, carbohydrates, vitamins, minerals — as well as hundreds of trace elements — to function properly and to retard premature aging. The best mix of these substances, and sometimes the only place they can be found, is in the foods supplied to the body. We now know that, for adults, fruits and vegetables are more important than ever!

Yet, dieticians tell us it is almost impossible to get all needed nutrients from the foods most people eat. If the diet does not contain enough leafy green vegetables, the body may be short of the folic acid needed to protect it from heart attack and stroke. A shortage of a tiny amount of a trace element can affect the emotions. If vitamin E, such as is found in wheat germs is in short supply, the risk of developing Parkinson's and Alzheimer's diseases may rise. The selenium in foods such as garlic help fight cancer and the beta carotene in cantaloupe and carrots is an antioxidant that soaks up free radicals that age the body.

Free radicals are particles left over from food digestion. These oxygen-rich substances damage body cells in the same way they make iron rust, vegetables rot and oils rancid. Free radicals can cause cells to lose their ability to function properly, or even die. Antioxidants such as flavonoids, carotenoids, vitamin C and vitamin E are the body's defense against free radicals. These protectives are found in fruits and vegetables. Some of the very special things that happen when lots of fruits and vegetables are added to the diet include:

- A daily dose of pectin (the amount found 2 or 3 apples) may be able to lower cholesterol — by as much as 25% or more.

- Even when a diet contains more fat than doctors feel is healthy, extra fruits and vegetables can help lower blood pressure. And the benefits begin in as little as two weeks!

- Adding garlic to the diet can reduce the likelihood of getting an infection. It fights 17 different kinds of fungus.

- Eating lots of both garlic and onion has been linked to lower levels of cholesterol.

- The carotenoid in tomatoes has twice the antioxidant power of beta carotene!

Chapter Three

The Vinegar Diet

CAN THE VINEGAR DIET BRING NEW HEALTH TO YOUR LIFE?

VERY PROBABLY!

Eating better with The Vinegar Diet is about a whole lot more than vinegar! It is a complete way of living and feeling better about yourself. And best of all, you can begin today. Eating better and feeling better is as simple as filling your plate! Never again count calories, weigh food or struggle with measuring cups. The Vinegar Diet is as easy as filling your plate, as pleasant as eating your favorite food, and as good for you as sunshine in the morning!

The Vinegar Diet combines what we have always instinctively known about eating with the best of today's biochemical research. It is good food for a healthy body without:

- Confusing calorie counting.
- Complicated rules.
- Depressing restrictions.
- Fad foods.
- Expensive supplements.

Fifty years ago your Grandmother said, "Eat your fruits and vegetables." Twenty-five years ago your Mother said, "Eat your fruits and vegetables." Today's best scientific research confirms their wisdom. Best health only comes when you eat your fruits and vegetables!

Fruits and vegetables are the heart of healthy eating. And, many believe a daily vinegar tonic is also a good idea! Vinegar is an essential building block for the body. It can also help the body absorb the calcium it needs to ward off osteoporosis because calcium needs stomach acid to be absorbed well. Yet, many of those who desperately need calcium, those over 60, have reduced amounts of natural stomach acid.

THE VINEGAR DIET

Traditionally, vinegar and honey are taken with a full glass of water 30 minutes before the two largest meals of the day.* Taken this way they help control appetite, aid digestion and supply trace amounts of a spectacular

*See Chapter One

THE VINEGAR DIET

Sweets

Oils

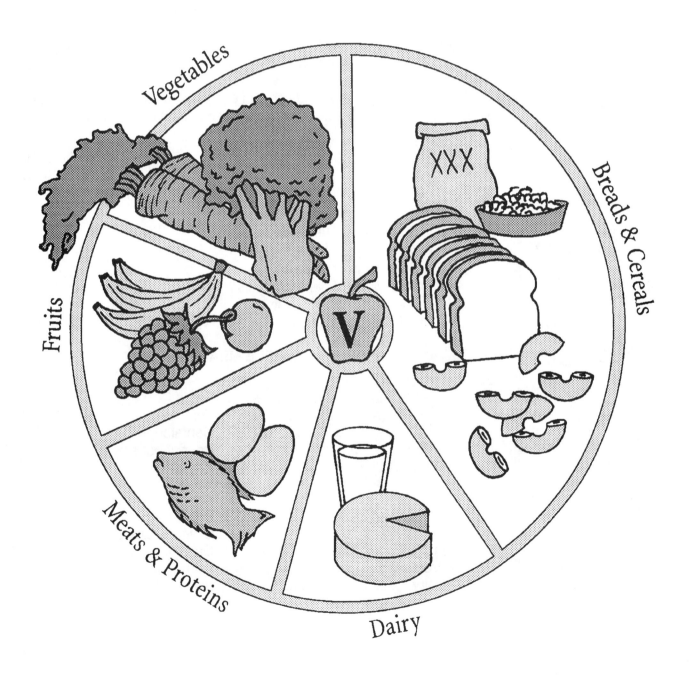

number of nutrients. (If you take a vinegar tonic on a daily basis, use a straw so tooth enamel is protected.)

THE SECRET TO THE VINEGAR DIET IS PROPORTION!! Each time you eat, use the drawing on the opposite page. It shows you how much of each food group to eat at each meal. It is essential to use these proportions every time you eat! Every day, you need to include foods in your diet from all five food groups:

- Grains & breads - includes rice, potatoes, pasta, beans, baked goods.
- Vegetables - includes broccoli, squash, green beans, corn, tomatoes.
- Fruits - includes oranges, bananas, grapes, pears, berries, melons.
- Proteins - includes meat, fish, peanut butter, beans.
- Dairy - includes milk, yogurt, cottage cheese, buttermilk.

If you are eating a big meal and heap up lots of food on the bread and grain section, then you must also heap up lots of food on all the other sections. This way, the food you eat stays in proper proportion. If you go back for seconds, you must eat some of each food group, in the proportions shown. If you are only eating a snack, fill each section sparingly.

Add fats and sweets sparingly to the foods above and drink six to eight glasses of water a day. To maintain an average weight and to get the nutrients your body needs each day, you need:

Emily Says

Healthy goal = 30% (or less) calories from fat.

- 6 to 11 servings of breads and grains
- 3 to 5 servings of vegetables
- 2 to 4 servings of fruits
- 2 to 3 servings of protein
- 2 to 3 servings of dairy products
- A few splashes of oil or fats
- A bit of sugar or sweets

SAMPLE MEALS

Breakfast:

Breads and grains	Bagel
Vegetables	Tomato
Fruit	Cantaloupe
Protein	Peanut butter
Dairy	Yogurt

Full meal:

Breads and grains	Pasta and a dinner roll
Vegetables	Green beans and beets
Fruits	Orange
Protein	Fish
Dairy	Skim milk

Light meal:

Breads and grains	Rice
Vegetables	Broccoli and carrots
Fruits	Grapes
Protein	Chicken
Dairy	Skim milk

Snack:

Breads and grains	Crackers
Vegetables	Cucumber
Fruits	Cherries
Protein & dairy	Cottage cheese

Make sure the amount of food for each food group fits inside the space allotted for it. Each helping must fit on its place on the sample plate. If the total amount is more food than you want, adjust the size of portions rather than allowing yourself to skip an entire food group.

For example, if an entire plateful of breakfast is more food than you want, serve yourself 1/2 a bagel, a couple of cherry tomatoes, a small sliver of cantaloupe, a teaspoon of peanut butter and 1/4 cup of yogurt. If you want a hearty breakfast, serve yourself an entire bagel, a large tomato, 1/2 a cantaloupe, a tablespoon of peanut butter and a cup of yogurt.

Occasionally, one section of a meal may overlap another. When this happens, make up for it at the next meal. For example, if a piece of fish overlaps its section at one meal, you may skip the protein section on the next meal and fill that area with extra vegetables or fruits. And remember, many kinds of beans can do double duty because they are good sources of protein.

Keep fats and oils to a minimum by trimming meats and avoiding fried foods. Limit sugar and sweets by replacing them with fruits.

Fortified vinegars can help you increase the amount of vegetable and fruit nutrients you get. They are also good ways to get your daily servings of vinegar. For example, in the sample full meal, serve the fish topped with lemon or garlic fortified vinegar. In the sample snack, apple fortified vinegar is a smooth, tasty way to add flavor, nutrients and excitement to the cottage cheese.

COLOR MATTERS

Good food comes in a healthy rainbow of colors. Always look at your plate of food and check that you have included many different colors. If the plate is mostly white, faded and colorless your food is probably over-processed and short of nutrients. Your diet should be a joyful mix of color. Check for a variety of colors at every meal, every day. Include foods that are red, orange, yellow, purple and green because:

- Red foods can contain lycopene that fights cancer; others have betacyanin that fights bacteria. Red foods include radishes, tomatoes, strawberries, cherries, raspberries, grapes, peppers, beans, watermelon, cranberries, beets and apples.

- Orange foods can contain beta carotene, which lowers the risk of getting some cancers. Orange foods include squash, carrots, oranges, pumpkins, sweet potatoes, cantaloupe, papayas and apricots.

- Yellow foods can contain lutein to help preserve eyesight by fighting macular degeneration. Others have the antioxidant anthoxanthin, or an anti-inflammatory, antibacterial and antiviral substance called quercetin. Yellow foods include raspberries, cherries, peppers, grapefruit, squash, lemons, corn, beans, bananas, pineapple and apples.

- Purple foods can contain anthocyanin, a phytochemical that attacks free radicals while also dilating blood vessels to reduce the risk of stroke and heart attack. Purple foods include egg plant, red cabbage, blackberries, raspberries, grapes, blueberries, cherries and plums.

- Green foods can contain indoles that block some cancer causing chemicals. Green foods include broccoli, Brussels sprouts, kiwis, grapes, peppers, spinach, beans, apples, asparagus, celery, kale, okra and cucumbers.

BOOST THE HEALTH EFFECTS OF THE VINEGAR DIET!

You can multiply the benefits of The Vinegar Diet by drinking six to eight glasses of water each day and limiting coffee to one or two cups. Take an energy boosting "mini vacation" of 10 minutes from your usual day. Get outside into the fresh air. Move around a bit, let your mind wander. Never skip meals. Eat several small meals instead of one or two large ones that can make you feel sluggish and bloated. Give yourself a new routine by making changes in the way you do things during the day.

Learn to reward yourself in nonfood ways. Have a massage instead of dinner at a fancy restaurant. You will feel better, longer. Do some deep breathing exercises instead of eating a handful of cookies. Move around more to improve circulation. Wear brightly colored, soft comforting clothes. Sit in the sunshine, outside when the weather is nice, at a window when weather is bitter. But most important, begin right this minute! Put a smile on your face, think about something pleasant, and vow to yourself that you are going to begin eating for health with the next bite you take by following The Vinegar Diet plan!

VINEGAR DOES EVEN MORE

One of biggest jobs vinegar does in the human body is promote the growth of beneficial bacteria. They are needed to keep disease-producing germs at bay. For example, human intestines contain millions of good bacteria (such as bifidus and lactobicillus) to keep the gastrointestinal tract healthy and disease free. Helpful bacteria in the intestines also work to:

- Support the immune system.
- Help digest food.
- Discourage illness caused by E. coli and clostridia bacteria.
- Make some vitamins.
- Keep the intestines acidic.

Fruits and vegetables are storehouses of flavonoids, biflavonoids and carotenoids. These are wondrous antioxidants with the ability to neutralize free radicals that age the body. Of the hundreds of flavonoids in plants, more than 60 kinds (such as beta carotene) have been found in the foods we eat. For example, you can get your entire daily beta carotene needs in half a cantaloupe or half a carrot. The cantaloupe has the vitamin C of two small oranges.

CHOLESTEROL

Almost all body cells have some cholesterol. The body makes some, and it is found in all animal-based foods. Meat, fish, poultry, eggs and dairy products all have it. Some cholesterol is essential. The body uses it to build new cells, make hormones and as an aid in digestion. Too much contributes to clogging arteries and heart damage.

Vegetables, which are cholesterol free, are a very healthy way to get protein. Cold water fish help maintain low cholesterol, too. They bring cholesterol lowering omega-3 fatty acids to the body. (This is probably because of the way omega-3 fatty acids act on platelet aggregation and lipid metabolism.)

FIBER

Vegetables and fruits bring fiber to the diet. Fiber helps regulate digestion, absorbs cholesterol and dilutes toxins that cause cancer. Foods containing soluble fiber include rye, oats, legumes and fruits such as apples. Food containing insoluble fiber include whole wheat, bran and most fruits and vegetables.

CARBOHYDRATES

High doses of sugar hurts cells, ability to fight disease. Complex carbohydrates in fruits and vegetables stay in the digestive system longer, and are fed into the blood stream more slowly than refined sugars. This slow, steady digestion keeps essential nutrients in the bloodstream. They bathe cells in healing antioxidants for long periods of time. A cell which is bathed in nutrients will go a long way in healing itself.

A low fat, sugar and cholesterol diet may be helpful in fighting infection. So is eating enough protein. The risk of many chronic disease of elder years is increased by poor eating habits in younger years. And poor nutrition makes recovery from illness take longer.

THERMOGENSIS — A WORD YOU NEED TO KNOW

Thermogensis is the process by which the body turns food into energy. This energy is used to warm the body, make muscles work and power the brain. And, some is used to repair and replace worn out tissue. When you eat, think about what kind of nutrients that particular food is giving your body. If it is a very fatty food it may supply more energy than the body can work off, without giving it the vitamins and minerals it needs to repair injury. The result is fat added to the body.

FOOD MYTHS

- There are no calories in cottage cheese.
- Pickles and milk at the same meal will make you sick.
- Bread sticks have very few calories.
- Brown eggs are better than white eggs.
- Ice cream is the secret to losing weight.
- Hot food is healthier than cold food.

Good health and a youthful appearance go hand in hand with a good diet. It has been said that the body's real age is tied closer to the health of its immune system than to its calendar age. Nutritious food is the best way to empower the immune system, to bring a healthy glow to your face and to put a spring into your step. You can improve your appearance by feeding your body everything it needs. This includes eating a wide variety of foods.

Promise yourself you will begin today to make better choices.

ET SAYS   **IS THE VINEGAR DIET FOR YOU?**

Ask your doctor before beginning any changes to your usual diet. The suggestions offered in The Vinegar Diet may be appropriate for healthy adults — they are not intended for children, the frail elderly, those taking medications or with chronic health conditions — without the approval of a medical professional!

Chapter Four

Lose Weight The Vinegar Way

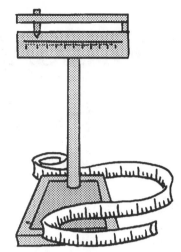

CAN VINEGAR MELT AWAY POUNDS AND INCHES? Doctors tell us when calories are restricted as a way to lose weight 95% of diets fail! Harsh dieting, with strict calorie reduction, is harmful to the body and an unnatural process. When you are hungry the natural thing to do is eat! Strict "dieting" can affect the immune system, making it unable to do a good job fighting off disease. People who spend a lifetime gradually putting on pounds should not expect to take it all off overnight.

SO, CAN YOU REALLY USE THE VINEGAR DIET TO MELT FAT AWAY?

YES!

There is a way for you to eat all the food you need to feel full and create the slimmer body you have always wanted! If weight loss makes you look drawn and ill you are losing weight too fast. Losing weight is a very complex process. You can win the war against unwanted pounds, but it is important to not lose important nutrients along with the weight.

What is the very best diet of all? The one that works for you — The Vinegar Diet! It can help you keep off unwanted pounds for life. Its slow and steady weight loss means you never need to "go on a diet" again. You will feel better about yourself and have more energy from the very beginning. It is a way of living, a plan for a healthier life!

HOW TO BE THINNER, LOOK YOUNGER, FEEL MORE VIGOROUS!

Depriving yourself of food, being constantly hungry or even having to count calories is not the way to create a healthy new body. To begin using The Vinegar Diet to help you lose weight, review vinegar and honey use in Chapters One, Two and Three. Follow The Vinegar Diet eating plan at every meal and every time you eat a snack.

THE VINEGAR WEIGHT LOSS DIET

Sweets

Oils

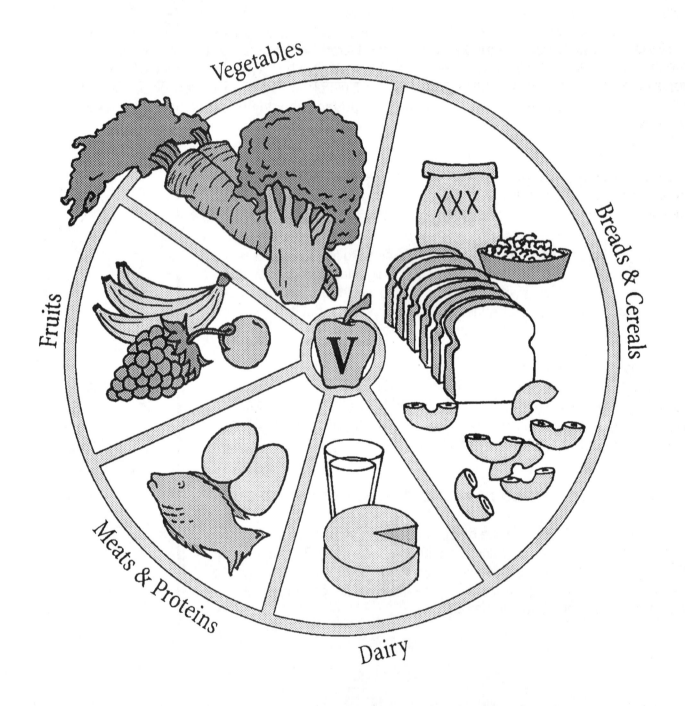

Vegetables

Breads & Cereals

Fruits

Meats & Proteins

Dairy

THE SECRET TO LOSING WEIGHT WITH THE VINEGAR DIET IS PROPORTION!! Each time you eat, use the drawing on the opposite page. It shows you how much of each food group to eat at each meal. It is essential to use these proportions every time you eat ! And, just as in the regular Vinegar Diet, you must include foods from all five food groups in your diet each day:

Grains & breads .. includes rice, potatoes, pasta, beans, baked goods.
Vegetables .... includes broccoli, squash, green beans, corn, tomatoes.
Fruits .... includes oranges, bananas, grapes, pears, berries, melons.
Proteins .... includes meat, fish, peanut butter, beans.
Dairy .... includes milk, yogurt, cottage cheese, buttermilk.

Resist the urge to pile up your plate with huge amounts of food at one time. If you are very hungry, fix a medium-sized plate of food using the proportions shown on The Vinegar Weight Loss Diet plate. Then wait a few minutes to decide if you are really hungry for more food. If you are, refill your plate, being sure to select food from each food group and in the proportions shown.

Add fats and sweets very sparingly and drink at least eight glasses of water a day. Even if you are determined to lose weight as rapidly as possible, every day your body needs at the very least:

- 4 to 6 servings of breads and grains
- 3 to 4 servings of vegetables
- 3 to 4 servings of fruits
- 2 to 3 servings of protein
- 2 to 3 servings of dairy products
- A splash of oil or fat
- A sprinkle of sweetness

You need to eat at least the number of servings of each food group listed above every day. Any less food and your body will be at risk for a nutrient deficiency. Depending on the foods you choose and how much fat and sweets you add, this diet should provide you with between 1200 and 1600 calories.

DO NOT EAT LESS WITHOUT A DOCTOR'S SUPERVISION!

Limiting fat is the simplest way to control weight. As a bonus, you decrease the risk of stroke, high blood pressure and diabetes. Your goal, for the most successful, longest lasting weight loss is to begin your vinegar diet by keeping the number of calories you eat each day about the same as you are eating right now. Simply switch fat calories to calories from fruits and vegetables and begin to increase the amount of exercise you get.

SAMPLE MEALS

Breakfast:

        Breads and grains .... Puffed wheat
        Vegetables .... Tomato
        Fruit... Cantaloupe
        Protein .... Slice of turkey breast
        Dairy .... Skim milk

Full meal:

        Breads and grains .... Sweet potato
        Vegetables .... Green beans, beets, salad
        Fruits .... Orange, kiwi
        Protein .... Fish
        Dairy .... Skim milk

Light meal:

        Breads and grains .... Rice
        Vegetables .... Broccoli, carrots
        Fruits .... Grapes, apple
        Protein .... Chicken
        Dairy .... Yogurt

Snack:

        Breads and grains .... Crackers
        Vegetables .... Cucumber, celery
        Fruits .... Cherries, grapefruit
        Protein & dairy .... Cottage cheese

Emily Says

When fat is burned to make heat it is called thermogenesis.

    Make sure the size of each helping of food fits on its place on the sample plate. Compared to the standard Vinegar Diet, the Vinegar Weight Loss Diet gives you slightly smaller portions of breads and grains and slightly larger portions of vegetables and fruits. The protein and dairy sections are exactly the same. If the diet seems to offer more food than you want, adjust the size of portions rather than skip an entire food group.

    For example, if breakfast is more food than you want to eat, serve yourself 1/2 cup of cereal, a couple of cherry tomatoes, a small sliver of cantaloupe, a very small piece of turkey and a glass of skim milk. If you are very hungry, serve yourself a full cup of cereal, a large tomato, 1/2 a cantaloupe, a small slice of turkey and drink a full glass of skim milk.

If a meal does overlap one section, make it up at the next meal. For example, if a piece of fish overlaps its section at one meal, you may skip the protein section at the next meal and fill that area with extra vegetables or fruits.

As you can see, The Vinegar Weight Loss Diet is very similar to the regular Vinegar Diet. And that is the magic of this eating plan! You lose weight by eating extra vegetables and fruits and increasing how much you move around.

You will protect the health of your heart and arteries, and lose weight, by eating very small amounts of fats and oils. Limit sugars and sweets, too. Use fortified vinegars to increase the amount of vegetable and fruit nutrients you get, and as an alternative to drinking vinegar in water.

For example, in the sample breakfast the cantaloupe is delicious topped with fortified raspberry vinegar. In the sample light meal fortified carrot vinegar can be served over the broccoli. Or, spoon warm garlic fortified vinegar over both the broccoli and carrots.

Emily Says

To the body most "diets" seem like a deadly famine.

Several times a week substitute legumes, such as beans, for animal sources of protein. Many kinds of beans do double nutritional duty because they are good sources of protein. You will eliminate cholesterol loaded fats and be able to eat much larger portions for the same calories. And, beans make you feel full for hours longer than many other foods. To use the plate diagram for plant-based sources of protein (such as beans) use both the bread and grain and protein sections when filling your plate.

THERMOGENSIS — A CONCEPT FOR LOSING WEIGHT

The body thinks of food as fuel. So, its first instinct is to turn it into energy. Some energy is used to power muscles and the brain. A lot of energy is used to heat the body and a tiny bit is used to replace worn out or damaged cells. Only after doing all this does the body make fat.

If there is a sudden reduction in the amount of food the body gets it panics and thinks a famine has started. To protect itself from dying in this famine all available calories are turned into fat. And, worst of all, the body sends urgent signals of hunger to its appetite control center.

Little wonder many doctors tell us nearly all of the weight lost by conventional calorie reduction "dieting" is soon regained! The very best way to begin a weight loss program is to lower total body fat and increase lean body mass, while keeping actual weight steady. Muscle takes more calories to maintain, even at rest. This means the body uses more calories, so total weight is gradually reduced.

This thermogenic weight loss happens because muscles have a higher metabolic rate than fat. And, muscles weigh more than fat for the same bulk. So, for the same total weight, extra muscle means a slimmer body. And, increased muscle tone will enable you to have a firmer abdomen and stronger back muscles, which will make you appear slimmer. As more and more fat is replaced with muscle, the higher metabolic rate will need enough extra calories that the body will begin using up its stored fat.

The second part of thermogenic weight loss is based on the fact that the body's biggest use of calories is to make heat. What is left over goes to fix worn out body parts and allow muscles to do work. Only after all this is fat produced. If the cycle is interrupted anywhere along the way, there is no fat to store.

Thermogenesis, turning food into heat, can be increased by diet choices. You can feel it begin when you eat a big meal and your body gets hot as it burns food. Some foods do this longer and better than others. They encourage the body to burn calories faster by increasing metabolism. By adding these foods to the diet and by moving around more you lose weight without reducing the total number of calories in the diet.

If you suddenly restrict calories, the body slows down its metabolic rate. Food is stored as fat instead of being used as energy. When the rate of metabolism is high, more food is burned and less is available to make fat. (When the rate of metabolism is very low it is almost impossible to lose weight, even on a severely restricted calorie diet.) Cold, food and exercise speed up thermogensis. Increasing the number of calories the body burns is a sure, safe and lasting way to lose weight.

COLD When the body is chilled, it has to work harder and burn more calories to keep warm. Some researchers believe cooling off the body helps increase its metabolic rate. For example, they feel always wearing a heavy sweater could help the body stay fat by reducing the amount of calories it needs to burn to stay warm.

EXERCISE Exercise turns up the body's fat-burning metabolism. This faster burning of calories continues for hours after exercise has ended. For this reason some researchers suggest spreading exercise out over the entire day, rather than limiting it to a single session. To practice this, get moving early in the day. Make your body wake up and begin using calories as soon as possible. Follow up with frequent short exercise periods.

Emily Says

When fuel is low the body's thermostat is turned down.

208

FOOD Some foods, such as capsicum-containing peppers increase metabolism. They burn off more calories than they contain because they stimulate the body. Thermogenic agents such as hot peppers and chili powder also have lots of vitamins C and E, carotenes and antioxidants. They even have substances to fight the bacteria which causes some diarrhea. Fennel is another good "diet" food. Fennel can be of great help in a weight loss program because it helps tone and stimulate the gastro-intestinal system and reduces the gas that can be produced by a diet high in vegetables and fruits.

THE SECRET TO LOSING WEIGHT

The real secret to losing unwanted pounds and inches is to get the body to increase the amount of fuel it burns without sending it into panic anti-famine mode. To do this it needs a reasonable amount of many kinds of food and an adequate amount of exercise. Count your nutrients first. Then, calories tend to take care of themselves. And, when you eat healthy and move around a bit, your weight tends to take care of itself!

DANGER IN REDUCING CALORIES

Calorie restriction diets usually cause the loss of important muscle tissue as well as fat. The ratio can be significant. For many dieters, half of their weight loss is muscle or bone. Only half of it is the unwanted fat. Even with heavy exercise calorie restriction usually results in at least one-fourth of the weight coming from lean body mass.

It is important to eat some protein, as it is an important part of the system that tells your body when to stop eating. Some diets distort the value of protein by encouraging the dieter to eat huge amounts of it. These diets cause the body to lose a lot of water, rapidly. This can make it seem as if there has been a sudden weight loss. Too much protein can increase the amount of precious calcium lost in the urinary tract and has been linked to more frequent bone fractures.

Emily Says

To begin, keep calories steady and increase movement.

The healthiest way to eat protein is in proper proportion to other food. The protein space on The Vinegar Diet drawing shows you the proportion of protein the U.S. Department of Agriculture recommends in its Food Guide Pyramid.

WATER WASHES AWAY POUNDS

Water is especially important when losing weight. Drink at least eight full glasses a day. Coffee, tea and colas do not count as part of this. Extra water helps the body wash away toxins. It also encourages you to eat less. For variety, try water with a twist of lime, a wedge of lemon, a drop of vanilla or a dash of herbal vinegar. When you think you are really hungry it can help to drink a glass of water and wait a few minutes. You may find you are not so hungry after all!

VINEGAR IS ESSENTIAL

Vinegar, as acetic acid, is used by the body in the process by which it burns both carbohydrates and fat. It is naturally present in most plant and animal tissues. The human body even makes it. Vinegar also plays a role in how the body stores fat. When vinegar enters the blood stream it is carried to the kidneys and muscles. There, it either becomes energy or is used to make body tissues through its role in making essential amino acids. It even facilitates the process which forms the red blood cells that supply the body's oxygen!

FAST START TIPS

When you follow the vinegar weight loss plan for healthy eating your weight loss may not be sudden, but it will be permanent! You can give up yo-yo dieting that takes off a few pounds one week and puts them back on the next. The Vinegar Diet encourages you to eat a balanced diet, including food from all five food groups.

Bring out the good taste of these foods with healthy splashes of plain or flavored apple cider vinegar. It has only two calories in an entire tablespoon. Or, increase their nutrient content dramatically with fortified vinegars. If you follow this plan you will not have the overwhelming fatigue that goes with many diet plans. Actually, you should have more energy! Some other ways to get your weight loss program off to a fast start follow:

- Eat a raw vegetable or fruit half an hour before a meal.
- Eat only lean meats, and eat them less often.
- Add more cold water fish to your diet.
- Use small plates to serve your meals.
- Stop eating when you are full, even if food remains on your plate. You do not have to "clean up your plate."

- Substitute pureed pumpkin or apple sauce for half of the fat or oil in baked goods.
- Use only low fat dairy products.
- Bake or simmer in no-fat sauces and broil rather than fry.
- Eat slowly because it takes about 20 minutes for the body to be able to judge when you are really full.
- When you really want something you know is not good for you, eat at least one bite of it. In the long run you will be less likely to pig out on it!

VITAMINS & OTHER SUPPLEMENTS

Plants contain thousands of different substances. There is no way a pill can duplicate the exact effect of eating a fresh orange or a ripe tomato. The only way to get all the nutrients needed for a healthy body is to eat a variety of good foods. Regular exercise and enough pure water are also needed. This is a plan that is safe, sure and will bring results that last for life!

Many doctors recommend a daily vitamin and mineral supplement. This is partly because so many of the foods most people eat are so heavily processed. And, it is because so few people eat the five servings of fruits and vegetables recommended for good health.

As you make changes in your diet, do a little bit at a time. Use fats sparingly. Remember, all animal fats (and some vegetable fats) are associated with atherosclerosis. Do not shock your system with sudden changes in the way you eat or exercise. Strict calorie reduction can cause fatigue, and it makes the body's fat-burning mechanism slow down to conserve fuel. Even good things need to be done gradually!

Concentrate on high bulk, high fiber foods rather than concentrated sources of nutrients. Baked beans, for example, have lots of fiber, protein and are low fat. Mushrooms contain about 60 calories in an entire pound (25 calories in a cup). They are high in fiber and contain biotin, one of the complex of B vitamins involved in the digestion of fats and proteins. Some of the nutrients in mushrooms are only available to the body when they are cooked. Cooking also inactivates hydrazines in mushrooms that can increase the risk of getting cancer.

SPOT TONING

Yes, you can reduce places on your body that are especially troublesome to you! Exercise which tones a particular set of muscles can give the appearance of spot reducing. For example, tummy toning can be achieved by increasing the strength of the abdominal muscles. These stronger muscles will hold a sagging tummy in and up, even if total fat mass stays the same. Strengthening back muscles can help you stand up straight and appear thinner, too.

FAT MAKES FAT!

If there is too much fat in your diet your body will use it instead of burning the body fat you want to lose. One way to use less fat is to substitute vinegar-based toppings for fatty sauces and spreads. It also helps to use butter or margarine at room temperature so you can spread it thinner. Apply it with a small spatula and you will use even less! Other ways to cut down on the fat in your diet follow:

FATTY FOOD	BETTER CHOICE
Sour cream	Whipped cottage cheese
Cheese omelette	Egg substitute scrambled with vegetables
Granola	Oatmeal with raisins
Beef & cheese nachos	Bean burrito
Fettuccine Alfredo	Spaghetti with tomato sauce
Sweet & sour pork	Pork stir fry
Hamburger, fries, milk shake	Salad, baked potato, tea
Loaded pizza	Vegetarian pizza
Packaged microwave popcorn	Air-popped popcorn
Danish	Fruit
Whole milk	Skim milk
Deep fried chicken leg	Broiled, skinless chicken breast

Emily Says

Cream cheese is a fatty food! Croissants & muffins are weighty food!

LOSE A LITTLE, GAIN A LOT!

Why lose weight? Because even a small weight loss can give you a lot of benefits. Diabetes, high blood pressure, atherosclerosis, heart disease and cancer are all tied to extra body fat. Even a little weight off can decrease risk of osteoarthritis, even in your hands. (Researchers think a chemical in stored fat increases the progression of osteoarthritis.)

Where and when you gain matters, too. Extra pounds on your stomach are more serious than weight carried on the hips and thighs. And, if you have gained more than 10 pounds since becoming an adult it is more of a problem than if you have always carried the extra weight. This "middle-of-life" weight gain is especially dangerous for women. A mere 10 pounds can raise the risk of heart attack by 25%. (25 pounds may triple it!) Gaining weight as an adult tends to increase blood fat, pressure and sugar levels.

VISUALIZATION

Put your daydreams to work for you and they will become reality! You can use visualization to reshape your body. It makes any weight reduction program more effective. Some say you can even increase your metabolism this way. Put a picture in your mind of your new thin self. Enjoy the way it will feel. Do this before you get out of bed in the morning, during meals, and as you drop off to sleep at night. Soon it will be real.

AROMATHERAPY

Smell is 90% of the body's sensation of taste. Researchers are using this to help people lose weight. They have found that, for some people, smelling banana, peppermint or apple allows them to keep from overeating. Average weight loss using aromatherapy is about a pound a week. These smells probably work by making the body think it has eaten. Fennel may also be an appetite suppressant.

VARIETY! VARIETY!

We know the body needs a variety of smells and tastes at each meal to satisfy its food cravings. Be sure to include sweet and sour, salty and tangy foods in your diet, along with a range of colors.

Experiment with new and different foods at the supermarket. Try a pre-made salad, tiny baby carrots or a prepared selection of vegetables such as broccoli and cauliflower. They may be more expensive than your usual way of buying vegetables, but compared to eating out or a packaged "diet food" meal they are cheap. Their wonderful nutritional benefits are worth it if this is the only way you are going to eat these healthy foods.

THE FRENCH CONNECTION

Wine and France have an inescapable connection. It is home of some of the great wines of the world. And wine is one of the substances from which an excellent vinegar is made. Wine, like vinegar, is an acidic liquid, much like the chemistry of the body. It has long been recognized as an aid to digestion. Now it is said to do even more!

Many believe a small glass of wine with or before meals can have a definite effect on weight. It does this because is seems to reduce the total amount of fuel the body desires. The effect is especially noticeable when compared to the effect of unsweetened liquids.

Red grapes, from which red wine vinegar is made, have been found to contain a very special antioxidant. This substance, proanthocyanidin, is extremely effective at fighting free radicals associated with degenerative diseases and ageing.

FASTING — IS IT FOR YOU?

A weight-loss fast is a period of time where only liquids are taken. It can bring about an immediate small amount of weight loss, but because it throws the body into famine protection mode it is of very limited long term value. Weight lost through fasting inevitably returns, often within a day or two. It is not a way to permanently lose weight.

Arthritis sufferers sometimes use a fast to control pain. It has been found that fasting changes immune cells, so some kinds of arthritis may be calmed by a fast. Although fasting may bring temporary relief, it must not be overused. A low fat and protein diet that has lots of vegetables and fruits may work just as well.

If you decide to fast while on the vinegar weight loss diet be sure to supplement the vinegar and honey tonic with large amounts of vegetable and fruit juices. And, keep the fast short. Prolonged fasting can cause serious damage to the body!

ET SAYS   IS THE VINEGAR WEIGHT LOSS DIET FOR YOU?

Ask your doctor before beginning any changes to your usual diet! Feel free to show your health care provider the drawings that show you how to fill your plate for the vinegar weight loss diet. And please remember — suggestions offered in The Vinegar Diet may be appropriate for healthy adults — they are not intended for children, the frail elderly, those taking medications or with chronic health conditions — without the approval of a medical professional!

Chapter Five

Build Up Your Body With Vinegar

The Vinegar Diet can help you create the stronger body you have always wanted! With its help you can gain strength, energy and vigor.

Many older adults, particularly those who live alone, are at risk for becoming too thin. If body weight is too low the immune system may not be getting all the nutrients it needs to keep the body healthy. Frequent colds and bouts of flu, having several allergies, slow healing of cuts and scrapes and being tired every day could mean you have a weak immune system. Because very low body weight can lead to greater susceptibility to disease, if you are thin it is extra-important to eat some food, each day, from each food group.

The Vinegar Diet can be a healthy beginning for building up a frail, too thin, undermuscled or flabby body. If you are underweight or disabled, you – most of all – need the nutrients of vegetables, fruits and whole grains. Use the drawing in Chapter Three every time you eat. It shows you how much of each food group to eat at each meal.

It is essential to use these proportions every time you eat ! THE SECRET TO BUILDING UP YOUR BODY WITH THE VINEGAR DIET IS PROPORTION!! Every day, you need to include foods in your diet from all five food groups.

Add healthy oils for extra calories and smooth taste, fortified vinegars for concentrated nutrients, a few sweets, and drink six to eight glasses of water a day. To maintain an average weight and to get the nutrients your body needs each day, you need:

* 6 to 11 servings of breads and grains
* 3 to 5 servings of vegetables
* 2 to 4 servings of fruits
* 2 to 3 servings of protein
* 2 to 3 servings of dairy products

- Enough oil or fats to maintain weight
- A bit of sugar or sweets

To build up your body, choose foods with concentrated calories and nutrients. Eat bananas instead of grapes, avocados rather than watermelon, corn or beets rather than lettuce or mushrooms. All beans are good for you because they are rich sources of the protein you need to build up a damaged or frail body. You may tolerate small meals every three hours better than three large meals.

FATS

Fats are the most concentrated fuel for your body, as well as being an essential part of the taste, flavor and texture of food. For the same bulk, fat has more than twice the calories of other food. Because saturated fats, such as those from meats, may be associated with a higher risk of clogged arteries, choose healthy vegetable oils. Hazelnut, walnut and flaxseed oils are good choices for mixing with vinegars. So are monounsaturated corn, safflower and soy oils. For cooking, use oils that are resistant to heat, such as canola or olive.

Emily Says

Fat has 9 calories per gram, protein and carbohydrates have 4.

EXERCISE

Exercise is as important for normalizing weight as diet! It increases energy and lifts your mood. Your first goal should be to increase endurance and flexibility. To begin, stand up straight and breath deeply. Get oxygen flowing to all parts of your body. Short walks throughout the day help do this.

Regular, gentle exercise will increase the body's ability to move and bend and firm up flabby muscles. Begin by doing several repeats of light exercises, rather than trying to do heavy exercises too soon. Twenty minutes of exercise, three times a week can add years to your life. It is not necessary to do all 20 minutes at once. It is often better to start out exercising a few minutes at a time, spread out during the day.

When physical problems slow you down exercise may seem like the last thing you need to do. Actually, it is probably more important for those with physical problems to exercise than for others. Move the parts of the body that you can. If you use a walker or cane, you still need to move your body as much as possible to retain balance and coordination. Do a lot of stretching and range of motion exercises to keep joints mobile.

Exercise is needed for bones to retain their calcium. Only about 1/00 of the body's total calcium circulates in the blood, so tests can show a blood level that is normal, even when the bones are honeycombed by loss of calcium.

Mild exercise is especially important for those with fibromyalgia or any other type of arthritis. Gentle exercise is needed to strengthen tendons and ligaments around joints. Those with mild high blood pressure may find exercise lowers it into normal range.

IS THE BEST WAY TO FITNESS TOO EASY?

The President's Council on Physical Fitness and Sports calls walking the slower, surer way to fitness! Walking burns about the same number of calories as running, for the same distance. The best news of all is that the less you weigh, the fewer calories you burn and the more you weigh, the more calories you burn in this easiest of exercises. Many researchers believe walking is better than running for overall body conditioning. Generally, those who walk regularly even sleep better.

For best results swing your arms while you walk. It is also a good idea to do stretching exercises at the beginning and end of your walk. Take it slowly at first. If walking makes you too breathless to talk, you are going too fast. Getting some exercise is more important than how fast you go or how far. The biggest benefits come when those who do not usually exercise begin moving. Advantages to walking for exercise include:

- No lessons are needed, almost everyone can do it without training.
- You can do it most any time, anywhere.
- It is free.
- No special equipment is needed.

Expensive "sports drinks" are unnecessary. A teaspoon each of vinegar and honey stirred into a quart of water makes a good substitute. Or, plain water will do fine!

Exercise tends to normalize appetite. The body goes on burning more fuel for hours after exercise. Firm, healthy muscles burn more fuel, even at rest, than soft, flabby fat.

FATIGUE

Chronic fatigue is not a natural part of aging. It is a sign something is wrong, perhaps that the immune system is not functioning at its peak level. To find out why you are overly tired, decide when it happens most. When are you exhausted? Keep a chart for a week and write down the time you are really tired each day. Then, look back and see how this relates to your eating habits.

Be especially aware of your use of caffeine, too. It may increase fatigue symptoms. Low levels of the B complex of vitamins reduces endurance and results in feelings of tiredness. Using music to help energize your body and lift your mood may also help.

You may need to add a protein, carbohydrate and calcium rich snack for an afternoon energy boost. Cheese and crackers, with a rich honey and strawberry fortified vinegar to dip them in tastes great. Or, try a slice of chicken on half an English muffin and a spoonful of cooked prunes drizzled with cucumber-celery fortified vinegar. A short afternoon nap may help, too.

If you are very thin, use the principals of thermogensis and help the body conserve heat. Be sure to wear a heavy sweater when it is cool so the body does not need to burn a lot of calories to stay warm.

Fight fatigue by eating healthy food, getting daily exercise and taking an active interest in the world around you. This plan will help you stay fit so you can manage your daily life.

Chapter Six

Recipes For Success

If weight is a problem, you need a better way of eating, not another "diet!" We have come a long way from the days when it was thought food left on the table overnight fed the fairies, thus ensuring good fortune for the household. We now know it is the cook who shapes the fortunes of the household by preparing healthy food!

Hundreds of foods make use of the preservative and unique taste qualities of vinegar. It is an essential ingredient in catsup and mayonnaise, and is one of the original preservatives for meats and eggs. The rich, vivid taste sensation of fortified vinegar can help stimulate an appetite which has become dulled with age or depression.

Vegetables have fiber, vitamins and minerals. They are low in salt and most are fat-free. Beta-carotene rich vegetables fight colon, lung, bladder and esophagus cancer. A special carotenoid (lutein) fights deterioration of the retina. All foods with soluble fiber, such as the apples used to make apple cider vinegar, are good for preventing heart disease. A few recipes for using vinegar in a healthy diet follow:

EASY YOGURT To 1/2 gallon skim milk add 1 tablespoon each apple cider vinegar and plain, live culture yogurt. Mix every well, cap lightly, and set in a warm place for about 24 hours. Drain off excess clear liquid and you have a mild yogurt. Or, shake the mixture for a cultured buttermilk drink. This is a great way to use milk that is a bit old.

NO-FAT COLE SLAW Sprinkle 1/4 cup sugar over 4 cups shredded cabbage. Let set overnight. Add 2 cups cucumber-celery fortified vinegar and mix well.

HOT ORANGE BEETS Simmer 1/2 cup champagne vinegar, 1/2 cup beet juice and 1 teaspoon cayenne pepper until reduced by half. Add 4 cups canned, sliced beets and 2 cups chopped fresh orange. Simmer until just warm and top with 1 teaspoon parsley. Serve warm or chill overnight.

PEACHY FISH Baste fish fillets with fortified peach vinegar and bake or broil until well done.

CUCUMBER BOATS Cut a cucumber lengthwise and scoop out the seeds. Fill with a mixture made of equal parts fortified vinegar, yogurt, diced tomatoes and celery.

VINEGAR SUNDAE Top your favorite ice cream with a fortified fruit vinegar for a super-delicious sundae. Thick, fruity vinegars make an interesting change for topping pancakes or French toast, too.

RASPBERRY SLIPPER Put 1 tablespoon fortified raspberry vinegar in a tall glass and fill with cold water. This is a good way to get your daily vinegar and add water to your diet. This bit of sweetness before mealtime helps control the appetite and is just plain good!

TANGY CHERRIES Steep pitted sweet cherries for 3 hours in enough wine to barely cover them. Then add enough champagne vinegar to double the volume and simmer, uncovered for 15 minutes. Remove from heat and top with generous dashes of hot pepper and cinnamon. Add honey if a sweeter mixture is desired.

SALADS

Top salads with a dressing made of vegetable stock and vinegar instead of using oil. For a fat-free stock simmer a mix of diced summer vegetables in lots of water. When they are tender, puree the mix in a blender. For a darker, more intense stock, brown vegetables before simmering. Use herbal vinegars for variety, fortified vinegars for bolder flavors and extra nutrients.

PASTA & TUNA SALAD Toss together a can of well-drained tuna, 1 cup diced celery, 2 cups cooked pasta, 1 cup halved seedless red grapes, 1/2 cup white raisins, 1 cup diced, unpeeled apples. For the dressing, use 1/4 cup yogurt mixed with the liquid from the tuna.

FULL MEAL SALAD Combine 1 cup each of the following cooked vegetables: green, yellow wax, pinto and lima beans. Add 1 cup each chick peas, green peas and diced potatoes. Mix in 1/2 cup onion and 1/4 cup parsley. Toss with vinegar blended half and half with liquid from cooking the vegetables.

POTATO-CARROT SALAD Mix 2 cups boiled, diced potatoes and carrots. Toss with a dressing made of 1/4 cup apple cider vinegar, 1/4 cup tomato paste, 1 teaspoon chili powder, 1 tablespoon parsley.

CITRUS SALAD Peel and chop 1 cup oranges and 1 cup grapefruit. Top with raspberry, blueberry or strawberry fortified vinegar.

RECIPE TIPS

Get meals off to a healthy start with homemade soup. Good choices include chicken, celery, pumpkin and vegetable. In clear soups, use the liquid from canned vegetables or the water used to cook fresh ones. It can contain nearly one-third of the total nutrients. Pep up mild chicken soup with a splash of herbal vinegar or a bit of fortified garlic vinegar. Rinse cooked meats for soups (such as hamburger) in water to remove their fat. Prepare healthy cream soups by using skim milk made with twice the normal milk powder.

Use mustard, ketchup or apple butter on breads and rolls instead of fatty spreads. Better yet, drizzle them with fortified vinegar or cottage cheese blended with apple cider vinegar.

Cook stuffing outside a chicken or turkey to avoid the risk of salmonella germs. As a bonus, it will be lower in calories than the exact same stuffing cooked inside fowl! (If cooked in the bird, stuffing soaks up melted fat.) For a healthy change try white or brown rice instead of bread for stuffing. Use tomatoes, corn, mushrooms and red and green peppers, too.

Skip the salt in boiling pasta and vegetables. Substitute a splash of apple cider or herbal vinegar.

Make lighter corn muffins and brownies by replacing half the oil with apple sauce, mashed pumpkin or sweet potato.

An easy, tasty dessert can be made by baking bananas, pears or apples with cinnamon and nutmeg.

Add a bit of peppermint to salads for a fresh taste. It is said to sharpen the memory and stimulate circulation.

Skim milk tastes better with a tablespoon or so of dry milk stirred into each glass. A dash of vanilla or honey makes it even better. Add dry skim milk to mashed potatoes, cooked cereal, gravy, ground meats, casseroles, and baked goods to increase the amount of calcium you eat. Be sure to finish the milk at the bottom of the cereal bowl because many nutrients dissolve into it. For a fruity milk treat mix 3/4 cup very cold skim milk, 1/4 cup frozen orange juice concentrate and 1/4 cup crushed ice.

FOOD FACTS

Olive oil is graded by flavor as extra virgin, virgin and fine. There is no difference calories. Canola oil has linolenic acid, an omega-3 fatty acid (usually found in cold water fish) for a healthy heart.

One green pepper has much more vitamin C than a large orange. When peppers fully mature and turn red, their beta carotene content increases dramatically.

Sweet potatoes and white potatoes have a similar number of calories, sweet ones have lots of vitamin C and beta carotene.

Avocados contain more fat than other vegetables. Dry roasted nuts have most of the calories of regular roasted nuts.

Spinach and other flavored pastas are not good sources of vegetable nutrients. There are just enough vegetables added to make them have interesting colors. Usually this is a tablespoon or less in an entire pound of pasta!

FOOD CAUTIONS

Some foods need to be used with caution. Tofu can develop a bacteria that causes gastrointestinal distress if it is not stored in the refrigerator.

Limit the amount of liver you eat because it collects and stores any toxins the animal may have eaten.

Salmonella contamination is becoming very frequent in meat and eggs. E. coli (Eschericnia coli) can be found in meats, milk and juices which have not been pasteurized. For best health, never eat raw meat, fish or eggs. This includes cookie dough, uncooked eggnog and cake batter. Disinfect utensils used on these foods by soaking them in white vinegar. And, keep cold foods cold, hot foods hot.

Chapter Seven

Ageless Beauty & Glowing Skin

The Vinegar Diet does more than energize the inside of the body. This healthy regime will help the outside of the body look its very best. Your increased energy level will give your skin the glow of fresh health because when you are good to your insides, your outsides will show it!

For hundreds of years vinegar has been the basis for home remedies to beautify, cleanse and soothe the skin. Some of the most helpful ways that have been suggested, through the years, for using vinegar follow:

SOOTHING BATHS

Add a generous splash of apple cider vinegar to bath water to help keep the skin soft and smooth. Vinegar helps soothe itchy skin, while discouraging germs. Make bath time super-special by using an herbal scented vinegar. Especially nice vinegars for the tub include rose, lilac, geranium, lavender, rosemary, thyme and mint. (Some scented vinegars are only appropriate for external use.)

A few tablespoons of honey added to apple cider vinegar in a tub of warm bath water helps moisturize skin.

FACIALS

Blend together 1/2 cup apple cider vinegar and 1/4 cup well-cooked rice and 1/4 cup cooked oatmeal. Spread this mixture on the face, neck and shoulders. Allow to dry for 10 minutes, then wash off and pat dry with a soft towel. Skin will be soft and smooth.

For a refining facial, combine 1 tablespoon apple cider vinegar, 1 tablespoon honey and 1/2 a mashed banana. Apply a generous coating and after five minutes your skin will feel revitalized. Strawberries or a peach may be used in place of the banana.

Make a paste of dry yeast and warm water. Pat this onto the face and allow to dry. Rinse off with warm water. Then, rinse again with a quart of cool water to which a tablespoon of apple cider vinegar has been added.

HANDS & FEET

Thoroughly blend 1/2 cup olive oil and 1 cup mashed potatoes. It should have a cream-like consistency. Rub this mixture onto hands and feet to smooth and moisturize rough skin.

Eating lots of cauliflower fortified vinegar will give the body extra amounts of biotin. This plant-based nutrient helps it grow strong nails.

Clean and soothe work roughened hands with a paste of apple cider vinegar and cornmeal. After a minute or two rinse with warm water and apply a soothing lotion.

For silky feeling hands, wet them with apple cider vinegar. Then, rub them very gently with sugar. When the sugar is dissolved rinse hands in warm water. They will feel extraordinarily soft and velvety.

Condition hands and feet by soaking them for 15 minutes in 1 cup cooked oatmeal, 1/2 cup milk and 1/2 cup apple cider vinegar.

Banish foot odor by soaking feet in strong tea. Follow with a rinse made from 1 cup warm water and 1 cup apple cider vinegar.

Vinegar has been used to control more than foot odor. It was once considered an underarm deodorant! And, vinegar has been used as a gargle to deal with unpleasant breath. Herbal vinegars are said to be especially helpful. Vinegars which are especially good breath fresheners include rosemary, sage, clove, thyme, cinnamon and any of the mints. Because too much exposure to vinegar can hurt tooth enamel, always rinse with clear water after using it in the mouth.

SUNBURN, CANCER & CAROTENOIDS

Carotenoids, those amazing substances in vegetables and fruits, can reduce sunburn damage by UV rays! New research indicates eating carotenoid rich vegetables and fruits can be a preventive against skin cancer. It has been suggested that supplements of carotenoids, taken before going out in the sun, may be as effective as sun screens. This is another reason to use fortified vinegars to increase the amount of these foods in your diet!

Chapter Eight

Vinegar & Disease

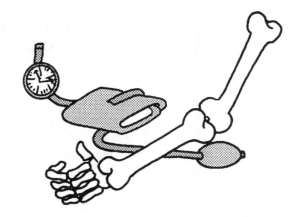

An ancient proverb assures us "Diet cures more than doctors." Combine this age-old wisdom with the importance of vinegar and you have — The Vinegar Diet!

The Vinegar Diet brings together the goodness of vinegar and eating habits needed for continuing health. The balance of food in The Vinegar Diet furnishes your body with what it needs to resist disease and be vital and vigorous well into old age.

THE VINEGAR DIET IS SOUND NUTRITION FOR A HEALTHY HEART!

Basics of The Vinegar Diet have been follow by health conscious individuals for decades. What is new, is scientific confirmation that there is a direct association between food and specific diseases. Substances in foods are now linked with arthritis and rheumatism, asthma, allergies, colds and flu, Alzheimer's Disease, diabetes, blood pressure, cancer, heart and cardiovascular disease. Improper eating habits can lead to a depressed immune system and even to more rapid aging!

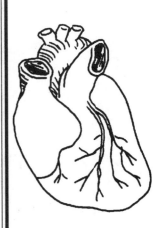

Twenty-five national health and aging organizations, including the American Dietetic Association, National Council on the Aging and American Academy of Family Physicians issued a report on Medical Nutrition Therapy. They propose using foods as medical treatment because many elders' eating habits put them at risk for malnutrition. They suggest preventive health care in the form of nutritional intervention would result in an older population with better immune function, resulting in:

• Fewer medical complications.
• Shorter hospital stays.
• More elders being able to live independently, in their own homes.
• Savings of more than 100 million dollars a year in medical expenses.

Vegetables and fruits are storehouses of antioxidants such as beta carotene. This wondrous antioxidant has the ability to neutralize free radicals. So, it is no surprise degenerative diseases of aging are less likely to develop in those with high blood levels of the more than 50 carotenoids in vegetables and fruits.

Each carotenoid seems to protect a particular part of the body or type of cell. They also have different ways of providing this antioxidant protection. Some foods, and what they contain follow:

Cantaloupe, carrots & pumpkin — alpha carotene.
Apricots, carrots, pumpkin & sweet potatoes — beta carotene.
Oranges, peaches & tangerines — beta cryptoxanthin.
Apricots & tomatoes — gamma carotene.
Red peppers, mustard greens & corn — lutein.
Tomatoes & watermelon — lycopene.
Beet tops & kale — zeaxanthin.

Emily Says

Antioxidants in vegetables and fruits attack free radicals.

ILLNESS & DIET

General aging of the brain has been linked to damage caused by free radicals. Specifically, confusion and memory loss can be caused by too little vitamin B-12 or folic acid. Some depression is associated with a deficiency of folic acid, calcium, iron, copper, magnesium or potassium. Protecting the mind from aging and depression to eat a diet high in antioxidant containing fruits and vegetables!

Macular degeneration is fought by the lutein and zeaxanthin in kale, spinach and several kinds of peppers.

Dark green and orange vegetables are rich in carotenoids that the body converts to vitamin A. It is needed by the body to make rhodopsin. This substance is essential to night vision and helps cut the risk of developing macular degeneration, one of the most common causes of blindness.

Prostate, breast and endometrial cancers seem to be restrained by lycopene. It is a carotenoid in tomatoes, pink grapefruit, apricots and watermelon.

Calcium loss from bones and menopause symptoms can both be reduced by estrogen-like isoflavones in soybeans.

Psoriasis is less common in those who eat lots of fresh fruit, carrots and tomatoes.

Urinary tract infections are inhibited by phytocompounds in blueberries and cranberries.

Emily Says

Phytocompounds = substances found in plants.

ARTHRITIS, ALLERGIES & MORE

Food allergies can cause a feeling of extreme fatigue after meals. Foods can also cause bloating, congestion, itching, cramping, headaches and mood swings. Food sensitivity, a less dramatic reaction, has been linked to fatigue and joint pain.

The existence of allergic arthritis shows how very much food affects the immune system. Researchers are constantly adding to the medical community's knowledge of how food allergies can cause the body to produce chemicals that trigger inflammatory reactions.

Those with arthritis may be particularly susceptible to food reactions because their immune systems already react in inappropriate ways. Zinc, magnesium, copper, vitamin B-6 and folic acid help regulate the immune system and may also minimize the side effects of anti-arthritis drugs.

Many seasonings do more than make foods taste better. Arthritis pain may sometimes be eased by the actions of cayenne, ginger or turmeric. (No, hot foods such as cayenne peppers do not cause ulcers.)

Foods affect the bacteria naturally present in the digestive system. Some have been linked to making rheumatoid arthritis symptoms worse.

Mushrooms contain polysaccharides, complex carbohydrates that stimulate the body's natural immune response to both bacteria and viruses. They have been used for thousands of years in Eastern medicine to fight disease.

Doctors are searching for better ways to fight deadly infections, such as tuberculosis, with diet changes. One day they will confirm the existence of specific foods that have the ability to regulate the immune system. In the meantime, most recommend a low saturated fat regimen that features lots of vegetables and fruits and a minimum of animal protein.

Alfalfa has been proved to induce systemic lupus erythematosus. This inflammatory disease of the connective tissue can be brought about by eating large quantities of alfalfa sprouts, seeds or tablets. And, those who already have lupus, but are in a remission, can reactivate the disease by eating alfalfa. Researchers suspect a non-protein amino acid in alfalfa (L-canavanine) may cause blood changes in those predisposed to lupus.

UN - CLOGGING ARTERIES

"Coronary artery disease can be stopped in its tracks, even reversed, without drugs!" That is what researchers say about an eating plan very much like The Vinegar Diet. Their studies suggest the nutrients found in abundance in vegetables and fruits can improve the condition of arteries. Nutrition therapy can help even if there are no obvious signs of deficiencies. Extra amounts of vitamin C, chromium, magnesium, selenium, niacin and potassium are especially helpful.

New studies report those who eat a salad every day have fewer heart attacks. When eggplant is eaten with foods high in vitamin C it seems to protect the body from developing fatty plaques in the arteries. Vegetables are excellent foods, but they do not take the place of fruits. Eating both fresh fruits and vegetables, every day, has been linked to a significant reduction in fatal heart attacks and strokes.

Ginger is very good for artery health. It helps lower cholesterol and seems to discourage cells from sticking together to form clots.

FIBER

A low fat, high fiber diet helps deter heart attacks, strokes and cancer. One way fiber fights cancer is by quickly pushing toxin laden food through the colon. Fiber helps reduce the likelihood of developing stomach ulcers because food and its digestive acids spend less time in the body. Its bulk eases constipation and its water absorbing capabilities moderates diarrhea.

Soluble fiber in legumes such as pinto, navy, kidney and soy beans protects good HDL cholesterol and lowers bad LDL. They begin their cholesterol lowering work almost immediately.

Fiber, particularly the soluble fiber in foods like oatmeal, helps remove cholesterol from the body. Too much fiber, such as is in some supplements can interfere with calcium absorption.

The membrane holding together sections of grapefruit is an especially healthy fiber. Half of it is soluble to soak up cholesterol, half is insoluble to fight constipation and colon cancer. Two grapefruit have a full day's fiber needs.

Vinegars fortified with apples or sweet potatoes are high fiber foods that can help ease hemorrhoids.

Diabetes is at least as deadly for adult women as breast cancer! A high fiber, low fat, diet and exercise are the recommended preventatives.

CANCER

More than half of women's cancers can be traced to diet. Breasts seem to be particularly sensitive to food toxins such as pesticides and partially hydrogenated oil preservatives. This is probably because these oil soluble chemicals tend to be stored in breast fat.

Lower the risk of breast cancer by eating soy products for their phytoestrogens (plant estrogens). Eat broccoli, cauliflower and kale for their effect on the way the body uses estrogen.

Garlic is considered an anti-cancer food because it stops the activity of some substances which are known to cause cancer. It seems to work on both existing cancers and as a preventive against new ones. Garlic lowers the risk of developing many diseases because it strengthens the immune system.

FAT

All fuels produce by-products when they are burned. Some of these by-products are more harmful than others. Foods high in saturated fats produce more toxic chemicals than vegetables, fruits and whole grains. Some fat is necessary for good health, even the body makes a bit of cholesterol.

The healthiest diet seems to be one with a small amount of the right kinds of oil added to it.

Polyunsaturated oils such as flaxseed, corn, safflower and soy are good for use in cold dishes. Flaxseed is a rich source of the omega-3 oils also found in cold water fish.

When polyunsaturated oils are heated they produce toxic lipid peroxides. So, for cooking, the oleic acid containing monounsaturated oils are best. Two good heat and light resistant monounsaturated oils are olive and canola.

Fat substitutes are used in many processed foods. Simplesse is one that has been used for many years. Avicel is a cellulose gel. N-Oil is a tapioca based dextrin. Olestra, one of the newest fat substitutes, is calorie free, but may inhibit fat soluble vitamins such as A, D, E and K. It may also interfere with the absorption of important carotenoids.

WEIGHT LOSS DRUGS

Weight loss drugs work in several ways. Some of the newest ones affect the way serotonin, a neurotransmitter, is handled by the brain. This is thought to be helpful for some people because neurotransmitters affect the way the body's appetite control mechanism works. A few weight loss drugs that are available now, or are being tested, and some things you need to know about them, follow:

REDUX is the trade name for dexfenfluramine. It raises brain levels of serotonin and so produces results similar to anti-depression drugs such as Prozac. Redux can complicate the condition of those with high blood pressure. Its manufacturer recently sent letters to 300,000 health care providers to warn of newly documented side effects, including primary pulmonary hypertension, a potentially deadly reaction.

PONDIMIN is a trade name for fenfluramine. IONAMIN and FASTIN are trade names for phentermine. These drugs are not recommended for anyone taking blood pressure lowering agents, antidepressants, or anyone who has a history of alcohol or drug abuse. Their side effects can include insomnia, headache, diarrhea and nausea.

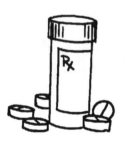

Fen-Phen is the popular name for the combination of fenfluramine and phentermine, two appetite suppressing drugs.

Drugs being tested include orlistat, sibutramine and leptin, a hormone found in fat cells. Researchers have been working with leptin for more than 10 years in the hope of developing an obesity fighting drug. It still seems linked to insomnia, constipation and increased blood pressure. And, patients tend to regain lost weight when it is discontinued.

Some widely publicized drugs for weight loss have had problems with the Federal Drug Administration (FDA). Some injections of adrenal cortex extract have been linked to serious bacterial infections. They are the subject of a Federal Drug Administration alert. The FDA has tried to ban the use of Co-enzyme Q-10, a substance that is associated with the body's regulation of metabolism.

The FDA warns that those who take many of the prescription appetite suppressants increase their risk of developing primary pulmonary hypertension by as much as 20 times. Diarrhea, dizziness, memory lapses and depression are common short-term side effects of weight loss drugs. Long-term studies on safety and effectiveness have not yet been completed.

Experts agree, when dieters stop taking drugs most can expect to gain back the weight which was lost. They are then faced with the need to take the drugs on and off for the rest of their lives. (Plus the cost of repeated doctor visits and about $50.00 a month for the pills.) For most people the risks "out weigh" any weight problem!

A nonprescription supplement, chromium picolinate, seems to have fewer known side effects than some other weight loss agents. But there have been no long term tests to confirm this. And, it has not been proven effective for most people.

Caffeine is the most popular stimulant drug in the world! Until 1991 caffeine was used in over-the-counter weight loss products. The FDA no longer permits this, as it as been deemed to have no long term effect on weight. Colas, regular tea, coffee and chocolate contain caffeine.

Caffeine increases metabolism, especially when combined with aspirin. Unfortunately it also encourages brittle bones. It is estimated that one six ounce cup of coffee pulls about five milligrams of calcium from the body. Replacing this calcium takes the equivalent of the concentrated power of two tablespoons of yogurt.

Cafestol and kahweol are in the oils in ground coffee. They are not in instant or filtered drip coffee, but remain in percolated coffee. Drinking even four cups a day of oil-containing coffee may significantly increase the risk of heart disease.

One thing all weight loss drugs share is that when they are stopped, any weight lost tends to be regained! Considering their many, often dangerous, side effects they are a poor substitute for a healthy diet and a little exercise.

FOOD & CHEMO-PREVENTIVES

Tumeric is a very safe, anti-UV radiation, antioxidant. It has even been shown to help prevent chromosome damage.

Rosemary contains substances that act against free radicals. It also protects the liver from the damage that can be done by some toxins. Rosemary's phenolic compounds, carnosol and carnosic acid do this antioxidant work. These flavonoids can be used as preservatives for fats in foods.

Ginger has substances to help protect the liver. It is also useful against platelet clumping, which contributes to heart attacks.

Apples, onions and tea contain flavonoids, antioxidants to reduce the risk of heart disease.

Carotenoids, those amazing substances in vegetables and fruits, can help limit the spread of breast cancer. Tests are being conducted on using them to stop the spread of lung, stomach and colon cancers, too.

Beta carotene helps maintain healthy eyes. When taken at the same time as aspirin, it may prevent some side effects, such as stomach distress.

Garlic has substances that energize the immune system. One of these, selenium, has been found to lower the risk of cancer of the colon, lung, prostate and rectum.

All weight loss drugs carry some health warnings. Vegetables, fruits and whole grains do not. Whenever a product has dangers attached to it, proceed with great caution. You may not need to take that risk. The Vinegar Diet, with its use of fortified vinegars to add all the goodness of vegetables and fruits to your diet may be what you need.

No matter what scientists finally decide about vinegar's usefulness in the diet, people have instinctively felt, for untold centuries, that vinegar was good for them. It is truly a living substance, capable of bringing health benefits far beyond the ability of today's medical world to fully comprehend!

Chapter Nine

Questions &
Answers

Question: I have diabetes, a heart condition, arthritis, etc. Is it safe for me to take vinegar every day?

Answer: If you have a chronic medical condition ALWAYS check with a health care professional before adding anything, including vinegar to your diet.

Question: I take medication. Can vinegar be taken with it?

Answer: If you take medication, including over the counter drugs, ALWAYS check with a health care professional before adding vinegar to your diet.

Question: Will vinegar pull calcium from my bones?

Answer: No. Vinegar in the digestive system does not come into direct contact with your bones. It works in other ways to aid health.

Question: What kind of vinegar should I use?

Answer: Use white vinegar for cleaning and to pickle light colored foods. Use apple cider vinegar for tonics and most recipes. Rice, champagne, wine and other vinegars can also be used in recipes.

Question: Where can I find herbal vinegars?

Answer: More and more supermarkets now carry a line of herbal vinegars. For the freshest, most robust flavor make your own by adding a few tablespoons of an herb to a good supermarket vinegar.

Question: Where can I find organic vinegar?

Answer: A few supermarkets now carry organic vinegar, as do many health food stores. Some mail order speciality houses sell organic vinegar, too.

FREE HEALTHY-EATING PUBLICATIONS

For information on how the chemicals in plants (phytochemicals) fight disease send a stamped, self addressed, business sized envelope to:

American Institute for Cancer Research
1759 R Street NW
Washington, D.C. 20009

For facts on how to use food nutrition labels ask for "New Food Labels to Choose Healthier Foods," Publication Number (FDA) 94-2276. Write to:

FDA, Office of Consumer Affairs
5600 Fishers Lane, HFE-88
Rockville, MD 20857

Get answers to questions about food safety by calling the USDA's Meat and Poultry Hotline at 1-800-535-4555. Or, write to them at:

Eating for a Healthy Heart
FDA
HFE-88
Rockville, MD 20857

YOU CAN HELP DOCUMENT THE EFFECTS OF THE VINEGAR DIET!

Would you like to add your experiences to my register of Vinegar Diet results? Simply follow the guidelines in Chapter Three, Four or Five for at least three months. Be sure to eat lots of fruits, vegetables and grains, limit fats and sweets, and begin a walking or other program of gentle exercise.

Then write and let me know how the diet affected you. I want to know if it helped you move your weight into a healthier range. Be sure to tell me exactly how much difference The Vinegar Diet made to your weight and to your general health. If you shared the plate drawing with your doctor, tell me what reaction you received. Send your Vinegar Diet results to:

Diet Survey
% Emily Thacker
718 - 12th Street
Box 24500
Canton, OH 44701

REFERENCES

"Action Almanac" UFCW Action. March- April 1993: p 14

ALIAS C. and Linden G. "Food Biochemistry." Professors of Biochemistry, University of Nancy, France: Ellis Harwood Series in Food Science and Technology: 1991.

AMELLAL, M. et al. "Inhibition of Mast Cell Histamine Release by Flavonoids and Bioflavonoids," Planta Medica. Stuttgart: Georg Thieme Verlag, vol 49, 1985: pp 16-19.

AMERICAN Heart Association, "Brand Name Fat and Cholesterol Counter." Bristol-Myers Squibb Co. NY, NY: Times Books, 1994.

ANDERSON- Parrado, Patricia; "No Mater How You Slice 'Tomato' You'll Get Lycopene in Every Bite." Better Nutrition Dec. 1996: p 14.
"An Interview With Durk Pearson and Sandy Shaw:" pp 1-5

ANTOL, Marie Nadine. "Healing Teas" Garden City Park, NY: Avery Publishing Group;1996.
"Arthritis Update." Nov-Dec 1996, vol III/no 6

BOWERS, Jane. "Food Theory and Applications." NY, NY: Macmillan Publishing Co. 1992.

BRODY, Jane E. "Midlife Weight Gain is Very Dangerous to Your Health." Health Confidential, vol 9/ no 5: p. 5.

CARPER, Jean "Food-Your Miracle Medicine." NY NY: Harper Collins Publishers, 1993.

CHAITOW, Leon. "Amino Acids in Therapy." Northamptonshire, England: Thorsons Publishers Limited, 1985.

CHOTKOWSKI, L A., MD, FACP. "What's New in Medicine: More Than 250 of the Biggest Health Issues of the Decade." Santa Fe, NM: Health Press, 1991.

CONNOR, Sonja L., MS, RD., & Connor, William E., MD. "The New American Diet System." NY, NY: Simon & Schuster, 1991.

DEAN, Ward, MD, et al. "Smart Drugs II: The Next Generation." Petauma, CA: Smart Publications, 1993.

"Delicious. Your Magazine of Natural Living." vol/no 1, Jan 1997.

"Does Leptin Trigger Puberty." Science News vol 151, Jan 25, 1997: p 58.

DOLBY, Victoria. "Rise to the Challenge: Reduce Your Cancer Risk with Garlic Protection." Better Nutrition Dec 1996: p 22.

DUKE, James A. Handbook of Phytochemical Constituents of Gras Herbs and Other Economic Plants. CRC Press, 1992.

ELLIOT, Rose & Depaoli, Carlo. "Kitchen Pharmacy." London, England: Tiger Books International Plc, 1994.

"Environmental Nutrition." vol 19/no 11, Nov 1996.

"Environmental Nutrition." vol 20/no 1, Jan 1997: pp 1-8.

"Environmental Nutrition." vol 19/no 12, Dec 1996.

FACKELMANN, Kathleen. "Rusty Organs: Researchers Identify the Gene for Iron-Overload Disease." Science News Jan 18, 1997: pp 46-47.

"FDA Consumer." Nov 1996: pp 4-5.

FORD, Norman D. "Natural Remedies: Techniques for Preventing Headaches and the Common Cold." NY, NY: Galahad Books, 1995.

FOSTER, Steven. "Phytomedicinals: The Healing Power of Plants." Better Nutrition Dec 1996: pp. 44-49.

FREMES, Ruth & Sabry, Dr. Zak. Nutriscope. Stoddart Publishing Co. Ltd, 2nd ed, 1989.

GARLAND, Sara. "The Complete Book of Herbs and Spices." Pleasantville, NY: The Readers Digest Assoc. Inc., 1993.

GROMLEY, James J. "Saturated Fat- From 'Enemy' to Essential: A Balance of Fat is Key." Better Nutrition Dec 1996: p 12.

"Growing Older Eating Better." FDA Consumer Magazine Reprint: Mar 1996.

"Harvard Women's Health Watch." Harvard Medical School Dec 1996 vol IV/no 4.

"Health News." The New England Journal of Medicine Dec 10, 1996.

HEINERMAN, John. "Heinerman's Encyclopedia of Fruits, Vegetables and Herbs." W. Nyack, NY: Parker Publishing Co, 1988.

"Help Build Strong Bones 8 Ways." Consumer Reports on Health, Dec 1996: pp 135, 138-139.

HENDLER, Sheldon Saul, MD, PhD. "The Purification Prescription." NY, NY: William Morrow & Co. Inc., 1991.

HIKINO, H. "Antihepatonic Actions of Ginerals and Diaryihepataroids." Journal of Ethnopharmacology, vol 14, 1985: pp 31-39.

HORTON, Sara K. "Lose Weight and Keep it Off." Journal of Personality and Social Psychology, vol 70, no 1.
"Housecalls." Health Sept 1996: p 128.

JACOBSON, Michael F., PhD, et al. "Safe Food: Eating Wisely in a Risky World." Los Angeles, CA: Living Planet Press, 1991.

JARVIS, D.C., MD. "Arthritis and Folk Medicine." NY, NY: Rinehart and Winston, 1960: pp 40, 54-55.

JARVIS, D.C., MD. "Folk Medicine: An Almanac of Natural Health Care." NY, NY: Galahad Books, 1958.

KEVILLE, Kathi. "Herbs; An Illustrated Encyclopedia." Michael Friedman Publishing Group, Inc., 1994.

KIKUZAKI, Hiroe & Nakatani, Nobuji. "Antioxidant Effects of Some Ginger Constituents." Journal of Food Science, Institute of Food Technologists, vol 58/no 6, 1993: pp 1408-1410.

KURTZEIL, Paula "Taking the Fat out of Food." FDA Consumer July/Aug 1996: pp 7-13.

LALANNE, Elaine. "Eating Right for a New You." NY, NY: Penguin Group, 1992.

LAMM, Steve MD. "Safe, Lasting Weight Loss: Breakthrough Drug Regimen Makes It Possible," p. 9.

LANGER, Steven MD. "When It Comes to Vitamins, 'Cs' Make the Grade." Better Nutrition, Dec 1996: pp 40-43.

LEBER, Max R., RPh, BS, et al. "Handbook of Over-the-Counter Drugs and Pharmacy Products." Berkeley, CA: Celestial Arts Publishing, 1994.

LIEBERMAN, Laurency MRPh. "The Dieter's Pharmacy." NY, NY: St. Martin's Press, 1990.

"Low- Fat Diets: Moderation and 'Good' Foods Are the Key." UT Lifetime Health Letter Apr 1995: p 7.

"Manganese." Better Nutrition Dec 1996: p 58.

MARIANI, John F. "The Dictionary of American Food and Drink." NY, NY: Hearst Books, 1994.

MCLEOD, Kate. "Stepping Up to healthy Living." Health pp 105-108.

MINDELL, Earl, RPh, PhD. "Earl Mindell's Anti- Aging Bible." NY, NY: Simon & Schuster, 1996.

MORGAN, Brian L.G., PhD. "Nutri- Tips." Stamford, CT: Longmeadow Press, 1991.

NAVARRO, Concepcion M. 'Free Radical Scavenger and Anti-hepatotoxic Activity of Rosmarinus tomentosus." Planta Medica, Stuttgart: Georg Thieme Verlag vol 59, 1993: pp 312-3114.

"Novel Antioxidants May Slow Brain's Aging;" Science News Jan 25, 1997: p 53.

"Nutrition Action Health Letter." Center for Science in the Public Interest. Jan/Feb 1997.

"Nutrition and Your Health: Dietary Guidelines for Americans." U.S. Department of Health and Human Services and U.S. Department of Agriculture Dec 1995.

"Olestra and Other Fat Substitutes (Revised)." FDA Backgrounder Nov 28, 1995: pp 1-2.

PAPAZIAN, Ruth. "Should You Go on a Diet." FDA Consumer Magazine May 1994.

PARSONNET, Mia MD. "What's Really in Our Food." NY, NY: Shapolsky Publishers, Inc., 1991.

PEARSON, Durk and Shaw, Sandy. "The Life Extension Companion." NY,NY: Warner Books, Inc., 1984.

PERCHELLET, Jean-Pierre, et al. "Inhibition of DMBA- Induced Mouse Skin Tumorigensis by Garlic Oil and Inhibition of Two Tumor- Promotion Stages by Garlic and Onion Oils." Nutrition and Cancer vol 14/no 3-4, 1990: pp 183-193.

"Prevention Magazine's Complete Book of Vitamins and Minerals," Wings Books and Rodale Press, Inc., N.Y., NY, 1988: pp. 134-137, 348, 372, 383.

"Prevention's Healing With Vitamins," Ed. of Prevention Magazine Health Books. Emmaus, PA Rodale Press, Inc., 1996.

SANTAMARIA, L et al. "Chemoprevention of Indirect and Direct Chemical Carcinogenesis by Carotenoids as Oxygen Radical Quenchers." NY, NY: Annals of the New York Academy of Sciences; 1988: pp 584-596.

SOMER, Elizabeth, MA, RD. "Food and Mood." NY: Henry Holt and Co., 1995: p 16.

SRINIVAS, , Leela, et al. "Tumerin: A Water Soluble Antioxident Peptide from Turmeric (Curcumalonga)." Archives of Biochemistry and Biophysics vol 292/no 2, Feb 1992: pp 617-623.

SRIVASTAVA, K.C. and Mustafa, T. "Ginger (Zingiber Off Icinale) in Rheumatism and Musculoskeletal Disorders." Medical Hypothesis vol 39, 1992: pp 342-348.

STEINMAN, David: "Diet for a Poisoned Planet," NY, NY: Harmony Books, 1990.

STERNBERG, S. "Can Selenium Ward Off Deadly Cancers?" Science News Jan 4, 1997: p 6.

"Tea for Two: Less Cancer, Less Heart Disease." Consumer Reports on Health Dec 1996: pp 135, 138-139.

"Walking for Exercise and Pleasure." The President's Council on Physical Fitness and Sports 1994: pp 2-4, 11.

WEBB, Denise, PhD, RD. "Foods For Better Health: Prevention and Healing of Diseases." Lincolnwood, IL: Publications International, Ltd., 1995.

"Weight Loss Drugs." New England Journal of Medicine Dec 31, 1996: p 7,

WELLS, Valerie "Think Thin." San Francisco, CA: Chronicle Books, 1992.

WERBACH, Melvyn R., MD. "Nutritional Influences on Illness," A Source Book of Clinical Research. New Canaan, Conn: Keats Publishing, Inc., 1987.

"Working Out the Facts: The Truth Behind Ten Common Myths." Consumer Reports Dec 1996; pp 48-49

ZERDEN, Sheldon "The Best of Health: The 101 Best Books." NY, NY: Four Walls Eight Windows, 1989.

No one book could ever contain all the useful remedies and health secrets of the good people I've met through my travels. Most likely you, too, know about healing remedies that have been passed down from generation to generation.

And so, I would love to hear from you. If you have a remedy, or other useful advice, you would like to share with others, please use this page (or a sheet of plain paper) to share it with me. If I am able to use it in an upcoming edition of a remedies book, I will send you a free copy of the new book.

Thank you, and my best wishes for a long and healthy life,

Emily Thacker

_____

_____

_____

_____

_____

Please indicate (yes or no) whether I may use your name if I use this helpful advice:

❑ YES, please credit this remedy to _____
                                                            (Please Print)

❑ NO, please use my remedy, but do not use my name in the book.
(Either way, Yes or No, if I use your remedy, I'll send you a free copy of the new edition of home remedies!)

My favorite chapter in "Emily Thacker's Collected Works" is:

_____

_____

The helpful remedy I most appreciated in "Emily Thacker's Collected Works" appears on page _____, and tells how to: _____

_____

_____

What I liked best about "Emily Thacker's Collected Works" was:

_____

_____

_____

If you have any comments or experiences to add to the information you've read in this collection, or if you have information for subsequent editions, please address your letters to:

Emily Thacker
718 - 12th Street N.W., Box 24500
Canton, Ohio 44701

- -

Use this coupon to order "Emily Thacker's Collected Works" for a friend or family member -- or copy the ordering information onto a plain piece of paper and mail to:

Emily Thacker's Collected Works
718 - 12th Street N.W., Box 24500,
Dept. TVCW3206
Canton, Ohio 44701